The
Debt
Threat

If you want to make debt relief for
the world's poorest nations
really happen, go to

TheDebtThreat.com

where you can get involved in the campaign,
send a message to Washington,
or tell a friend about *The Debt Threat*.

Also by Noreena Hertz

The Silent Takeover

The Debt Threat

HOW DEBT IS DESTROYING THE DEVELOPING WORLD

Noreena Hertz

HarperBusiness
An Imprint of HarperCollinsPublishers

THE DEBT THREAT © 2004 by Noreena Hertz.
All rights reserved. Printed in the United States of America. No part of
this book may be used or reproduced in any manner whatsoever without
written permission except in the case of brief quotations embodied
in critical articles and reviews. For information address HarperCollins
Publishers Inc., 10 East 53rd Street, New York, New York 10022.

HarperCollins books may be purchased for educational, business, or
sales promotional use. For information, please write to: Special
Markets Department, HarperCollins Publishers Inc.,
10 East 53rd Street, New York, New York 10022.

Designed by Nicola Ferguson

Library of Congress Cataloging-in-Publication has been applied for.

ISBN 0-06-056052-5

04 05 06 DIX/RRD 10 9 8 7 6 5 4 3 2 1

To Jonathan, Arabel, and David
Thank you so much.

5/05

Contents

Acknowledgments

There are many people who helped make this book happen. In particular I would like to thank:

Ed Victor, superagent extraordinaire, who has been a fantastic source of support and wisdom throughout; Marion Maneker, whose belief in me was integral to getting this project off the ground; Caroline Michel, whose care for me as an author has made the publication process so enjoyable; Mitzi Angel, whose commitment to the project is so appreciated; and Philippa Harrison, whose considered comments have been of such great help.

Bono and Bobby Shriver, for their selfless commitment to the debt cancellation cause, and the enthusiasm they have shown for my project right from the start.

Larry Summers, Jose Maria Figueres, Sheryl Sandberg, Stephanie Flanders, Sonny Callahan, Jamie Drummond, Karl Ziegler, Ann Pettifor, Gary Klesch, Paul Ladd, Ashok Sinha, Caitlin Zaloom, Martin Powell, Justin Forsyth, John Clark, Demba Moussa Dembele, Benjamin Mkapa, and Theogène Rudasingwa for sharing their insights and experience from "the field."

Philip Gould, for setting me on this writing track all those years back now, and for being so supportive throughout. David Held for being the best intellectual sounding board I could have ever hoped for, and also for being a great friend. Len Blavatnik for his continued care and consideration. Christos Pitelis for being such a great colleague at CIBAM and Sandra Dawson for being such an inspiration herself.

Bruce Rich, Richard Segal, Reza Dana, Chris Stout, Saqib Qureshi, Christine Eberlein, Alex Wilks, Derek Yach, Tommy Helsby, Gerd Leopold, Igor Fuchsman, Mike Rowson, Robert Wade, Mary

Kaldor, Ajit Singh, Jeffrey Sachs, Celia Szusterman, Martin Varsavsky, Mark Weisbrot, and Justin Alexander, for invaluable feedback on individual chapters.

Jan Pronk and Sir John Vereker for sparing the time to read through drafts of the entire manuscript, for their always extremely helpful comments, and for believing so firmly in what I have tried to do. And Peter Ntephe for not only being so smart but also so generous with his time.

The many researchers who helped me gather material for this book. Especially Peter Abbott, my first reader, Aaka Pande, Armida de la Garza, Sony Kapoor, Mark Sivarajah, Adam Quinn, and Sergey Radchenko. But also Monika Thakur, Rashmi Singh, Romilly Greenhill, Valerio Cerretano, David Palfrey, Daniel Nieto-Michel, Duncan Elliott, Gherardo Girardi, and Maria Volpe.

My friends, who once again amazed me in terms of how supportive they are. Especially James Brett, Daniel Levy, Dambisa Moyo, Tony Juniper, Emmanuel Quartey, Richard Symons, and Billy O'Donnell. But also Mark Barrett, Francesca Joseph, Gina Bellman, Wendy Goldsmith, Stacy Meyrowitz, Kinky Friedman, Juliet Cassidy, Abby Turk, Joshua Ramo, Alex Cooke, Craig Cohon, Gary Baddley, Theo Phanos, Omar Salah, Nicolas Topiol, Diane McGrath, and Alexis Johansen.

Charles Pither, David Curtin, David Oakley, Julie Masonic, Shoshana Gellman, Pat Lilley, and Mira Lajanska, for being there for me throughout.

And finally my father, Jonathan, and sister, Arabel; I couldn't have done this without you.

The Debt Threat

1

Rock the Vote

And
ye shall hallow the
fiftieth year, and proclaim
liberty throughout all the land
unto all the inhabitants thereof: it
shall be a jubilee unto you; and ye
shall return every man unto his
possession, and ye shall return
every man unto his family.
—*Leviticus 25:10, as partially
inscribed on the Liberty Bell*

Who's the Elvis here?" asked the rock star impatiently. The question reverberated through Leslie Gelb's book-filled office in the beaux arts brownstone that houses the Council on Foreign Relations. The exasperated tone came from a man accustomed to addressing stadiums filled with fans hanging on his every word and syllable, but it was far from an arrogant question.

Gelb had just finished his tutorial on the American power structure by laying out the great chain of influence—from David Rockefeller to UN ambassador Richard Holbrooke to U.S. treasury secretary Robert Rubin to former chairman of the Fed Paul Volcker to a number of key Republicans—that led from Wall Street to Washington and back again. Which only served to remind Bono that he was aiming to play in a very different league. Paul McGuinness, U2's manager, had only just admonished him that it was one thing to lobby for the debt cancellation cause at music industry events but quite another to pilot the issue through the American political process. With those words still clearly ringing in his ears the star tried to find a shortcut toward his goal.

"You know I've got a day job?" asked Bono, half jesting. It was entirely possible that the decidedly unhip Gelb, then president of the United States' premier foreign policy think-tank—a place that played host to many self-important investment bankers, foreign service officers, journalists, and academic wonks but no conventional celebrities—had no idea why the young man was important.

But Bono's attempt at humor cut him no slack; Gelb leaned across to him and repeated in rasping tones (he had lost his voice that day) that any one of the names he'd just listed "could basically stop this idea from getting off the ground." And if Bono truly wanted to get the United States to cancel all the debts owed to it by the world's poorest countries, not to mention get the U.S. to provide funds to cover monies owed to the World Bank, the International Monetary Fund (IMF), and regional development banks, he would need the support of every one of these American dignitaries—and that was just the beginning. Gelb broke the news that there was no single figure with enough clout to pull off such a complicated—and politically inert—maneuver. Developing-world debt was a diverse issue with many constituencies. For the U.S. government to orchestrate debt cancellation would require the kind of unanimity rarely seen in such a partisan climate. "There is no Elvis," Gelb finally answered, and ushered the rock star firmly out the door.

Gelb had been right: there was no Elvis and there were no shortcuts. Eventually Paul Hewson, the Irish singer revered by millions as Bono, would travel back and forth across the Atlantic Ocean thirty times, painfully assembling a coalition from some of the world's least sentimental politicians. After a year and a half of beseeching and cajoling, he arranged for a dozen prominent Democrats and Republicans in Congress and the Clinton administration to support a package that pledged to cancel all the debts owed the United States by the world's thirty-three poorest nations, as well as cover part of what they owed the World Bank and IMF. It was the culmination of the first—and last—serious attempt by the ordinary people of the West to force politicians to address the painful legacy of Third World debt.

But what was it about the debt of developing countries that motivated Bono to go to so much effort? Aren't *all* countries in debt? The United States certainly is. It owes $3 trillion, around ten times what Africa owes, but Bono wasn't campaigning to cancel that.

The difference is this. The United States may be the world's most highly indebted nation, but it can afford to service its loans, for now at least. The world's poorest countries, in Africa, Asia, and Latin America, cannot—because to do so they have to pay an unacceptably high price, mainly at the expense of their poor or sick. Botswana, in which 40 percent of adults are now HIV-positive, pays more today on debt servicing than it can afford to pay on health care or provision. Niger, the country with the highest rate of child mortality in the world, continues to spend more on debt servicing than on public health. Countries that can't afford to provide basic health care, education, or shelter to their people have to use their pitiful resources, including, in many cases, *all* their aid flows, to repay debts typically racked up by authoritarian, unelected regimes long since gone. Children in Africa die every day because their governments are spending more on debt servicing than they are on health or education. The injustice of this situation made Bono mad.

It made him mad too that most developing countries had become so indebted only because the world's superpowers had callously used them as pawns in the days of the cold war. And that the rich countries of the world continue to lend to dictatorships and corrupt regimes in the poor, despite the fact that it is the ordinary people living under them who bear the cost. It made him even angrier that the West continues to lend monies to the developing world under the condition that they use them to buy arms or military hardware. And that to the traders on Wall Street and the vultures who hover over highly indebted countries, debt is just another product to be bought and sold, regardless of the damage their actions so often cause.

But this still doesn't explain why a rock star turned political lobbyist. Bono could have kept his politicking confined to music biz events and still played a part.

To understand that, we must understand the state of the debt cancellation movement in 1999, the year Bono and Gelb met. In Europe, it enjoyed a very high profile. From inauspicious beginnings at Keele University in central England, in just a few years it had evolved into a broad-based alliance—the Jubilee Coalition—which counted churches, the Mothers Union, the British Medical Association, trade unions, and aid agencies among its members. In Britain, 500,000 "Cancel the Debt" postcards had been sent to Gordon Brown, the British chancellor of the exchequer, including one from his own mother; in Italy, rival soccer teams wore debt relief T-shirts; on the same day that Frank Sinatra died, 70,000 Jubilee supporters formed a human chain around the G8 summit of the world's wealthiest democracies, to protest against the shackling of the developing world by its rich-world creditors.

In the United States, however, despite the support of various religious groups, the Jubilee Coalition had almost no profile, and its campaign—to get the world's richest countries to commemorate the millennium by canceling the debts owed them by the world's poorest countries—had completely failed to take off. But without the United States making a serious commitment to debt relief, the whole Jubilee campaign would falter. The $6 billion debt owed to the United States by the poor countries was an albatross around their already scrawny necks. More critically, there could be little progress toward canceling the $70 billion the world's poorest countries owed the World Bank, the IMF, and regional development banks unless America played a major role.

Jamie Drummond, a young British debt campaigner, who had been charged with getting the United States more engaged, decided to push the envelope. He saw that there wasn't time to rally the kind of mass public support that had proven so effective in getting debt onto the European political agenda. It was early 1999 and the mil-

lennium clock that marked the deadline for the Jubilee campaign
was ticking very loudly. And so he decided to go a completely different route.

In the States, celebrity was, he figured, the quickest way of opening doors and ramping up support. And Bono, the Irish singer,
whose band U2 had sold over one hundred million records, and who
was known for his staunch support of human rights, the environment, and development issues was, Jamie believed, his man.

Luckily, Jamie's father had a useful neighbor on the west coast of
Ireland. Through Chris Blackwell, the legendary founder of Island
Records, Drummond managed to reach Bono.

Bono was excited. He cared about Africa. After headlining at
Bob Geldof's revolutionary Live Aid concert in 1985, which raised
$70 million for famine-stricken Ethiopia, he and his wife, Ali, spent
a summer working in an orphanage there. Bono had seen firsthand
the immense strain of repayment of debt and thought it absurd that,
for every dollar of government aid the West sent to developing nations, several times that amount was coming back to them in debt repayments. But perhaps what clinched it for Bono was that he was
also, despite his rock-and-roll pedigree, a deeply religious man, and
the biblical notion of jubilee, the idea that you have the right to
begin again, appealed to him with its combination of moral force
and profound simplicity.

"Great ideas have a lot in common with great melodies," recalls
Bono. "They have a certain clarity, a certain inevitability, and an in-
stant memorability. And I couldn't get this one out of my head. I
knew it was right, and that the time was right for this and I couldn't
let it go."

But while the pierced and sunglasses-wearing rock star might
have been able to fill giant stadiums, Bono was a nobody as far as
American politics was concerned. If he was to play a part in putting
debt relief on the U.S. political agenda, he needed help. So he phoned
a woman he thought might be able to do just that. Bono knew Eunice Shriver—the founder of the Special Olympics, and daughter of
Rose and Joseph Kennedy—from a charity recording project; he de-
scribes her as a "Hibernophile," a person who knows more about

Irish culture and politics than most Irish people. She told him that she'd love to help and suggested that he get in touch with her son. "I think Bobby would be good at this," Bono recalls her saying. "And I knew Bobby but hadn't thought to ring him. And he *was* good. He was more than good."

For while Bono had passion, Bobby had political savvy. Shriver immediately knew that in order to get the United States to really commit to debt cancellation, it was essential that not just the Democrats but also the Republicans, right-wing journalists, and most important, Wall Street, blessed their proposal. With this in mind, one of the first things Bobby did was set up the meeting between Bono and the well-connected Gelb.

But Bobby also knew that Bono couldn't just go and meet the men on Gelb's list until they both knew their subject inside out. "I had been minding my own business," Bobby recalls, "making records, producing movies, when I got Bono's call. I knew *nothing* about debt, but I did know I wasn't going to Washington with him, or to see anyone at all, unless we really knew what we were doing. We *really* had to know what we were doing." So Shriver picked up the phone and called "a guy I knew who was doing a lot of work on this subject." That guy was Jeffrey Sachs, one of Harvard's most famous economics professors.

"I called Jeff up and I said, 'I have this friend that I did the Christmas record with, a musician called Bono, and if he comes over to Cambridge, will you spend a couple of days with him and try to get him up to speed on the actual numbers?'"

Sachs was forthcoming. "Sure, I wanted to meet Bono," he recalls. But debt cancellation had been something *he* had been advocating for years, to little avail, and he was skeptical of the impact the musician could have. "It's never going to work," Bobby remembers him saying. "No one in Washington will pay any attention to you. We can't get anyone to pay attention to this issue."

But by the end of their two-day cram session, Sachs felt differently. Shriver recalls Sachs's palpable excitement. "He said, 'This guy is a very persuasive guy, you know; maybe something *can* be done.'"

With Bono thoroughly briefed, it was time for Shriver to start spinning his Rolodex.

His first call was to James Wolfensohn, the head of the World Bank, a man whom Bono had been trying to meet ever since Jamie Drummond had first approached him, but with no luck. Shriver, however, had worked for Wolfensohn some ten years back, in between leaving law school and entering the music business. "So I called Jim and his office put me through to him in London, and I said, 'I'm sure you've heard of this Jubilee debt relief thing?' And he said, 'Of course.' And I said, 'I have this friend who's a singer, who is a sort of activist on this debt thing—and he'd like to meet you.' And he said, 'Oh no, I don't have time for that.' And I said, 'Jim, he's in Dublin. You're in London. Why doesn't he come over tomorrow? It's Sunday. You have nothing to do on Sunday.' And he said, 'Okay, tell him if he can be at the Berkeley Hotel at noon, I'll have lunch with him.' I called Bono, and said, 'If you can be at the Berkeley at noon tomorrow, Wolfensohn will have lunch with you.' And Bono said, 'Wow, can I bring Geldof [the knighted lead singer of the Boomtown Rats and founder of Live Aid]?' and I said, 'It's up to you, man. It's your lunch. Whatever you want.' And I called Wolfensohn back and said that Bono would be there at twelve and was going to bring this other guy."

The lunch was a disaster. "Afterwards Wolfensohn called me," recounts Bobby, "and he was furious because Geldof had yelled at him the whole time." Bono confirms it. "Yeah, Bob was like, you fucking this and you fucking that, and how can you fucking sit here in your fucking seat, you prick. And Jim Wolfensohn is a real debonair sort of gentleman, and he looked over at me with that look of 'help' on his face. But we got on."

"He liked Bono," says Shriver. "He thought he was bright. And said that if he wanted to work on trying to get money for debt relief he would do what he could to help."

Game on.

Next up was the highly influential central banker and former chairman of the Federal Reserve, Paul Volcker. "Volcker laughed at me when I first raised the idea of debt cancellation," recounts Bono.

"Just laughed out loud—ha ha! He said, 'I hate this idea. I hated it in 1968, I hated it in 1972, I hated it in 1985, and I hate it now. You're from Ireland, aren't you? You should stick to fishing.' " But Bono would not rise to the bait. He patiently explained that the Jubilee campaign was different. It wasn't just about canceling the debt, he told Volcker; it was a one-time opportunity to level the playing field, to put right the relationship between North and South, a relationship that had been wrong for far too long. His patience paid off. "At the end of a very long meeting," Bono recalls, "Volcker said 'Give me your phone number.' And he not only made a few calls on my behalf. He helped. It may have been behind the scenes, but he actually helped."

After Volcker came David Rockefeller, the wise old man of Wall Street, and former chairman of Chase Manhattan Bank. "That meeting went really well," Bobby remembers. "We discussed then-current initiatives, and the problems with these. We corresponded back and forth for several months." And after Rockefeller came Richard Holbrooke and after Holbrooke, Bob Hormats, vice chairman of Goldman Sachs.

Bono and Bobby were ready to hit D.C.

Robert Rubin, the U.S. treasury secretary at the time, was evasive. "I just couldn't get to him," recounts Bono. "I even said I would swim to wherever he was at one point." Rubin was a devotee of Alexander Hamilton, America's first treasury secretary, who famously insisted after the War of Independence that the individual states repay all their debt. Rubin, not surprisingly, was dead set against debt cancellation. But when they did eventually meet, thanks to Hillary Clinton's intervention, Rubin, although clearly never going to be an advocate, indicated that he would not stand in their way.

Word got to Bono and Shriver that Larry Summers, the treasury secretary–designate, might be more proactive. Summers had formerly been the chief economist at the World Bank, and development was a known passion of his. But, again, just getting the meeting wasn't easy.

"I didn't particularly see why I had to hang out with a singer I'd never heard of," Summers recounts. "But the young women on my staff told me I had to see him."

"It's true. Larry had no idea who Bono was, nor had he heard of U2," confirms Cheryl Sandberg, Summers's chief of staff at the time. "It was a cause of great hilarity in the office. But I was his chief of staff, which meant that requests came through me, and I would then make recommendations as to who the secretary should or should not see. As a cabinet member, your time is the only commodity you have, so we took the scheduling process very seriously. And when this request came in, I was, like, we're doing this meeting, we're not going to have a normal conversation."

But Summers wanted to lie low. About to be sworn in as treasury secretary, the last thing he needed was a gossip item about him meeting a pop star, perfect ammunition for his political enemies already labeling him a liberal flake. The meeting could not take place in his office. Instead, it was set up in the White House offices of Gene Sperling, the head of the National Economic Council, across the street from the Treasury.

"There were about six of us around the table when Bono walked in, wearing jeans and sunglasses, which is not what you'd expect in the White House," recounts Sandberg, "especially as Larry didn't really get that he's, like, a rock star."

"I didn't feel I had a very good meeting with Larry," says Bono now. "I didn't think the pitch went very well. It wasn't one of my better days, and he was drumming on the table with his fingers while I was talking, distracted."

But those at the meeting remember it differently. Stephanie Flanders, Summers's former speechwriter, was impressed. "He was massively informed on the subject," she recalls of Bono. "He was referring to a lot of turgid studies—documents on the debt issue, reports for Congress. Everyone was really impressed."

Sandberg agrees: "He knew what all the acronyms were, he knew how the debt flows worked, he knew about capital risk." Summers himself sums it up: "He turned out to actually know a ton about debt."

Finally, when the meeting was winding down, Bono, looking

Summers straight in the eye, said, "I've been all over the world, and every single person says if I can get Larry Summers, I can get this done. Because if *he* wants this done, it'll be done. So I'm here to get *you*."

Sandberg remembers the surprise on the faces around the table. "It was kind of just like, 'whoa,' she recalls. "Very few people come in with that much force and speak to the secretary of the treasury in that way. And it was very inspirational. I think we all wanted to believe that something like this could happen, that it was worth fighting for."

"Bono had an effect on me," admits Summers. "His presence suggested there was a big constituency out there who cared about debt." So although his response at the meeting was a noncommittal "let me think about it," Summers turned to Flanders when Bono had left the room, and said, "I think the administration has just had its consciousness raised. This guy's right. We have to fix this."

The first step was getting President Bill Clinton to pledge to cancel 100 percent of the debts owed to the United States by the world's poorest countries—a goal that Professor Sachs had persuaded Bono to push for. Although various debt-relief programs had been in place for the past few years, thanks largely to the British treasury's championing of the cause, they had required that creditors cancel only a percentage of what they were owed, rather than the whole amount. Debtor countries, therefore, never actually received what they needed to become solvent.

One hundred percent debt cancellation would send a clear signal to the international community that the to-ing and fro-ing on debt relief wasn't working. It would also set the standard for other creditors to follow suit.

"Cancellation," not "relief," of the debt was a distinction that had been made explicit a few months before, after Bono met with Sandy Berger, Clinton's national security adviser, the morning the United States had gone into Kosovo. "He hadn't been to bed," Bono remembers. "He'd been up all night, he was bleary-eyed, and Clinton had sent me down to meet him, you know, talk to him about it. So I'm sitting there and he was scrunching his red eyes, saying, 'Run that by me again? Debt relief, debt relief. God, that just sounds so wrong in this environment. You're a songwriter—can't you come up with something better than that?' And I said, 'Debt cancellation,' and he said, 'That's better. Relief sounds like a handout. Cancellation sounds like justice.' "

Selling the idea of canceling debt to Clinton wasn't hard. The president had just come back from the G8 meeting of the richest developed nations in Cologne, where debt relief had been high on the agenda. He had already pledged to contribute to funding the IMF's and World Bank's debt relief efforts, and also to increase the amount of American debt that would be canceled. But canceling *all* the debts owed to the United States was another matter. Could the United States really afford it?

It was up to Summers to convince the president.

"I remember a frantic weekend in which Larry, Gene [Sperling, who'd facilitated the first meeting with Summers], and Gene's niece, who he was minding, had come in on the Saturday to do the numbers and try to make it happen," recounts Bono. "Busy, busy people coming in on a Saturday to get shouted at and reasoned with. Trying to work out what it'd actually cost to cancel these debts. The extent to which they could be written down so that we could meet the 100 percent cancellation objective." (For, given that there was no real possibility of their ever being repaid in full, these debts could be discounted so as to reflect a realistic market value.)

"And we did it," says Summers with a smile. "In the last thirty-six hours we worked out that we could afford to do this." By writing down the value of their loans by approximately 90 percent, the real cost to the United States of canceling the $6 billion debts owed would amount to only around $600 million.

On September 29, 1999, in a speech at the World Bank, with Summers's numbers in his back pocket, President Clinton announced that the United States would cancel 100 percent of the $6 billion debt owed it by the world's poorest thirty-three countries— the first country in the world to make such a huge commitment.

Bono was in France when he heard the news of Clinton's announcement. "I got a phone call from Bobby and it felt like, you know, just the biggest thing ever. We had been working so hard, I was jumping up and down. It was a real breakthrough. One hundred percent, no nonsense, no games. The United States was stepping out in front. Okay, it was only thirty-three countries [Jubilee had been calling for the cancellation of the debts of fifty-two poor countries], but it was a clear melody, a clear-cut idea."

It seemed as though they were on track. But when Bono started to hear the critics say that Clinton was only doing this because he knew it wouldn't get past Congress, that Congress would never fund the scheme, he was reminded of just how complicated his mission was—because in the United States, it is Congress and not the administration that holds the purse strings. And Congress was controlled by the Republicans. If the money to fund Clinton's 100 percent debt cancellation pledge, as well as meet the commitment he had made at Cologne to contribute to bailing out the IMF and World Bank—$545 million in the first instance—was to be found, it was Republicans who were going to have to vote for that amount to be released.

Getting $545 million allocated to what was essentially foreign aid was, in a Republican-controlled Congress, never going to be easy. Giving money to poor countries doesn't tend to poll well for American politicians. "It was very hard even for people who wanted to be for this, to be for this," explains Sandberg. "Debt relief for Africa? The United States just doesn't do this."

It was time to get the Terminator involved.

Bobby Shriver, who had done such a majestic job in getting the bankers, liberals, and cognoscenti on board, wasn't the man when it came to bringing the Republicans around to his side: his Kennedy lineage got in the way. His sister Maria, however, was married to someone who helped him get over that problem. Arnold Schwarzenegger, the movie star and Bobby's brother-in-law, was already, five years before becoming governor of California, moving in Republican circles.

"Bono and I explained the idea to Arnold," remembers Bobby, "and Arnold thought about it and said, 'I know a guy who might help you. A friend of mine who's the congressman from Columbus, Ohio, John Kasich.' "

Kasich, whom Schwarzenegger knew through the Arnold Classic Body Building Contest, which is held in Columbus each year, was, at the time, the chairman of the Budget Committee in the House of Representatives, a very influential position. He was no namby-pamby liberal. "John was a hard, right-wing guy," says Shriver, "and someone who was very smart. Not book smart like Larry. But, you know, street smart. Smarter than most people in Congress. And he got what we were talking about. He had traveled overseas and could see that people did not like Americans. This was before 9/11. And he didn't like that. And he saw that canceling their debts for what, in his view, was a relatively small amount of money was a way to say to people, 'Look, we're not just a bunch of pricks flying B1 bombers over your country.' "

Kasich came on board, and his support was key. Not only did he bring with him other important members of the Republican leadership including House Speaker Dennis Hastert and House Majority Leader Dick Armey, but also lower-profile but equally essential Republican politicians from both House and Senate.

And, in November 1999, two months after Clinton's historic pledge, Congress agreed to appropriate $110 million.

Although this *was* a start, the $110 million was far less than the $545 million the campaigners had been after. This would cover only the first year of America's own debt cancellation schedule, and it didn't cover any financing for the participation of the regional development banks in the debt cancellation initiative; nor provide for the IMF and World Bank, the poor world's major creditors, to cancel any of their debts. If the Cologne international initiative was not to crumble, an additional $435 million had to be found.

"I called Bono," recalls Sandberg, "and said, 'If you want to help get this through, you've got to come back to town.' We needed him. Bono could get in to see any member of Congress, and we needed to rally support. He said that he was recording his new album and making a documentary, and couldn't come to town over the next few weeks because they were filming. And I said if you can't come now it'll be too late. Two days later, he was here. And once he landed in D.C., he was a machine. He went around from member to member telling them that they could change the world if they got behind us. He would get up early in the morning, and would walk the halls and work it all day. And then we would have dinner late at night and he would still bring a member of Congress or some staffer. He was tireless. And when you think of the combination of a rock star who can get in to see anyone and someone who knows as much as some staffer who works on it full-time and can speak with the kind of passion that he speaks with, well, the world had never seen anything like it."

But although politicians from every end of the political spectrum were falling under the Bono spell, one key man continued to hold out. Sonny Callahan, the libertarian conservative congressman from Alabama, was chairman of the Foreign Operations Subcommittee of the House Appropriations Committee, and he held the checkbook. It was up to him to recommend how much money to allocate to debt cancellation. And Callahan wasn't having any of it. He believed that the additional monies being asked for "would encourage the World Bank and others to continue to make bad loans and leave poor countries to have to borrow and get into debt all over again." As far as Callahan was concerned, debt cancellation was "money down a rathole."

Shriver got his feelers out and tried to influence Callahan through an old fishing friend, but to no avail. And, in June 2000, Callahan's committee recommended to the House of Representatives that Congress fund only $69 million of debt relief that year, even less than Congress had agreed to in November, a sixth of what the campaigners had been gunning for, and an amount, effectively, that meant Clinton would have to renege on both what he had pledged at Cologne and the 100 percent debt cancellation he had announced at the World Bank in September.

"We had basically failed," says Shriver. "With the committee reporting that, it was basically over. It's almost never the case that Congress overrides a committee recommendation."

There was one last avenue available. If they could stage, and then win, what is colloquially known as a "floor fight" in Congress, a challenge on the floor of the full House of Representatives against what the committee had recommended, the recommendation could be stopped from going through.

But to win that fight they would need even more Republicans on board. And they would need to work fast—the House and Senate would make their decision on how much to appropriate for debt relief by the beginning of the new fiscal year, October 1.

With less than four months to go, the campaigning shifted up to an even higher gear.

"John Kasich [Arnold Schwarzenegger's friend, the Republican chairman of the National Budget Committee] took the lead and agreed to launch the fight. But we needed to ensure that when he got up and said, 'We're not going to accept the committee's recommendation,' others would get up and say, "John is right—I agree with him. Let's not accept these recommendations, let's do the full $435 million,' " Shriver recalls. "So we met with Jim Leach from Iowa. We met with Clinton's staff. We started calling everybody who could help challenge Callahan's recommendation. And then we called them back again and again. We got Volcker to call them; we got the president to call them. We were like animals; we would not leave them alone."

Bono flew from Europe to Washington eight times that summer. "He came back and forth like a tired old dog," says Shriver. "I would do the red-eye from Los Angeles, meeting him there [in Washington]. We were pretty bedraggled. It had become beyond a full-time thing for the both of us. And when we weren't meeting face-to-face, we were back on the phone and writing to people and having conference calls, and asking people to write stuff, and finding out names of newspaper editors in key states, and then placing articles in papers."

"It was kind of like the theater of the absurd," remembers Bono, who was supposed to be delivering a new album, *All That You Can't Leave Behind,* while all this was going on. "There were even times that Bobby used to hide outside meetings that I would have with Republicans. I would go in and he would hide, stay outside. He'd say, 'I'm a Kennedy. You don't need me around here.' He would have flown from L.A. and be hiding outside."

The Bono-Shriver commitment, tenacity, and good humor encouraged their allies to try harder too.

Kasich pulled his considerable weight. "He was soundly determined," Shriver says. "And he's one of those fellows who when he
gets very determined you know you really don't want to cross him.
People knew that he would just, to put it bluntly, fuck them if they
didn't go along with him."

So they did.

Larry Summers went all out for them too. "He went to those
meetings at a time of hostility that is hard to imagine," remembers
Bono. "This was after the Monica Lewinsky affair, when there was a
terrible stink in the city, and he batted for us." Professor Jeffrey
Sachs hosted a prominent conference on debt cancellation in Washington and Gene Sperling played an integral part. "He was always
on the phone, always with great ideas of how to get things done," recounts Shriver. Democratic congresswomen Maxine Waters and
Nancy Pelosi did their bit to rally support, as did Republican congressmen Spencer Bachus and Jim Leach, Republican senator Orrin
Hatch (whom Shriver had got on board early on), AFL-CIO president John Sweeney, Ray Offenheiser of Oxfam America, and Jim
McDonald of Bread for the World. The U.S. affiliate of the Jubilee
campaign did a lot of legwork on Capitol Hill to educate congress-
people and their staff, producing form letters for their supporters to
send to their representatives, and providing e-mail addresses of
swing senators and representatives that campaigners could send out.
And big business was brought on board—Goldman Sachs, Motorola, Bechtel, Caterpillar, and Merck all signed an open statement
calling for the full $435 million to be found.

But if the congressional floor fight was to succeed, they'd need yet
more support. Various key Republicans were still holding out, and
Callahan needed to be, at the very least, out of the way.

It was time to call upon Jesus.

And it was Eunice Shriver who had his number. She was pals with
the Reverend Billy Graham, the TV evangelist with a virtual congre-
gation of hundreds of millions. Graham agreed to make a video for
Bono and Bobby that they then sent around to recalcitrant members

of Congress, a two-minute, no-bells-no-whistles video in which he asked them to support Bono's Jubilee cause.

Jesse Helms, the notoriously conservative, hugely influential Republican senator from North Carolina and chairman of the Senate Committee on Foreign Relations, a man who symbolized opposition to foreign aid of any sort, wasn't sent a video—he was, after all, Graham's own senator, and knew him well. But Graham's office played an important part in enabling what became a critical meeting between Bono and Helms—they vouched for Shriver. And with this endorsement, Helms agreed to the meeting.

"Bono connected with him in a spiritual way," recounts Shriver. "The two talked about the vast gulf between Africa's misery and America's prosperity. About the Bible, children, and so forth. And Helms was very moved by Bono's sincerity and evident knowledge. Not only in terms of the Scripture, but in terms of the financing. He said he would come on board."

Helms's support was what Bono had been waiting for. His entry into the fold gave permission to all those politicians who were in his anti–foreign aid camp to stop opposing debt cancellation. What's more, the very public way in which Helms joined the team, with stories of the hard man of American politics in tears during his meeting with Bono doing the rounds, meant that the final laggards—people like Phil Gramm from Texas, who might have opposed any challenge to the committee's recommendation—could now safely be counted upon not to do so.

Sonny Callahan was the last holdout.

"It was a story Harry Belafonte told me that made me go for Sonny's bishop," recounts Bono. "Harry Belafonte said that he remembered being with Martin Luther King and a group of Dr. King's key supporters when Bobby Kennedy was made attorney general. The team around Dr. King was very depressed, because at the time Bobby was known to be quite reactionary on civil rights. They saw it as a very black day for the civil rights movement, and they were all bitching about Bobby Kennedy, about what a hopeless case it was. And Dr. King told them to stop bitching and said, 'Look, there must be one redeeming thing about this guy—give me one redeeming thing.' And they said: 'Look, I'm telling you, Martin, there's nothing redeeming about him. He's an Irish racist.' And Dr. King closed the meeting and said: 'Come back when you've got one redeeming thing.' And when they met again two weeks later they said, 'We've found something.' 'What?' said King. 'His bishop. He's very close to his bishop. He's a religious guy and he really listens to his bishop.' So they went and met with the bishop. And then Harry tells me, in this incredible voice that he has, 'When Bobby Kennedy lay in a pool of his own blood in Los Angeles, there was no greater friend to the civil rights movement.'

"He moved. Any man can move one hundred and eighty degrees. Harry had told me this as a sort of way of steering my way, and I have used the story many times as a guide. But in the case of Sonny I used it literally.

"There were priests in the pulpit. Priests and pastors sermonizing on debt relief on Sundays, telling their congregations to tell Callahan to take care of this, including my own bishop. Eventually I gave in," concedes Callahan. "What else could I have done?"

When the floor fight finally did take place in early September and Kasich got up as planned and voiced his objections, Callahan didn't stand in the way. Members from both sides of the aisle, in a rare moment of bipartisanship, voted to override the committee's recommendations.

And on October 25, 2000, Congress agreed to provide $435 million for debt relief, the entire amount the campaigners had hoped for.

The Herculean efforts of Bono and Shriver are a beacon to what the civic community *can* achieve and leave us with a permanent hope that we *can* get politicians to act. But did the great American gesture inspired by Bono and Shriver actually resolve the developing world's debt crisis? Did the Cologne initiative that they had been backing ever provide the world's poorest countries the opportunity to make a "fresh start"? Were the IMF and World Bank loans ever canceled? Was the $435 million the start of a renewed commitment on the part of the United States and other countries to funding development? Or were the difficulties in securing it a warning of how hard it would continue to be to raise money domestically for foreign aid?

And what about less poor but still highly indebted countries like Brazil or Turkey or Pakistan, which were not included in the debt cancellation program? How likely is it that emerging markets such as these, if their debts continue to build up, will also reach crisis point and be forced to call a default? And how destabilizing to the world economy would such a scenario be? With what political consequences?

And how about the two issues that most threaten the stability of our future—the environment and terrorism? How connected are they to the debt story? Is debt an issue that should be of concern just to financiers, number crunchers, and churchgoers? Or should defusing the debt threat be of utmost importance to us all?

But first, how on earth had most of the developing world at the end of the millennium ever get into a situation where it was so visibly drowning in debt? How had debt, surely a positive instrument for development, ended up becoming the cause of so much desperation and despair? What had gone so dreadfully wrong?

The
Background

2

It's Politics, Stupid

Imagine
your bank
manager saying to
you, "I'll lend you as
much money as you
want, as long as you'll
be my friend."

Debt-endency

"Eat, sleep, and shit" was all Mao Zedong said he did while in Moscow in December 1949, his first ever trip abroad. He should have added "and wait." Because in between crapping, snacking, and napping, that was primarily what he did. Ensconced in virtual seclusion in one of Stalin's dachas, in a birch forest a few miles to the west of Moscow with nothing but biographical films of Stalin to watch, Mao Zedong waited for weeks to be received by the "Steel Man" whom he had traveled 5,300 miles by train to see.

The purpose of his trip was twofold: first, to ask Stalin for a $300 million loan on behalf of the newly established People's Republic of China (Mao had no other source of hard currency)—the United

States wouldn't lend to China and China's economy was in difficulty); and second, to establish a new Sino-Soviet treaty of alliance.

Given that the Soviet Union was itself strapped for cash and in the process of trying to rebuild its own war-torn economy, $300 million was a huge amount for it to lend out. Moreover, Stalin needed time to work out whether an alliance with Communist China was really in the Soviet interest, and more specifically whether Mao, a man he considered a "cave Marxist," someone with no real understanding of socialism, was a necessary ally. Would he be an asset or a liability?

Eventually, Stalin buried his doubts. China was too important to risk losing. A number of countries, including India, had officially recognized the People's Republic, and Stalin was worried that continued procrastination would risk alienating the Chinese Communists. Stalin also realized that by lending to China, the Soviet Union would be able to bank a favor it could later call in. He agreed to establish the treaty and authorized the loan.

The wisdom of the decision was soon vindicated. Only a few months later the Korean War erupted, and within weeks of the American landing at Inchon, the Russian-backed North Korean army was on the verge of annihilation. An anxious Stalin requested Chinese intervention and Mao, partly prompted by his desire to prove that Soviet support of China had been justified, obliged. Ironically, and much to Mao's irritation, almost all of the $300 million Soviet loan ended up being used to buy Soviet weapons to fight a prolonged war in Korea on Stalin's behalf.

Four years later the question of debt reared its head once more in Sino-Soviet relations. In 1954, Stalin's successor Nikita Khrushchev, in a show of "fraternal" support, offered another $500 million to Mao Zedong—at a very low interest rate of only 2 percent. The loan was meant to be paid back between 1966 and 1967, but this time China returned the debt ahead of schedule, much to Khrushchev's surprise. As he told the Central Committee Plenum in February 1964, the Chinese could have reaped great financial rewards on such a low-interest loan. In fact, the Soviets had made this clear to Beijing. But Mao insisted on repayments. "Can any of the economists understand this?" Khrushchev asked. "It is difficult to understand. Only Mao Zedong can understand this."

Mao had insisted on repaying the Soviets so quickly because he understood all too clearly that the cost of debt cannot be measured *only* in financial terms. He saw that loans from other governments often also come at a huge political cost: binding countries to each other and creating a dependency that first establishes and then serves to reinforce preexisting power asymmetries, and he didn't want to risk being so dependent on the Soviet Union that he lost political maneuverability and endangered his own sovereignty. This was a conclusion similar to that reached by Simon Bolívar, the liberator of the Andean Spanish colonies (a rough amalgam of Venezuela, Colombia, and Ecuador as they are today) over a hundred years before. "I despise debt more than I do the Spanish!" Bolívar had said to his comrades-in-arms, explaining that "it threatens the independence that had cost so much in blood." And this was echoed much more recently by the Indian government in 2002, when it paid off its most expensive multilateral loans (loans to the IMF, World Bank, and regional development banks) early, and again in 2003 when Prime Minister Atal Behari Vajpayee announced to twenty-two donor countries that he did not want to receive their aid on a government-to-government basis anymore as India was no longer willing to accept the conditions that came with it. It was echoed again by Thaksin Shinawatra, prime minister of Thailand in 2003 when he repaid a year before it was due the $12 billion loan his country had secured from the IMF in the wake of the Asian financial crisis. Against a backdrop of a massive national flag and with patriotic theme songs blaring, he swore to his audience that this was "the last time the country would be indebted to the IMF," while reminding them of what a "pain to the nation" the debt had been.

But the responses of Mao, Bolívar, and Vajpayee and Shinawatra are not typical. Most developing countries have not and do not take a stance against borrowing. Instead, developing world leaders have on the whole accepted, indeed in many cases *embraced,* loans from whichever government has proffered them. We will come back to the reasons later on.

It's a Cold War

At no time in recent history have loans been proferred as "generously" as during those not so distant days of the cold war. It was a money-for-influence circus with China, the Soviet Union, and the United States all pursuing communism around the ring; a time of two political and economic ideologies and three camps—the capitalist bloc under the auspices of the United States, and the Chinese and Soviet socialist blocs—with each camp seeking to win the allegiance of the greatest number. It was a time when loans to countries and regions shot up in direct proportion to their perceived geopolitical influence or ideological loyalties and when loans were used as a means of securing powerful allegiances and ensuring political stability.

In 1960, for example, when South Asia and the Far East were perceived as the main "Red threats," 50 percent of all U.S. aid (loans and grants) was sent to key "domino" countries like South Korea, Vietnam, Thailand, India, Pakistan, and Iran. Between 1945 and 1952, when the Soviet penetration of Europe was perceived by the Americans as their greatest threat, it was *Europe* that received $13.3 billion in U.S. aid (in that case mainly grants) while other regions had to make do with significantly less.

The Bay of Pigs fiasco, in which the United States attempted and failed to overthrow the Communist regime of Fidel Castro, moved Latin America onto America's list of preferred borrowers. In a speech soon after the invasion, John F. Kennedy spoke of "the struggle in many ways more difficult than war . . . a struggle . . . taking place every day, without fanfare, in thousands of villages and markets . . . and in classrooms all over the globe." It was a struggle that needed, Kennedy believed, foreign financial assistance to win. Why? Not for the sugarcoated reasons laid out in his inauguration speech only a few months before.

> To those people in the huts and villages of half the globe struggling to break the bonds of mass misery, we pledge our best efforts to help them help themselves, for whatever period is required, not be-

cause the Communists may be doing it, not because we seek their votes, but because it is right.

But, rather, it was because if the Americans didn't provide loans, the "Reds" would. As Kennedy proclaimed later, in an address at the Waldorf-Astoria hotel on a blustery winter night just weeks after the resolution of the Cuban missile crisis:

> Less than a month ago this Nation reminded the world that it possessed both the will and the weapons to meet any threat to the security of free men. The gains we have made will not be given up, and the course that we have pursued will not be abandoned. But in the long run, that security will not be determined by military and diplomatic moves alone. . . . Aid is a method by which the United States maintains a position of influence and control around the world and sustains a good many countries which would definitely collapse or pass into the Communist bloc. . . . Really I put it right at the top of the essential programs in protecting the security of the free world.

And, indeed, Latin America's external debt increased from $12.6 billion (thousand million) to $28.9 billion between 1960 and 1970, a 230 percent increase, the majority of which was provided by the American government and the World Bank, the institute set up after World War II to aid *world* economic stability, but which throughout the cold war was blatantly used by the United States as a conduit of *its* foreign policy. Among loans made by the Bank were those to Nicaragua's U.S.-friendly Somoza regime, and to Yugoslavia once it broke from the Soviet bloc and the United States had recommended that the West offer the country "discreet and unostentatious support." Among loans withheld by the Bank were those to Poland in 1948, because the United States didn't want money going to a Communist country, and to Salvador Allende's Chile at a time when Richard Nixon had given orders to "make the enemy [Chile] scream." The lending to Chile resumed a few months after Allende was killed in a military coup.

Everyone's At It

The rivalry during the cold war was not just between America and the Communist "other." Throughout, China and the Soviet Union also battled each other for who would prevail in the Communist world, often also using loans as a means to hold sway.

In 1965, for example, during the Vietnam conflict while Moscow was bankrolling Hanoi's purchases of arms and ammunition, Deng Xiaoping reportedly offered an enormous loan of 4 billion yuan ($1.6 billion) if Vietnam agreed to abandon economic ties with Moscow.

Or take Soviet lending to decolonized Africa in the late 1950s and early 1960s. Initially this had almost nothing to do with the cold war rivalry between Moscow and Washington. Nor was this an altruistic act. Instead it was a direct outcome of an intensifying competition with the Chinese for the leadership of the international Communist and national liberation movements: securing influence in Africa was seen as greatly important in that quest, and if it took hundreds of millions of dollars in loans to do it—as it did—so be it.

In that case, however, the West soon also got involved. The patronage of Africa by the Chinese and the Soviets threatened *it*. As a British Foreign Office document of 1959 warned:

> If Africa is to remain loyal to the Western cause, its economic interests must coincide with, and reinforce, its political sympathies; and one of the major problems of the relationship between the West and Africa will be to ensure an adequate flow of economic assistance, and particularly capital, through various channels to the newly emerging states. On any reckoning the amounts required will be considerable; and, if the Western Powers are unreasonably insensitive to the economic aspirations of independent Africa, the Governments of the new states may be compelled to turn to the Soviet Union for the assistance that they will certainly need.

With that threat looming Washington launched a dual strategy to provide "friendly" African regimes with weapons and also to channel funds to them through their own development agency, US-AID, along with the World Bank and other international financial institutions. As one National Security Council memorandum recommended in 1965: "US-AID should be used as a political weapon with the major assistance going to African friends of the U.S."

This of course meant that now that the Sino-Soviet love affair with Africa was officially a ménage à trois; the Soviets started to lend even more to key countries in the region to ensure that the parties they were backing didn't switch camps. This led to the increasingly commonplace and clearly undesirable situation of rival groups within the same country being funded by either the East or the West. In Angola, for example, the Soviet Union provided loans for MPLA to purchase weapons, while FNLA and UNITA, MPLA's enemies, purchased their weapons with *American* dollars.

How ironic that loans made during the cold war in the name of security and peace even at the time were clearly engendering conflict and instability. And how indicative of one of the major ironies of cold war lending: that, in the pursuit of addressing immediate national security concerns, the world's superpowers played significant roles in laying the foundations for future insecurity and instability.

They did this in two ways. First, their profligate lending actively helped to jack up the debt mountain so that the Third World owed levels way above what many of its countries could realistically service, sowing the seeds of the crisis the developing world currently faces. And second, the frequent bankrolling of tyrannical, corrupt, or self-seeking regimes, regimes that never considered the needs of the majority of their people in their investment decisions, has left legacies of increasing levels of domestic poverty, conflict, unrest, and civil strife.

The corrupt regime of Mobutu Sese Seko in Zaire (now the Democratic Republic of Congo), for example, received half of all U.S. aid to black Africa in the late 1970s. Zaire's favored borrowing status persisted even after a damning internal memo was made public in 1978 by Karin Lissakers (later to become U.S. executive director of the IMF). The memo did not mince its words: "The corruptive system in Zaire with all its wicked manifestations is so serious that there is no (repeat no) prospect for Zaire's creditors to get their money back." Mobutu's spending sprees became quite legendary: Concorde chartered for private shopping trips to Paris; dozens of estates bought in Continental Europe; the building of the world's largest supermarket, and of a steelworks that one banker said the country needed "like it needs central heating," to name but a few. Yet despite the absolute clarity of the 1978 IMF memo and the progressive worsening of Mobutu's spending, in 1987 the United States (through the IMF) pushed through yet another loan in exchange for Mobutu making his territory available for U.S. covert action against neighboring Angola. Today the people of the Democratic Republic of Congo have to spend 37 percent of government revenues servicing their debt—not great for a country whose gross national income per capita is $90.

Another tyrannical regime, that of Saddam Hussein, was provided with loans amounting to around $100 billion, several times Iraq's GDP, during the 1980s by governments intent on serving their own geopolitical purposes. Half of this money came from Arab states, led by Saudi Arabia, in order to support Iraq's invasion of Iran. On top of this came $7 billion worth of credits from the Russians, $6 billion from the French, several billion from the Germans and British, and at least $10 billion from the United States, much of which was covertly pumped into Iraq throughout the mid-1980s through their export credit agencies—institutions we will be looking at in the next chapter.

While European loans to Iraq were made primarily to serve the interests of their domestic arms dealers, geopolitics played a significant part in the United States' decision to lend there. It emerged in the 1990 Iraqgate-BNL (Banca Nazionale del Lavoro) scandal, backed by hundreds of U.S. documents, that hundreds of millions of dollars of U.S. Department of Agriculture loans had been channeled to help Iraq build its military capacity: "BNL's loans to Iraq were part of a covert operation coordinated with Italian officials by the Reagan administration and continued by George Bush. The scheme was designed to finance the secret rearming of Iraq, both to balance the scales in the Iran-Iraq war and to gain bargaining leverage for 50 or so U.S. hostages who were at the time being held by the Iranians at the U.S. embassy in Tehran."

Clear geopolitical interest dictated lending policy throughout the cold war. This meant that both tyrannical regimes and regimes that didn't even pay lip service to the lenders' ideological beliefs were bankrolled by the West and the East to secure allegiance or to realize strategic goals. Zaire was lent money by the Americans although it never adopted a free market economy. Angola was lent money by the Soviets despite its insincere playacting at socialism. Saddam was lent monies by the West and Arab states up until the 1991 Gulf War despite the fact that his chemical gas bombing of the Kurdish city of Halabja in 1988, which killed 5,000 of his own people and wounded 10,000 others, was by then common knowledge. The Argentinian military junta of the 1970s was lent money by the United States despite the fact that it was known to be "disappearing" tens of thousands of people during its reign. As Lyndon Johnson famously observed in defense of Washington's support of Ngo Dinh Diem, the corrupt and brutal but Communist-fighting South Vietnamese leader to whom over $4 billion of loans and grants was given: "Shit, Diem's the only boy we got out there."

The superpowers gained an obvious advantage through these loans. But why did Third World countries borrow such huge amounts of money from other countries when the quid pro quo was so explicit? When in exchange they had to promise allegiance? It's not too difficult to answer that.

In the worst cases, it was because their leaders knew that they could easily ill manage, misappropriate, or divert funds—no bank manager would be peering over them, asking them on what they would be spending the money, or how they might pay it back.

In others, it was because the borrower country simply wasn't in Mao's or Bolívar's or Vajpayee's or Shinawatra's position—desperate for cash, these nations *needed* to borrow money from abroad. Domestic savings weren't sufficient to finance necessary investments for growth and development or in some cases even current consumption requirements. Exports weren't providing enough foreign exchange to fund imports and service existing debts. Commodity price shocks (such as the oil hike in the 1970s) meant that they needed to offset their impacts (just as a person might take out a loan to tide them over when they lose their job). Grants weren't available at levels of magnitude needed. And either loans weren't available elsewhere or the monies being offered by the bilateral (government-to-government) lenders were being offered at significantly better terms than other alternatives, often at well below market rates.

But more often than not, and why the amounts borrowed were often far above what was actually needed, it was because the battle for power between the East and West seemed as though it would never end. As long as the superpowers were fighting it out, most Third World countries believed that they could continue playing one off against the other, and that they would remain in the money. They believed that the "banks" wouldn't foreclose, and that the tap, which ensured that new loans were always forthcoming and that rescheduling was always an option, would never be turned off.

Although there were times when there was a real, legitimate, or proper need to borrow, the lending process had become divorced from sober economics (where a low-cost loan is put to sound economic use). Sometimes loans *were* used productively. Brazil, for example, took out many loans during the cold war to invest in developing its manufacturing industry; some of Africa's loans were used to invest in its infrastructure. And the lenders, for their part, were sometimes sensible enough to make loans to countries that were rich in oil, minerals, coffee, and other exportable resources. In other words, countries that were creditworthy. More often than not, however, the lending process was so distorted by geopolitics that the logic that underpins sound borrowing—that one incurs a debt in the hope of making an investment that will produce enough money both to pay off the debt and to generate economic growth that is self-sustaining—was simply absent. As too was the criterion that underpins sound lending—that the lendee will likely be able to repay the loan. And this isn't selective reporting. While it may be that good news is sometimes not reported, and there are undoubtedly more "positive" debt stories out there than I have highlighted, there is no question that in the vast majority of cases this is the way it was.

All Change

Once the cold war ended, things changed. The allegiance of strategically important Third World countries was suddenly perceived as unnecessary. Loans were called in overnight, and new lending (which was the way many countries had been able to service old debts in the past) was either curtailed or provided under far less generous or far more conditional terms.

Moscow, in its new post-Soviet guise and now suffering its own economic collapse, began harassing the former Soviet Union's satellite states for repayment of outstanding loans, having quite happily rescheduled them in the past. President Clinton started championing "trade-not-aid" policies, despite the fact that the by now aid-addicted countries were massively weighed down with significant debt burdens that they would never be able to service through trade alone, especially given the protectionist trade policies of the West, which meant that the very goods that the developing world could have hoped to export to the developed were as a consequence rendered uncompetitive.

Countries that had played off the superpowers so effectively during the cold war now saw themselves fast abandoned by their former sponsors. North Korea was so feted by the Soviets in the 1960s that the Russians, based solely on the North Korean argument "You must take into account that the Americans have already built an oil refinery in South Korea," even provided loans for a North Korean oil refinery, despite the fact that the country had no oil of its own. But by the early 1990s, the Russians had drastically cut back their support.

Regimes that had once enjoyed the benefit of blind eyes in the lending nations were now suddenly chastised. Zaire, for example, began receiving tough messages to combat corruption from its long-time donors—messages that had never been delivered when Mobutu's support had been valued.

With a lack of concern and seriousness that can only shock, aid was significantly cut back too. Between the last days of the cold war, and the last days of the millennium, development aid in general fell by 40 percent, despite the worsening financial and health conditions in much of the Third World, and despite the fact that countries were by now drowning in levels of debt to service. Entire regions were abandoned by their former "protectors": most of Latin America saw its U.S. backing disappear and Africa was hit hard. As the *African Research Bulletin* explained in 1994: "The Cold War's demise . . . has proven a setback for black Africa. Superpower rivalry once gave crucial purchase to poor lands with prized real estate for military bases, or a grip on maritime 'choke points,' or large reserves of strategic materials. . . . Africa's leverage has markedly weakened."

Many nations caught in the backdraft of the new global power vacuum were left to scramble for new loans, aid, and "patrons," in often quite poignant ways. In 1993, Vietnam made the extraordinary offer to take up the debts of the former South Vietnam hoping that honoring the repudiated wartime debt would help it to attract more Western loans. This was particularly poignant given that Vietnam, by agreeing to do so, was essentially agreeing to assume the debt burden of its former foe. Also, the country was (and continues to be) one of the world's most highly indebted poor countries. So when Vietnam eventually agreed to pay the United States $146 million of South Vietnam's wartime debt in 1997, that $146 million represented three-quarters of the nation's annual health budget. But as Nguyen Manh Hoa, director of the external financial division of the Finance Ministry explained: "We had to agree on old debts so we could have new relations, such as new loans and cooperation agreements."

By the mid-1990s, most developing countries found themselves having to face huge bilateral cold war–era debts, often ones that had been racked up by regimes long since vanished. In the new environment the lender had become much less understanding, and borrowers, in order to get their loans rescheduled or relieved, had to jump through many tortuous hoops (as we will see in later chapters).

Debts that had been warmly welcomed by Third World leaders as something they could use to their advantage, became in the post–cold war era a ball and chain weighing their countries down.

Of course, not all countries faced similar abandonment. Some retained their geopolitical importance, and continue to this day to receive loans and have their debts rescheduled or even canceled. Turkey's regular bailing out, for example, is testimony to its position as a "gateway to oil," as well as to its geopolitical importance to NATO. Even after its disagreement with the United States over the deployment of American troops during the war on Iraq, Turkey was offered up to $8.5 billion in loan guarantees to "relieve potential balance of payments needs that may result from hostilities."

Sometimes a country is considered too close physically to be allowed to fail. This is certainly what drove President Clinton to make Mexican president Ernesto Zedillo a $20 billion loan in 1995, despite the fact that 85 percent of the American public were at the time against the bailout. "Bob Rubin and [Lawrence] Summers told me if we don't do this, Mexico'll collapse, Brazil'll collapse. We had no option," Clinton now explains.

In other cases, the battle for a country's allegiance is still up for grabs. The Chinese and Taiwanese, for example, continue to mirror the bipolar world of the cold war by competing for diplomatic recognition in Africa and the Pacific on the basis of which can give the most aid, with their "clients" playing them off against each other as effectively as ever. Or a country is needed on your side to fight the twenty-first century's new wars. Pakistani president General Pervez Musharraf's support for the war on terrorism after September 11, for example, was rewarded with a $1 billion debt write-off, nearly a third of what Pakistan owed the United States. And on December 13, 2001, just two months after the attack on the twin towers, the Paris Club (the group of sovereign creditors to which a country must go to negotiate debt rescheduling) offered Pakistan a $12 billion "stock reprofiling" of loans for thirty-eight years under which it would have to pay nothing in debt service during the first fifteen years—terms that it would have never got a few months earlier. While in January 2003, Ethiopia saw a $30 million write-off of its U.S. debts over a year before this was due under the Cologne initiative. The timing was clearly chosen to serve the United States' own interests—this was, after all, precisely when America was looking to shore up support for the war against Iraq in the developing world.

On other occasions, a country is given a loan simply in order to maintain influence in a region. The French provided loans to the Habyarimana regime in Rwanda in 1992 to buy weapons including Kalashnikov rifles, antipersonnel mines, plastic explosives, mortars, and long-range artillery, in order to maintain its credibility and influence in French-speaking Africa. The United States tends to bail out countries that are facing financial crises not only if they are nearby but also if they are playing host to a U.S. military base. South Korea, with its large American troop presence, won U.S. help during the 1997–98 Asian crisis, for example, but Thailand and Indonesia did not.

To this day, the moral character of the borrower often remains an irrelevance. Turkey was offered the 2003 aid and debt restructuring package, for example, despite its continuing human rights abuses (although it has been making progress in its treatment of the Kurds). The French loans to Rwanda were made to a regime known to be highly repressive and were in all likelihood the monies used to buy the weapons used to commit the terrible 1994 genocide. America's post-9/11 debt relief package to Pakistan was made in spite of the fact that calls to Pakistan to reinstate democracy following the 1999 coup that brought Musharraf to power had not been heeded. And various central Asian countries continue to be provided with loans by the United States in exchange for their support in its war against terrorism, despite their own ongoing human rights violations.

It is abundantly clear that the lender is not an almsgiver in the world of realpolitik. The agenda is to serve the perceived self-interest of the lender, debt to be granted and withdrawn as he sees fit.

Under Their Thumbs

Just think how such naked self-interest could be interpreted by the borrower country's people. In many cases, these people never got any benefits from the monies borrowed, either because the loans were used by despots to retain their internal power base or because they were unwisely spent. And then add this: the thought of how easy it is to interpret debt as a tool of subjugation, whereby countries are kept in debt specifically to keep the weak weak, the poor poor, the powerless powerless, not only to maintain preexisting social and economic hierarchies but also to strengthen and reinforce them—something Mao Zedong, as we saw, so clearly feared.

Countries are usually given debt relief only if, as we will see, they conform to the rich world's own set of rules. Creditors are allowed to negotiate en masse, while the articles of the Paris Club explicitly deny that right to borrower countries. The U.S. Treasury did not even consider providing Nicaragua and Honduras with debt relief in the wake of Hurricane Mitch in 1998, Treasury Department officials actually admitting at the time that "loss of leverage" was their reason for refusing to consider comprehensive debt cancellation for the two countries. The United States decided in July 2003 to withhold military aid from countries that refused to exempt American soldiers from prosecution by the International Criminal Court. Many examples seem to give this interpretation credence. But the extent to which this interpretation is accurate is almost beside the point. The fact that debt can so easily be interpreted in this way creates very real problems of its own—problems that, as we will see in later chapters, can harm all of us, wherever we are.

For using debt as a highly effective mechanism of control will only serve to engender discontent in the very countries where the West seeks to exert influence, particularly given the heavy-handed way in which the lender often displays his dominance. When Yemen, for example, voted against UN Resolution 678, which authorized the first Gulf War, a senior U.S. diplomat commented on the occasion, "This will be the most expensive 'no' vote you have ever cast." A $70 million U.S. aid project for Yemen was subsequently canceled.

This despite the fact that Yemen was (and remains) one of the world's most highly indebted poor countries, and that life expectancy there was only forty-six. It was not surprising, then, that there were very large anti-American demonstrations in Yemen in 1991 and the U.S. embassy was attacked with small-arms fire.

So we begin to unpack the story of developing world debt. And what an unsavory chapter this one has been proven to be. It is true that there are a few cases where countries have tended to lend for relatively altruistic or disinterested purposes (Finland and the Netherlands spring to mind), but any general interpretation of lending to developing countries as being primarily motivated by a desire to help Kennedy's "struggling" masses would clearly be naive. For the story behind country-to-country lending is on the whole one neither of altruism nor even of enlightened self-interest. The self-interest is more usually myopic. The altruism is missing.

While it is true that in some cases, whatever motivated the lender, loans *did* result in high economic and social returns, all too often the outcome was one of bad guys getting benefits while the poor, marginalized, and vulnerable saw very little of the spoils.

As we have seen, some developing countries who could afford to have taken a stance against borrowing. Some others have had no choice and on occasion have used the loans for productive investment, but the majority have taken what they could get from the eagerly proffering superpowers. As a result, most of them, after the end of the cold war, are mired in impossible levels of debt repayment that profoundly damage their country's well-being. The lenders, for their part, not only provided the means, and sometimes the weapons, for internal and external wars; they also provided the means to shore up dictatorships and corruption in pursuit of immediate national security concerns.

This chapter has been the story of reckless borrowing and of profligate lending, the antithesis of a rational process of lending and borrowing where a loan is requested and granted in circumstances where it is believed that the investment will produce enough money both to pay off the debt and generate self-sustaining economic growth. It is also the story of a complete failure to understand long-term security considerations. The slashing of aid to the world's poorest countries after the end of the cold war, for example, under the misconception that this signaled the end of an era of high security risks, has undoubtedly played a contributory role in creating the insecure world we all now inhabit.

The shortsighted decisions created by geopolitical considerations devoid of humanity—or even intelligent self-interest—are a crucial component in the building story of the debt threat.

3

Backing the Bad Guys

> Imagine
> you went to your
> bank manager and said,
> "Can you lend me a few hundred
> million for a project that is
> environmentally unsound, highly
> corrupt, and unlikely to even
> materialize . . ." or alternatively,
> "How about a few hundred mil so
> that I can blow somebody's
> brains out?"

A Timeless Illustration

On February 5, 2003, Secretary of State Colin Powell presented a dossier to the UN Security Council with reasons for why the world should go to war against Iraq.

One reason was the existence of a chemical weapons plant, "chlorine plant Faluja 2," fifty miles outside of Baghdad, a plant that the United States claimed was a key component in Iraq's chemical warfare arsenal and that even the cautious Hans Blix, the former

UN chief weapons inspector, had reported to the Security Council might have to be destroyed.

Given that that dossier was used not only by the United States but also Britain as a justification for war, it is somewhat ironic that it was the British government that had been responsible for building the £14 million factory seventeen years before. In 1985, the British export credit agency ECGD, a government agency that funds or insures British corporations wanting to do business in high-risk areas, had provided insurance to a British subsidiary of a German company, Uhde Ltd., so that it could set up the plant in Iraq.

Did the British government know that this plant they were underwriting with British taxpayer money could be used to develop chemical weapons? Uh, yes. At the time, senior government officials wrote that there was a "strong possibility" that the plant was intended by the Iraqis to make mustard gas. Meanwhile, the British Ministry of Defense warned that the plant could be used to make chemical weapons, noting that the chlorine the factory would produce could "be used in the manufacture of phosphorus trichloride, a key nerve agent precursor." Richard Luce, a Foreign Office minister, went so far as to express concern that this deal would ruin Britain's image if news of it were to get out, and counseled, "I consider it essential everything possible be done to oppose the proposed sale and deny the company concerned ECGD cover." The Tory British trade minister at the time, Paul Channon, nevertheless revealed all too clearly where the British government's priorities lay. "A ban would do our other trade prospects in Iraq no good," he said.

Those "other prospects" turned out to be lucrative arms deals. The radio manufacturer Racal shipped several sophisticated Jaguar V radios to Saddam's army in 1985 thanks to ECGD insurance of £42 million, radios that enabled Saddam to overcome enemy jamming on the battlefield. In 1987, Marconi was given ECGD funding to sell Armets—the Artillery Metrological System, crucial for accurate artillery fire—to the Iraqi army; Tripod Engineering was given ECGD backing in 1988 to sell a fighter pilot training complex to the Iraqi air force; and Thorn EMI was given ECGD backing for a contract to ship Cymbeline mortar-locating radar to the Iraqi army. The British government even continued to issue export credits to Iraq after a British journalist, Farzad Bazoft, was executed by Saddam in 1990.

And it wasn't just the British whose export credit agencies (ECAs) were underwriting sales by domestic companies to dubious and dangerous projects in Iraq during Saddam's reign or even financing the entire deals themselves. Pretty much the whole world was at it.

At the same time that the British were smoothing the way for Uhde to set up a chemical weapons facility, the White House, for example, was pressuring *its* ECA, the U.S. Export-Import Bank (Ex-Im), to approve financing for a new oil pipeline in Iraq, a pipeline that Bechtel would build if the deal went ahead. "The State Department has exerted strong pressure on Ex-Im to make additional credits available, including for this pipeline," noted Bechtel official H. C. Clark in an internal memo on February 29, 1984. This despite the fact that the horrors of Saddam's reign were well-known, and reports of his gassing of thousands of Iranian troops with chemical weapons during the Iran-Iraq war had received public attention.

With Donald Rumsfeld, then Reagan's Middle East envoy, and George Schultz, secretary of state at the time (and former Bechtel president), both playing key lobbying roles, their efforts paid off. On June 21, 1984, Ex-Im's board of directors approved a preliminary commitment of $484.5 million in loan guarantees for the pipeline project.

But hang on a minute. Is there some connection between deals like those struck by Uhde, Racal, Thorn EMI, and Bechtel and our story of debt? Yes. Because when such deals go sour—following the commencement of hostilities in Kuwait, for example, the Iraqi government stopped honoring their contract with Uhde—the Western Export Credit Agency, the underwriter of the deal, pays the corporation almost all the monies owed it and assumes the debt itself. And then this debt is added to the outstanding bilateral debt owed by the debtor country to the country from which the ECA hails, thus becoming a significant part of the bilateral debt the developing world owes. Around 95 percent of the debt owed to the U.K. government by developing countries, for example, is export credit debt. While 65 percent of all debt owed by developing countries to official creditors is to ECAs.

Much like a department store that provides its own charge card so that people on credit can buy the store's own products, government ECAs facilitate loans for foreigners so that they buy the lending country's own products. The more the ECAs sell, the happier the domestic firms from the ECA's home country are, but also the more debts the foreign countries run up.

And Saddam's Iraq made Western arms dealers very happy. Of the $26 billion–plus currently owed by Iraq to the British, the French, the Germans, the Japanese, and the Americans, most of the debt was run up in the 1980s after Saddam came into power. Most of it undoubtedly resulted from military equipment procurement and weapons programs—funding the various international military manufacturers whose sales were underwritten by these creditors' respective ECAs.

And now the Iraqi people are being told to repay this debt, or at least that proportion of the debt that creditors feel they will realistically be able to squeeze out of them. The nation that suffered so much under Saddam that its cause became one of "liberation" is being told to repay debts that were racked up with the express encouragement of Western companies and Western governments for purposes of oppression, violence, and genocide. Debts that were clearly odious in nature.

But is the Iraqi situation an anomaly? How widespread are ECA loans in the first place? And how usual is it for them to be used so ill-advisedly?

As It Is

Let's start with some facts. Export credit agencies like the United States' Ex-Im, the German Hermes Guarantee, the Italian SACE, the Japanese Export-Import Bank, the Swiss ERG, the French CO-

FACE, the Canadian EDC, and the British ECGD are the largest source of public finance for private sector projects in the world. Between 1982 and 2001, ECAs supported $7,334 billion worth of exports and $139 billion of foreign direct investment primarily to countries of the developing world. In 2000 alone, ECAs provided a total of $500 billion in guarantees and insurance to companies operating in developing countries, and issued $58.8 billion worth of new export credits—with the two largest ones, the ECAs of Japan and the United States, in recent times approving on average new loans and guarantees worth $15 billion every year.

As overseas aid continues to fall, the importance of ECAs to developing countries continues to increase. Between 1988 and 1996, the worldwide value of new export credit loans and guarantees increased fourfold with approximately half of the new commitments going to the developing world. Eighty percent of financing for projects and investment in developing countries today comes from ECAs. And export credits are now at levels of between two and three times the amounts of aid provided by the World Bank, regional development banks, and countries of the developed world.

This is a trend that is likely to continue. The 2002 G8 Africa Action Plan stated: "We commit to . . . helping Africa attract investment, both from within Africa and from abroad and implement policies conducive to economic growth—including by . . . facilitating the financing of private investment through increased use of development finance institutions and export credit and risk-guarantee agencies. . . ."

Yet, rather than being used to bankroll projects that are "conducive to economic growth," export credits were and are often used to bankroll projects just as dangerous, dubious, or misguided as those in Saddam's Iraq. Time and time again, as we will see, export credits were and are used to pay bribes, support tyrannical or dictatorial regimes, or support environmentally unsound or socially undesirable projects.

And, once again, it is the ordinary people of these countries who are left to pick up the bill. ECAs are among developing countries' single largest creditors, and export credit debts account for about a quarter of developing countries' total long-term debt—in some countries even more. Gabon, Nigeria, and Algeria all owe more than 50 percent of their total debt to export credit agencies.

Why exactly are the governments of the developed world providing these loans? In some cases, it is to serve their geopolitical interests (as we saw in the previous chapter), but more often it is to serve the different, though related, interests of their domestic corporations, so manifest in the Iraq example. The United Kingdom's ECA, the Export Credit Guarantee Department, or ECGD, explicitly states that its goal is to "help exporters of UK goods and services to win business and UK firms to invest overseas by providing guarantees, insurance and reinsurance against loss."

ECAs also serve the interests of commercial banks. As Stephen Kock, the Midland Bank executive in charge of arms deals put it: "You see, before we advance monies to a company, we always insist on funds being covered by the [U.K.] government's Export Credit Guarantee Department. . . . We can't lose. After 90 days if [they] haven't coughed up, the company gets paid instead by the British government. Either way, we recover our loan, plus interest of course—it's beautiful." It's especially beautiful because the ECGD typically pays banks about 0.75 percent per annum on the total value of any ECA-backed loan it has provided so that the bank has an incentive to provide the capital to the British exporter.

And while 0.75 percent per annum may not sound like that much, on a $500 million project it amounts to around $3.8 million. And this is on a completely risk-free loan—the equivalent of lending to the Bank of England! No wonder banks spend serious amounts of money cozying up to big corporations. They want to be the bank through which the company secures its ECGD-backed loan.

From the point of view of a Western corporation, export credit arrangements are great because they enable them to pass some of the risk of doing business in developing countries on to their own governments. By providing lower fees, premiums, and interest rates than the private market can, and by backing transactions that the private market would refuse to back, ECAs are implicitly subsidizing their domestic exporters.

Export credit arrangements also offer companies the added bonus of harnessing a government's interests to their own. Once corporations have export credit guarantees they can rest assured that if things go wrong their government will protect their investments. "The Export Import Bank can be a powerful ally," Edmund B. Rice of the American pro-ECA corporate lobbying group Coalition for Employment through Exports, has said. "You've got the full weight of our U.S. embassy, our ambassador, the Treasury Department here and overseas the State Department all coming in."

No wonder corporations lobby hard for ECAs to continue their work. When there was a move to eliminate the U.S. Overseas Private Investment Corporation (OPIC) in the late 1990s—an agency similar to Ex-Im but focused solely on the developing world—Kenneth Lay, the now disgraced former CEO of Enron, wrote a letter to every single member of Congress staunchly defending the institution.

Why do Western governments want to serve corporate interests in this way? Typically, because they are so caught up in the "business interest serves national interest" myth that they don't stop to question it. They should. First, most economists remain highly skeptical that a nation can improve its long-term welfare by subsidizing its exports. Second, subsidies radically reduce the incentive for exporters to do all they can to ensure that the companies they are selling to will make good on their debts. In much the same way that many more homes would be built in flood-prone areas if their owners were compensated for flood damage by the government, ECAs provide exporters with incentives to maximize their exports in the knowledge that they will be bailed out if their deals go bad. Third, export subsidy policies have tended to be very costly for the exporting countries; many ECAs have suffered huge losses over the past two decades. And, finally, rather than benefiting the interests of their host country, ECA-backed companies often turn out to be benefiting only themselves.

Most of the companies that have received large amounts of Ex-Im support in the United States, for example, are companies that have ruthlessly shed jobs and have shifted production abroad to save money. Ex-Im's five biggest corporate beneficiaries in the 1990s—AT&T, Bechtel, Boeing, General Electric, and McDonnell Douglas—collectively cut more than three hundred thousand jobs during that time, shifting production away from the United States to India, Mexico, Japan, and elsewhere. Worse still, Ex-Im is extremely selective in the businesses it serves, choosing to benefit merely a small handful. In 2001, more than 60 percent of Ex-Im's loans and guarantees went to just three corporations, and almost 90 percent went to just ten. Similar trends can be seen in other countries.

Lining the Wrong Pockets

The lion's share of the subsidies is not, however, usually paid for by Western taxpayers despite the high failure rate of ECA projects. That burden more commonly falls on the peoples of the developing world—the masses in the developing countries who have to face the consequences of an increase in their debt burden as a result of the importer not paying up. For, as we have seen, export credit debt accounts for a significant proportion of the debt that developing countries owe to official creditors, and in some cases for almost all the debt they owe. And the interest paid on export credits is particularly onerous for developing countries because it corresponds to commercial rates of interest, not the lower rates incurred by bilateral or multilateral (the World Bank, IMF, or regional development banks) loans.

If it could be shown that countries now carrying ECA debt burdens were better off because of ECA-backed projects, a reasonable case could be made that the resulting debt burden was worth it. In many cases, however, the promised benefits never materialize, and a large number of projects do not even see the light of day. A former employee of HSBC told me that, of the export credit agency deals he worked on over a twelve-month period at the bank, every single one went bankrupt.

Moreover, billions of dollars' worth of ECA loans have ended up lining the pockets of corrupt government officials. Acres, for example, the company supported by the EDC (Canadian ECA), was convicted in a Lesotho court in September 2002 for having paid $260,000 in bribes to a Masupha Sole, the former CEO of the notorious Highlands Dam Project, a project that, besides being riddled with corruption, displaced hundreds of subsistence farmers and directly and adversely affected the lives of approximately twenty-seven thousand people. And it is commonplace for the prices of projects that receive ECA funding to be massively inflated so as to be able to cover the related "commissions." An investigation into power contracts in Indonesia in 2000, for example, revealed that most power transmission projects financed by foreign export credit agencies "smacked of mark up practices . . . [and] on average they cost 37 percent more compared to projects that underwent international tenders." This reflects similar findings by the corruption-fighting nongovernmental organization Transparency International. It revealed that it was common practice for the value of an ECA contract to have been inflated by between 10 and 20 percent to account for the "commissions" (otherwise known as bribes) necessary to secure the deal.

Yet rather than trying to screen out corrupt countries from export credit agency funding, some of the world's most corrupt countries—Indonesia, Turkey, the Philippines—continue to figure in the top ten markets for export credit support. As Transparency International has written: "The continued lack of action by export credit agencies to address the issue of corruption has brought some export credit agency practices close to complicity with a criminal offense."

Corruption, yet again, seems not to be a factor when governments of the rich world decide to which countries to lend. Indeed, it remains so pervasive in the world of the ECA that it can almost be thought of as a complementary export that our governments finance. One of Britain's most prominent contractors in Africa, a man who has built countless schools and hospitals using British ECA funding to do so, told me proudly that he has paid bribes of over $75 million to secure his contracts over the past ten years.

Of course, ECA loans aren't necessarily or always a bad thing.

Poor countries wouldn't be able to finance many projects without them, many of the projects they facilitate are beneficial or at least harmless, and even though the contractor in the story mentioned above did pay out tens of millions of dollars in bribes over the past ten years, he did at the same time build schools and hospitals. The bribes could be considered a kind of operating tax.

It is just that by lining the pockets of elites, ECA loans not only undermine the possibility of democracy, but also by essentially legitimizing corruption, can impede economic growth. Empirical study after empirical study has shown that corruption is a barrier to significant numbers of potential investors. Which means that the overall return on the debts incurred through ECA loans can be extremely low, or even negative.

There have been some token gestures made recently on the part of ECAs to appease mounting criticism—Britain, for example, has introduced a new warranty procedure that requires companies to state that they have not engaged in bribery. But in practice, reforms tend to be insufficient and unenforceable. Britain's ECGD still has no investigatory powers, and thus no way of ensuring compliance. As Transparency International has recently said: "None of the ECAs seem to seriously consider or even allow the possibility of denying access to export support to a country that has previously been shown to use bribery."

Morever, the projects ECAs choose to fund are often highly contentious. President Félix Houphouët-Boigny of the Ivory Coast built the world's largest church in Yamoussoukro, his birthplace, a cathedral modeled on St. Peter's in Rome with 118-foot-high stained-glass windows, a 280-ton dome twice the height of Paris's Notre Dame, and a 30-foot gilded cross, with $150 million worth of European export credit financing. This St. Peter's replica has air-conditioned seating for 7,000, standing room for 12,000, and an open-air piazza built to hold a congregation of 350,000 in a town with a population of 100,000 in a country where only 15 percent of the population is Christian, and still fewer Catholic. Worse still, Houphouët-Boigny built this huge edifice at a time when millions of people in the Ivory Coast were dying from disease, funding for immunization programs was nil, and AIDS was beginning to get out of control.

Or take the Bataan Nuclear Power Plant in the Philippines, built in 1976 for over $2 billion with loans largely provided by the United States' Ex-Im. The largest and most expensive construction project ever undertaken in that country, the loans taken out to build it are still costing the Philippines $170,000 a day to service and will continue to do so until 2018. This in a country in which GDP per capita is $4,000, 40 percent of the population live below the poverty line and annual per capita expenditure on health is only $30. And all this expense for a plant that never worked. "Filipinos have not benefited from a single watt of electricity," said the Philippine national treasurer Leonor Briones. Thankfully not, because the plant's design was based on an old two-loop model that had no safety record of any sort, and because the plant lies along earthquake fault lines at the foot of a volcano.

Paying for Pollution and Gun-Runners

ECAs not only finance self-aggrandizing or misguided projects or corrupt elites, they are, historically, rarely subject to *any* safeguards, even those designed to protect human rights or the environment. Most export credit agencies, for example, have no legal obligation to screen out projects with adverse environmental and social impacts, no obligation to ensure that their projects comply with a set of mandatory human rights and environmental and development guidelines, and no obligation to consider the environmental impact of their investments or the contribution they will make to local development. Attempts to get G8 countries to agree on minimal social and environmental standards for their ECAs have resulted only in a nonbinding arrangement, with companies now being asked to fill out questionnaires on their environmental and social impact. Once again, however, no procedures have been implemented to allow independent verification to take place. This clearly limited agreement was the compromise solution reached after Germany and France initially boycotted the talks, frustrated that their ECAs were losing their competitive advantage in the face of U.S. demands for higher standards—it is ironic that Green parties were part of governing coalitions in both France and Germany at the time.

In practice, what all this means is that many of the projects ECAs end up financing—leading favorites are big infrastructure projects and resource extraction projects such as mines, dams, oil refineries, and nuclear power plants—continue to be environmentally damaging and, frequently, socially undesirable as well.

The Three Gorges Dam project in China is a perfect example. Here is a project that will force the relocation of 1.3 million people and drown thirteen cities. It has been characterized by large-scale corruption and massive construction flaws, and has been protested against by numerous Chinese scientists, engineers, and journalists. Yet it has already received almost $1.5 billion in loan guarantees and insurance from various European ECAs. As one senior British official mused, "There was some problem about moving peasants there, wasn't there?"

Although the American ECAs are more strongly regulated than their European counterparts—President Clinton imposed mandatory standards in 1992 and 1997, which prevent them from investing in "projects that require large-scale involuntary resettlement" or "large dam projects that disrupt natural ecosystems or the livelihoods of local inhabitants"—Ex-Im and OPIC have also invested heavily in projects with dubious environmental credentials. From 1992 to 1998, for example, the two agencies between them underwrote $23.2 billion in financing for oil, gas, and coal projects around the world. Over their lifetime, these plants will release 29.3 billion tons of carbon dioxide, the equivalent of the amount of carbon dioxide produced by 24 billion round-trip New York–Heathrow flights, an amount that would need to be offset by the planting of 48 billion trees.

One of the American ECAs' biggest clients during the 1990s for these kind of projects was Enron. The Houston company's Cuba pipeline from Bolivia to Brazil, for example, cuts directly through the world's largest remaining dry tropical forest and also part of the Pantanal wetlands, damaging thirty-nine indigenous communities and several other nonindigenous communities on its way—as well as devastating the environment. It was a project the World Bank said it would not have financed. Many of OPIC's own staff recognized it was in violation of its own guidelines. Yet no one stopped it. Indeed, this was typical of the kind of project backed by Ex-Im and OPIC.

No wonder, as we will see in chapter 10, Ex-Im and OPIC are currently being taken to court in the United States for allegedly failing to conduct environmental reviews before financing projects that contribute to global warming. Although let's not forget that it's the industrialized rich world that is responsible for far more carbon dioxide emissions than the poor, a point we will return to in that chapter as well.

As Iraq illustrates, arms sales are another category of exports that account for large percentages of ECA loans. In the United Kingdom, between 30 and 50 percent of all export credits are allocated to cover sales by U.K. arms exporters—though not, since 2000, to facilitate sales to the sixty-three poorest countries in the world, thanks to an intervention by British chancellor of the exchequer Gordon Brown. This percentage is extremely high, particularly when one considers that defense exports account for only approximately 3 percent of total U.K. exports, while a third of France's export credits go to subsidize their arm exporters.

The question of how the arms might be used tends to be considered irrelevant. It's not only Iraq to which the British ECGD provided loans. In 1993, for example, it provided loans to the Indonesian authorities so that they could buy twenty-four Hawks from British Aerospace, and provided subsequent cover for a further sixteen Hawk jets three years later. Those same Hawks were later used by Suharto's armed forces to attack villages in East Timor and, more recently, to deliver what the Indonesian authorities called "shock therapy" against separatists in the Aceh province. A similar story can be told of Germany. On top of its "export über alles" policy regarding credits to Saddam, Germany offered $407 million in export guarantees to the Suharto government to catalyze the purchase of thirty-nine East German PT boats. When students protested against the purchase, the Indonesian government threw them into prison. France, as we saw in the previous chapter, provided export credits to its arms manufacturers to finance the weapons most probably used in the Rwandan genocide.

When the loans are used to buy arms, they frequently fuel conflicts, kill huge numbers of people, uphold repressive regimes, and subject citizens to internal repression. They also perpetuate a cycle in which arms manufacturers, with loans in tow, encourage war-crazy powerful elites to borrow more and more to fund the purchases of their own weapons.

By supporting arms sales, wealthy nations also encourage developing world governments to spend money on military equipment rather than on their health or educational needs. The money spent on one British Aerospace Hawk fighter jet, for example, could provide 1.5 million people with clean water for the rest of their lives. Export credits, deployed to serve the interests of the lender's domestic corporations, so often end up working to the severe detriment of the borrowing countries' populations. Those spared death from the barrel of a gun find their lives shortened by poor health care or famine.

And the dreadful irony is that the lender's weapons can end up being used against them. The U.S. military, for example, has had to face troops supplied with its own weaponry in Haiti, Somalia, Panama, Afghanistan, and Iraq.

Export credit agencies illustrate in shocking form one of the most serious imbalances in today's world. Not the geopolitical one in which countries with monies to lend wield power over those that need to borrow, or the imbalance within developing countries that can allow developing world leaders to take out loans without being held to account for their use. But an imbalance that lies at the core of developed nations themselves; an imbalance of power between corporate interests and the public interest, and among economics, politics, and society.

Subscribing to the myth that business interests serve the national interest, Western countries use ECAs for 80 percent of their investment in developing countries, subsidizing them and providing a risk-free bonus for the commercial banks that have lent the investment capital—and with no quid pro quo at all that the favored business employ the peoples of the subsidizing government, invest in its country, or fulfill any national interest.

The story of the ECAs is also a story of barefaced hypocrisy.

The rich world censures the poor for its high levels of military expenditure, yet continues to provide the funds so that it can buy its arms. The Europeans glorify multilateralism and sign on to a range of environmental conventions—Kyoto, the Convention on Biodiversity, and so forth—supposedly to protect the environment and slow down climate change, yet Europe's ECAs finance the very fossil fuels and energy-intensive projects that will lock in higher emissions in the developing world (thus re-creating there the same environmentally unsound development path these countries themselves followed). While in the United States the justification for rejecting Kyoto is supposedly in part because the Protocol does not require emissions limits for developing countries, countries in which American ECAs are financing the building of environmentally unfriendly power plants. The developed world unapologetically uses its ECAs to subsidize its exporters, yet demands in the name of "free trade" that developing countries do not protect their producers in any way at all. And, in the name of investment, saddles the developing world with yet more repayment of debt and debt at the higher rates of the commercial banks rather than the lower rates of the bilateral or multilateral loans.

The case of export agencies rams home the Janus-faced nature of the West. A developed world that espouses concern for human rights, transparency, and environmental issues on the one hand, yet on the other bankrolls projects that are at complete odds with any such concern. A developed world wedded to multilateralism, yet it defines this in a way that serves the narrowest of corporate interests.

So it is that the world's poorest countries sink further and further into debt while Western corporations grow fat from government-backed projects that fuel conflicts, harm the environment, and have built-in kickbacks. Rather than being a tool for development, ECA funds often serve to feed the vicious cycle of corruption, underdevelopment, conflict, and debt.

4

Pushers and Junkies

> Imagine
> a bank manager
> you didn't know
> came knocking on
> your door, begging
> you to borrow
> some funds.

Crossbones and Bananas

He must have been good-looking when he was younger, although now with his paunch and perma-tan, it's hard to imagine. But clearly there was a time when he was a player: the waterbed and hot tub are still there—I know because he pointed them out as he showed me around his spectacular, though crumbling, apartment. Stained-glass windows shipped in by the Rothschilds, wooden panels, galleried living room, and everywhere his own amazing photos of Africa, the continent in which he spent the best days of his life.

In 1969, the year man landed on the moon, Richard Nixon took office as president, and Charles Manson murdered Sharon Tate,

Karl Ziegler was twenty-six and just out of business school when he went off to Kenya with First Chicago to head up the bank's syndicated loans division.

The biggest loan he made was to Nigeria in 1975, a jumbo loan of $1.4 billion. It was the biggest loan, in fact, that had ever been made to that country. Four hundred million dollars of it went to the Wari Steel rolling mill (that part of the loan supported by Hermes, the German export credit agency) and the rest undesignated, a general-purpose loan to support Nigeria's balance of payments. Nigeria, he told me, was a good risk at that time. It was one of the world's major oil exporters and the oil price was high.

It was a good risk, true, in the sense that it wasn't likely to default, but it was not exactly the most salubrious of countries to lend to. Especially at the very time that Ziegler was working on the deal. Because right then the country was embroiled in a huge and highly visible scandal. A number of public officials and private contractors had imported over a million tons of cement at hugely inflated prices using central bank funds with the difference between the market price and the price they paid to be shared as a kickback between them. But rather than arriving in installments, the shipments arrived en masse. With hundreds of cement-carrying ships waiting to offload their cargo in a harbor that, at the best of times, could unload only ten ships a week, the shipments began to solidify in the hulls, rendering many ships useless, fit only to be scuttled. One and a half million tons of cement were left in vessels for fifteen months waiting to be unloaded, cement of such a poor quality that years later many of the buildings constructed with it had to be demolished. Building after building made with that material was simply collapsing.

Ziegler may not have known at the time about the inadequacy of the concrete, but he was well aware of the corruption that brought about the cement scandal. But back then cement wasn't the issue. "My job was to sell money," he told me. And his $1.4 billion deal was all about that: selling money, and making money, too. As the lead bank in the syndicate, First Chicago would make 0.25 percent of the $1.4 billion up front—$3.5 million. And if all went to plan, it wouldn't carry the risk. That would be passed on to other banks in the syndicate. "To some schmuck in Des Moines, or some smaller bank in the North," to quote Ziegler.

Doing the deal was, he explains to me now, what it was all about. "First Chicago came along and we won, and I felt eternally grateful for that," he told me. I asked him about the corruption. "It worried some of us more than others," he replied, but "it was great kudos. . . . The important thing was to win the mandate . . . [And when we did] . . . I was on a high. It was enormously exciting. . . . We were young guys with the world at our feet."

I pressed him on the corruption issue, and he smiled wryly, perhaps because he now heads a center whose mission it is to fight corruption and stamp it out. "As long as the country's flag wasn't black with a skull and crossbones on it or with a yellow banana on it," Karl tells me, "it was eligible for a loan."

Ziegler's experience wasn't unique. Throughout most of the 1970s, a host of banks—large banks (Chase, Citicorp, First Chicago, JP Morgan, Lloyds, Union Bank of Switzerland, the Banks of Montreal, Tokyo, Japan, and the French Banque National de Paris) and small rural American banks, too—lined up indiscriminately to push their loans to developing countries. It wasn't only the cold war players and other developed world governments getting in on the lending game.

With memories stretching back to the widespread defaults on Latin American bonds in the 1930s, commercial banks had, on the whole, stayed away from lending to the developing world since World War II. But, in 1973, the banks returned to those shores with a bang. Eurodollar syndicated loans to Latin America jumped from $2 billion in 1972 to over $22 billion in 1982: sixteen hundred banks were involved in loans to Mexico alone. Commercial lending to Africa was significantly more limited, never reaching the poorest sub-Saharan countries, but, by 1982, it accounted for 35 percent of regional debt.

Many countries that had already seen their bilateral debts rise earlier in the cold war now saw their financial obligations really explode. Argentina saw its debt rise by 544 percent, for example, between 1976 and 1983. And while, in 1970, the combined external public debt of Algeria, Argentina, Bolivia, Brazil, Bulgaria, Congo, the Ivory Coast, Ecuador, Mexico, Morocco, Nicaragua, Peru, Poland, Syria, and Venezuela was $18 billion (10 percent of their GNP), by 1987, once the commercial banks had entered the picture, these countries owed $402 billion (almost 50 percent of their GNP), with most of the monies being owed to the banks.

What accounted for this sudden desire to lend on the part of commercial banks? As in so many geopolitical cases, you just have to follow the oil. In the wake of the Yom Kippur War of 1973, oil-producing countries perpetrated a massive hike in oil prices, sending them skyrocketing by 400 percent, almost overnight. The oil producers were suddenly extremely rich, and the surplus was far too much for them to be able to spend in their own countries. Furthermore, Islamic sharia law forbade the practice of usury and prevented the Arab oil producers from earning interest in their own banks. They needed somewhere else to invest their petrodollars, and Western banks seemed the perfect choice.

This meant that overnight a huge new supply of credit emerged—$333.5 billion, to be exact. Forty percent went to banks in the United States and the United Kingdom, and the remaining, but still significant, portion to banks in France, Germany, and Japan.

The banks were desperate to put this windfall to productive use. The highly competitive banking industry of that time required the recycling of funds; it was absolutely key to staying at the top. Lending the petrodollars out again was a clear money spinner. Banks benefited doubly, from the fees they charged to arrange the loans and also from the interest they would make on the loans themselves.

But simply lending to the developed world wasn't going to satisfy the bankers given that the demand for loans from borrowers there had failed to keep pace with the expansion of available credit. So the banks actively sought out new lending targets in the developing world, especially in those places where they felt there was an opportunity to establish a close relationship with a burgeoning economy.

A market for commercial debt was created where there had not been one for decades. And once the big banks started lending, medium and smaller banks had no option but to follow suit.

It was another round of borrow, borrow, borrow—this time courtesy of the commercial banks. "The banks were hot to get in," Jose Angel Gurria, then head of Mexico's Office of Public Credit recalls. "All the banks in the U.S. and Europe and Japan stepped forward. They showed no foresight. They didn't do any credit analysis. It was wild. In August 1979, for instance, Bank of America planned a loan of $1 billion. They figured they would put up $350 million themselves and sell off the rest. As it turned out, they only had to put up $100 million themselves. They raised $2.5 billion on the loan in total." Other loans were similarly oversubscribed, and developing governments often found themselves offered more money than they had requested; that is, if they had even requested the loan in the first place.

The commercial loan pushers soon created commercial debt junkies. Money was lent under terms that were hard to turn down. In the mid-1970s loans actually had a negative real interest rate, which meant that a borrower could pay less than they borrowed, and although the rates were variable, no one expected them to rise significantly. Unlike funds from governments, which often had strings attached such as having to be spent on imports of that country's goods or having political colors firmly attached, these loans usually came obligation-free.

It was easy for developing countries to rationalize their new addiction. For some, the decision to borrow more was based upon a belief that they needed to incur these commercial debts in order to ensure their country's future development. During the nineteenth century, the United States went through a massive period of development, driven by a period of indebtedness to commercial banks, an example held up as a beacon for poorer countries to follow, despite the fact that many states never actually paid the loans back.

For others, like oil-importing countries who had suffered under the particularly harsh blow of oil price hikes, it was basically a huge relief to be offered these loans. What they were being offered by other governments didn't always suffice. As for the oil-exporting countries such as Colombia, Ecuador, Mexico, Nigeria, and Venezuela, the loans were a way to capitalize on their much improved financial status, at very reasonable interest rates. Likewise, African commodity exporters, seeing an increase in revenues thanks to the commodity price boom that initially accompanied the oil price increase, and anticipating a continuation of this enhanced income, were delighted to increase their level of borrowing.

For others, the fact that these loans were being sold so hard was just too much of an allure to be able to resist. A Latin American minister of finance in the 1970s put it this way: "I remember how the bankers tried to corner me at conferences to offer me loans. They would not leave me alone. If you're trying to balance your budget it's very tempting to borrow money instead of raising taxes to put off the agony." The surplus of offers was often overwhelming. And for poor countries in general, borrowing money made sense in theory at least, providing them with the potential to address the economic plight of their citizens.

Moreover the IMF, the World Bank, and the governments of the industrialized countries actively encouraged the developing world to borrow from these private banks, with the World Bank preaching "the doctrine of debt as the path towards accelerated development." The IMF, too, staunchly defended the system, claiming that higher foreign indebtedness was sound policy for both lender and borrower because the higher level of investment financed by foreign borrowing would eventually be reflected in additional net export capacity. As a result, commercial loans increased at much higher rates than those from governments or multilateral institutions during this period; while loans from official sources decreased from 54 to 34 percent between 1979 and 1981, the percentage coming from private banks rose from 25 to 30 percent.

Down the Hatch

And just as when governments lent out monies to serve their geopolitical interests or the interests of their domestic industries, commercial banks also turned a blind eye to how and where their money was spent. As long as the money kept on flowing, the bankers didn't care.

Most of the Latin American loans were granted "for general purposes," like the bulk of the Zielger Nigerian loan, rather than for specific projects. In the best cases, governments chose to use this money to invest in the structures needed to support growth. Argentina, Brazil, and Mexico, for example, used some of the monies for infrastructure—roads and transportation systems and communications. More often, the loans were used for debt servicing or supporting domestic financial policy, enabling the borrowing government to retain popular support by avoiding raising taxes, cutting jobs or increasing prices, even though such moves might have been in the long-term interest of the country and its currency. In the worst, but by no means atypical, cases, these loans were simply another type of borrowing being siphoned off by the ruling elites. Between 1974 and 1982, the external debt of Argentina, Brazil, Chile, Mexico, and Venezuela grew by $252 billion (most of which was owed to banks); about a third of that money went to buy real estate abroad and into offshore personal bank accounts.

Similar scenarios played themselves out in Africa, where much of the debt simply went unaccounted for, usually the victim of false invoicing, capital flight, or other techniques to send funds to "more secure" havens outside the country. In an alarming number of cases, the loans went into projects that had no chance of generating the income necessary to pay the loans back. Commercial banks lent monies hand in hand with ECAs, for a ghostly parade of white elephants. The Inga-Shaba hydroelectric project and power transmission line in Zaire, for example, originally estimated to cost $450 million—a loan for which the U.S. Export-Import Bank guaranteed the initial bill while commercial banks covered cost overruns—ended up costing over $1 billion, equivalent to 20 percent of Zaire's debt. "It's taking so long," one U.S. embassy official noted, "that a lot of the equipment they're putting at the two ends is deteriorating." In fact, by the time the project was finally completed, the need for power in Zaire's rich copper mines, the whole reason for the project in the first place, had already been met. The Belgians who were running the mines for the Zaire government had tapped their own sources of external finance, as well as locally available hydro-electric power, to keep themselves afloat.

In Togo, a combination of export credits and a loan syndicated by German commercial banks was used to build a steel mill. When the Togolese government realized that no iron ore was available to start production, it ordered the German technicians to dismantle an iron pier located at the port—a pier that had been constructed by Germany prior to World War I and which still functioned well. Once the steel mill had exhausted the pier as a feedstock, it closed down.

And, once again, dictators, tyrants, and military juntas were bankrolled by Western money. In Argentina, the debt contracted by the military dictatorship between 1976 and 1983 (the vast majority of which was commercial) went from $7.9 billion up to $45.1 billion, with half of the money lent by commercial banks between 1976 and 1983 remaining abroad, often with the knowledge of the lending banks themselves. In Brazil, it was also the military that contracted most of the roaring commercial debt—jumping from $3.9 billion in 1968 to $48 billion in 1978. In 1970s Africa, the corrupt Mobutu ran up $579 million of commercial debt.

How did these loans make it through the banks' due diligence? Investigations the banks carried out before they made their loans ranged from the minimal to the actively negligent. A loan is said to have been granted to Costa Rica in 1973 on the basis of a single *Time* magazine article on the country. Chase Manhattan and many other banks tried to lend to countries that were already in default to them: when Chase offered Bolivia a new loan in 1976, for example, it did so in complete disregard of the fact that it was a creditor on another loan for which Bolivia was already in default. Mexico was offered additional loans even though it had already committed 65.5 percent of its export revenues to paying debt service charges, which indicated a preexisting level of commitment that was already very high and extremely difficult to service. And many bankers making the loans just didn't know what they were doing. As one of the bank executives involved in the negotiations said at the time, "I am far from alone in my youth and inexperience. The world of international banking is now full of aggressive, bright but hopelessly inexperienced 29-year-old vice presidents with wardrobes from Brooks Brothers [and] MBAs from Wharton or Stanford."

Inexperienced they might have been, but they were sure making money. A Salomon Brothers' report, published in 1976, revealed that the thirteen largest U.S. banks had *quintupled* their earnings from $177 million to $836 million during the first half of the 1970s, with a significant share coming from developing country loans. By 1976, Citibank was earning 72 percent of its income abroad, Bank of America 40 percent, Chase 78 percent, First Boston 68 percent, Morgan Guaranty 53 percent, and Manufacturers Hanover 56 percent. In the 1970s, Banque National de Paris, one of the world's largest banking houses, profited more from its various African affiliates than from its extensive branch network in France. Nigeria alone came to account for up to 20 percent of the bank's after-tax earnings in the late 1970s.

All this lending appeared to have no potential downside at all. Walter Wriston, former president of Citibank and perhaps the greatest recycler of them all, famously said during the wild lending period that there was no danger in foreign lending because "sovereign nations do not go bankrupt." This was a maxim that essentially became the rallying cry for a whole generation of bankers. Lending, lending, and more lending was held up as a huge achievement. "It was the greatest transfer of wealth," Wriston said, "in the shortest time and with the least casualties in the history of the world . . . [it is] something to be proud of. It was a terrifically difficult thing to do. We did it. It was also hard to put the guy on the moon. We did that."

And this was the accepted position. "We reject the view that international lending activities of American banks are posing grave risks to the American economy or the banking system," said C. Fred Bergsten, assistant secretary of the treasury for international affairs, when he testified in 1977 before the House Banking Committee. "We believe to the contrary, that they have been remarkably successful in playing a vital role in helping to finance an unprecedented level of international trade, capital flows and payments imbalances—and that they continue to enjoy such success."

To some extent, this exuberance was understandable. Countries such as Argentina, Brazil, Nigeria, and Mexico had natural resources and enough trade to cope, at least initially, with a certain degree of indebtedness. Interest rates were low, which meant that servicing the debts should have been manageable in theory. Countries that could not pay back their debts were just given even more new loans to pay off the old ones. And even if countries couldn't service these loans, bankers believed that when push came to shove they would be bailed out, that geopolitical interests would as ever hold sway.

"Banks who lend too much too fast know there will be a bailout, no question about it," the officer of a large New York City bank said at the time. "They scoff at bankers who create large loan loss reserves and those who in general are more conservative. They know that come the revolution in Mexico, or wherever, their banks will have the highest earnings and pay the highest dividends, and that they personally will receive the highest bonuses."

Those who did recognize the precariousness of the situation and advised caution were viewed as doomsayers. The late senators Frank Church of Idaho, Clifford Case of New Jersey, and Jacob Javits of New York criticized the Ford and Carter administrations' "laissez-faire approach to petrodollar recycling" and warned that the American taxpayer would ultimately have to pay the price for the banks' lax lending. They were ignored. "As a loan officer," an ex-banker who did his share of lending at the time said, "you are principally in the business of making loans. It is not your job to worry about large and unwieldy abstractions, such as whether what you are doing is threatening the stability of the world economy."

But the bankers should have worried.

If they had studied their history books, they would have realized that the path they were taking was neither new nor safe. Since its independence from Spain and Portugal in the 1820s, Latin America, for example, had gone through several cycles in which it had borrowed extensively, seen long periods of economic expansion, and then in the inevitable postboom stagnation, found itself unable to service its debt obligations. In 1827, almost every Latin American government had defaulted on its debt. And this had happened again in 1873. The defaults of 1930 had been no anomaly.

And at the end of the 1970s the merry-go-round that enabled banks to keep on lending to Latin America and elsewhere, once again came to a screeching halt.

The Morning After

In 1979, the shah of Iran was deposed, an event shortly followed by the Iran-Iraq war. A second oil price hike occurred, with the price of oil more than doubling within two years. This put pressure on the economies of oil importing countries and created further demand for credit, which, in turn, created a new boost of lending. On the other side of the ledger, the added costs stretched the ability of borrowing countries to service the debt they had already contracted. In developed countries, the hikes caused prices of many consumer goods to rise, which triggered inflation.

To curb inflation, industrial countries, led by the United States, raised interest rates. There was an enormous global recession. The markets for developing countries' products shrank, which meant that those countries' capacity to pay back debts drastically diminished. Developing countries that had taken out loans with commercial banks had done so under variable interest rates. These now jumped up markedly—interest rates rose from an average of 0.5 percent on commercial bank loans to an average of 13.1 percent. Developing countries' debt payments skyrocketed. Argentina, to provide just one example, saw its interest payments rise from $1.3 billion in 1980 to $3.3 billion in 1984 and $4.4 billion in 1985. Projects that had originally made good economic sense now saw their costs go through the roof—the Brazilian-Paraguayan Itaipu Dam Project, which was supposed to cost $3.6 billion when planned, ended up costing $10.8 billion. Unable to repay their loans, developing countries were forced to take up even more loans to pay the interest. Meanwhile, export earnings dropped as commodity prices collapsed, falling by 28 percent between 1981 and 1982. Monetary reserves became depleted. Capital flew out of the region, as private investors, fearing a crash, pulled their money out—a pattern similar to what had prevailed in *all* of Latin America's preceding debt crises.

Then the debt junkies started overdosing. First came Mexico. On August 15, 1982, the Mexican government announced that it was going to default on its entire debt. It was an extreme action but the country was almost entirely out of money. Its Central Bank's resources were almost exhausted and commercial banks abroad had made it clear that they were now unwilling to refinance or roll over existing loans, on *any* terms. President Lopez Portillo had already tried a conciliatory approach, but with no success. Just before he announced the default, he had sent his finance minister Jesus Silva Herzog to the United States to request a loan for $1 billion to meet interest payments urgently due. Herzog had been turned down. And the president probably felt he didn't really have anything left to lose. Mexico already looked unlikely to have access to international sources of credit; whatever assets creditors might have attempted to seize would only have been worth a fraction of the debt outstanding, and capital was already fleeing the country. Besides, given the huge amount his country owed—$80 billion—Lopez Portillo speculated that Mexico would be in a powerful position when it came to the negotiations that would follow his default threat. Finally, since he was just about to retire, Lopez Portillo wouldn't have to deal with the consequences.

When Brazil, the next biggest debtor, assessed its situation in a similar fashion and announced that it too would issue a moratorium on its debt, the private banks suddenly woke up to how exposed they were. Of the $315 billion that Latin America now owed—a fourfold increase in just seven years—more than two-thirds was owed to banks. The size of the two debts was so great, there was a chance the banking system could not absorb the defaults and remain solvent. The possibility of a widespread banking collapse was suddenly all too real, sending down the share prices of the three hundred foreign creditor banks that were owed money by Mexico. The bank failures of the 1930s were foremost in people's minds, leaving export markets, financial stability, and even regional security threatened.

The world financial community soon realized that it had to act. Some of the world's biggest banks were in danger of being brought down. Inaction could also lead to serious geopolitical consequences. The *Economist* expressed its fears that "Mexico, which has until now been more or less stable . . . will become a new Iran or Argentina at the very doorstep of the US." The United States, as Lopez Portillo had gambled, quickly granted Mexico an emergency loan, crucial for the country's survival but still leaving it in enormous social and economic pain. But Mexico was only one country in a region now in freefall. A new scheme had to be devised quickly that would enable new loans to be procured so that countries could at least maintain their interest payments on their old loans.

The World Bank and IMF rolled up their sleeves and entered the fray to mediate between debtor countries and the banks. But rather than punishing or even chastising the banks for their role in the debt crisis, or safeguarding the developing countries' interests during this process, the Bank and the Fund made it clear that as far as they were concerned it was all about saving the banks.

And as Church, Case, and Javits had so rightly prophesied, the bailouts began. The IMF and World Bank devoted billions of dollars to "rescue packages." The United States and the Bank of International Settlements provided some bridge finance too, the burden of which was borne by Western taxpayers. But the money being poured in wasn't enough to get the banks out of trouble. Jacques de Larosiere, the managing director of the IMF at the time, told the banks that they would also have to bail themselves out, and put up a percentage of their existing total exposure to each country as new lending, so that the countries could pay at least the interest they owed.

This plan, while sound in theory, didn't work. The bank advisory committees established to negotiate the new terms soon became dubbed "adversary" committees by debtor countries as they adopted the conventions of the Paris Club by not allowing the debtor countries to negotiate *en bloc* while the banks themselves were allowed to act in concert as a cartel. Strong-arm tactics were employed, ranging from isolating recalcitrant debtors—making it difficult for them to take a united stand and negotiate better terms for themselves—to issuing threats that unless they accepted the terms laid down by the committees, further retaliation would be taken against them such as seizing their assets abroad or the use of trade sanctions. Trust broke down. Countries took in new monies but broke the agreements. Debt reserve payments were rescheduled almost continuously in a process that resembled nothing so much as "a poker game with the creditors hoping to recoup more in interest payments than they had to lay out in new money and the debtors gambling on the opposite."

The one-sidedness of the approach fast became counterproductive. Antagonism reigned. "Fuck you, I'm not forgiving," "Fuck you, I'm not paying" was the way most debt negotiations started. Meanwhile, the debt burden just continued to increase. Capital started flying out of developing countries at even more alarming rates. And as the debts continued to grow so did the view among radicals and opposition groups in debtor countries that they were unjust and ought to be repudiated, that the creditors' "divide and rule" tactics needed to be overcome, and that a collective stance was the only way to exact acceptable terms. "This debt is not only unpayable but also uncollectible," said Fidel Castro in a series of meetings in Havana in 1985. He was advocating that the region should now follow through on its early 1980s threats of default and not honor its debts. President Garcia of Peru, though less strident than Castro and not calling for a full repudiation, announced that he would limit payments on Peru's debt to 10 percent of export proceeds.

But most of the governments in the region did not seriously consider either of these options. They were unwilling to present the bankers with a collective ultimatum, preferring instead to continue to play by the creditors' rules. For the largest debtors, this decision was partly driven by the fact that they recognized that Washington, fearing serious political instability in the big Latin American economies, would grant emergency loans to bolster the position of those in the government who were in favor of continuing to pay, as it had in the Mexican case. But, significantly, it was also because many of those now in power in the region simply didn't want to piss the banks off. Many of the key decision makers as well as their countries' most affluent citizens had personally benefited from a pattern of growth that had been highly dependent upon access to international markets, and was highly unequal in its distribution, and they wanted to be able to do so again in the future.

Although a collective default was not going to happen, the situation remained dire. Latin American economies were clearly unable to deal even with the newly negotiated terms. New ideas were desperately needed. The United States couldn't just walk away—obligations from Latin America to U.S. banks alone amounted by now to some $82.5 billion, a sum equal to one quarter of all U.S. bank claims overseas. Nearly two-thirds of this was owed to the nine largest American banks alone, an amount well in excess of their total capital and assets, and it was clearly not in the interest of the OECD countries to let the international financial system collapse. To let the thousands of banks involved in these loans go bankrupt was simply unthinkable.

New plans were introduced in almost all countries that had debts with these banks. In October 1985, Secretary of the Treasury James Baker introduced his plan at the World Bank–IMF meeting, a plan that was configured under the assumption that countries faced only temporary problems of liquidity, which a restructuring of their debt and a rescheduling of repayments could address. To this end, the Baker plan offered a vast array of new options a country could take to repay, consolidate, or diversify its outstanding debt: debt-for-equity swaps (in which loans could be exchanged for shares in state-owned companies), debt-for-debt swaps (in which loans could be exchanged for new loans with new terms), cash buybacks (in which a debtor could repurchase its own debt on favorable terms), and various other options. What it didn't do was cancel or relieve much of the debt itself. So while the plan precipitated the rise of the secondary market for debt (we will look at this later)—the market where previously issued bonds can be bought and sold, which functions in a manner similar to the stock market, and in which the value of a particular bond varies constantly depending on supply and demand—a market that grew in size by 800 percent from an estimated $500 million worth of trades in 1983 to $4 billion just two years later, it didn't actually make any significant impact on the debt burden.

In fact, Latin American countries sank further and further into debt, and more and more of them ceased meeting their interest obligations. By 1988, more than half of Latin American countries were behind in their payments. Mexico saw its debt rise from $80 billion in the early 1980s to $112 billion in 1988, despite the fact that it had paid back $100 billion between 1982 and 1988.

In 1989, U.S. Secretary of the Treasury Nicholas Brady introduced his solution, thereafter known as the Brady Plan—at last acknowledging that the problem was not, after all, about liquidity but rather about solvency. In other words, Brady was getting everyone to admit giving these countries more time to pay their debts would never change the fact that their debts were too big to be repaid *ever*. In admitting that outstanding loans were unpayable, the Brady Plan called for a total reduction of about 20 percent of the global debt, rather than a restructuring or rescheduling. The IMF and the World Bank offered guarantees for the repayment of the other 80 percent.

In exchange, the debtor countries had to accept the IMF and the World Bank's ever more intrusive control over their internal economic policies, including issues of taxation, budget, the ownership of industries, and so on. But developing countries were by now in no position to argue. Owing to the long, drawn-out nature of the negotiating process, Latin America had been hemorrhaging for seven years. Alternative sources of funding had shrunk dramatically and foreign exchange reserves were drastically depleted, so that the prospect of attracting the new international credit and investment that the Brady Plan promised became extremely attractive. It helped that the ruling elites anticipated that they would be able to protect themselves pretty well from the austerity measures the IMF insisted upon. With few viable alternatives, developing countries accepted the path the IMF and World Bank had laid out.

In accordance with the Brady Plan, the remaining debt was converted into bonds—Brady Bonds—that were partially underwritten by the U.S. Treasury. This arrangement made it even easier for commercial banks to decrease their balance sheet exposure, and to launder their bad 1970s loans by transforming what were essentially illiquid assets into bonds that were tradable on the secondary market. By the mid-1990s more than $170 billion worth of Brady Bonds had been issued. And developing countries soon issued other bonds in their wake. Each issue offered a new business opportunity for the Western banks that underwrote them to take significant fees and also a new opportunity for the developing country to borrow again.

Global macroeconomics also played a part in the revival of these loans. The U.S. interest rate had decreased significantly during this period, making the yields on these bonds considerably higher than better-grade bonds, so further increasing the appeal of this new product for Western investors. Soon the secondary market for emerging debt began to come into its own. At its peak in 1997, secondary market trading reached $6 trillion, with Brady Bonds accounting for $2.5 trillion.

For banks, now much more cautious and risk-averse and seeking to reduce their exposure to emerging markets, the emergence of a bond market enabled them to continue lending to developing countries but with much less risk. In the loan market, the risk of loss was spread over a small number of banks, so that if a country defaulted, each would lose a large sum of money. In the bond market, however, the risk was shared among thousands of bondholders. Moreover, the yields paid on these bonds were adjusted for risk, making the returns spectacularly high.

And so the drama of debt continues to unfold, with commercial banks joining geopolitical concerns and corporations on the world stage.

What do we learn from this story? We learn that no matter who plays the tune, the song stays the same: loans were once again made irresponsibly with no care for how they would be used and borrowed fecklessly with no care for how they would be spent. Once again, shortsighted self-interest ruled the roost. Cocksure commercial bankers believing that their bubble would never burst and that the global financial system would always protect them, contributed to the enslaving of three-quarters of the world with yet more hundreds of billions of dollars of unpayable debt—an enslavement that would come, as we will see, to haunt us all.

But there are two quite new features in the story of the loans from commercial banks. First, there is a recognition of the impact that external factors—the oil crisis, the deposition of the shah of Iran, commodity price crashes—can have not only on the developing world but also on the developed. And, second, there is a foreshadowing of the power debtors could perhaps wield were they willing to act collectively, or were they able to leverage what they owed in an effective way—a sense that default, though never a decision to be taken lightly, could perhaps at times have benefits that outweighed its indisputable costs and be the right or at least the most popular strategic choice to make.

But the story is incomplete. The lending orgy of the 1970s and early 1980s served to set the stage for the rise of two new players, the bond market and bond traders at the extreme end of which are characters like Kenneth Dart, heir to the Styrofoam fortune, and Paul Singer from Elliot Associates, men for whom Peruvian debt and pork bellies alike are a staple diet. This is what the next chapter is about.

5

Traders and Vultures

Imagine
your creditors
trebled the interest
they demanded on your
loans without warning
and then all of a sudden,
all at once, called the
loans in.

Masters of the Universe

Lights flashing. Green type on jet-black computer screens blinking. Squawk boxes booming disembodied voices. A roar crescendos, then diminishes, and then rises up again and again. I am on the emerging-market bonds trading floor at one of the world's most prestigious investment banks, and it looks like a human battery farm. A group of men, packed in cubicles, all charcoal suits and receding hairlines, interspersed with the occasional and far more attractive sheer-hose–clad woman, sit crammed together side by side. Staring at the screens, Madonna-esque headsets on, these self-proclaimed "masters of the universe" buy, sell, and then buy again. "Buy Brazil." "Bid for half million for Manny." "Anyone got a price for Pakistan?" "Sell Argentina, sell, sell, sell!" The market moves fast and the traders stay in their seats, Pepsi cans, Starbucks coffee cups, discarded Chinese food cartons, and bento boxes piled up around them.

The traders talk as if in concert with the moving market, in response to their colleagues and their clients, and also in response to my many questions.

"What is the difference between emerging-market bonds and commodities?" I ask. "Developing-world debt or peanuts, it's all the same," a staccato voice fires back.

"How did you feel when Argentina was crashing?" I ask, referring to the days around Argentina's 2002 default. "Did you worry about what your selling was doing to exacerbate the situation? The panic it was creating in the market, the impact it would have on the Argentinian population if the crisis deepened?"

"No, I worried about my position, had I called it right or not, and if not, what did this mean for my bonus this year? My mortgage? My holiday? My job? If you own a bunch of Argentinian debt and it's going down at five points a day, and you called it wrong, that's what you'd be thinking about." The trader looked again at me and added, "Do you mean did I ever feel guilty? Hmmm. No. A trader can't feel guilt, he has to be unemotional. We're not here for charity, after all."

They certainly are not.

These Ritalin-deprived ADD sufferers (almost all the traders I have met with have some sort of twitch or tic) make huge amounts of money from buying and selling the debt of emerging countries. To give an illustrative example of just how much money can be made, the most expensive piece of residential real estate in New York City, a $45 million, twelve-thousand-square-foot condo in the AOL Time Warner Center was bought by David Martinez, a partner in Fintech Advisory Inc., which specializes in buying and selling developing-world debt.

It was the mid-1980s when Wall Street first acquired an appetite for the broader class of high-risk bonds, of which emerging-market or developing-world debt is a part. A now toupeed, later incarcerated, huge philanthropist by the name of Michael Milken had come up with the idea of aggressively marketing high-yield, high-risk, non-investment-grade corporate bonds known as "junk bonds" to folks with an above-average appetite for risk. His timing was great. The equity market was faltering, and while the interest rates being paid out on U.S. T-bills (short-term government bonds) were quite high, junk bond yields were significantly higher. Cutting-edge institutional investors and high-net-worth individuals (a euphemism for the immensely rich) immediately "got" what Milken was selling—some junk bond portfolios consistently returned more than 25 percent a year.

A host of investors started clamoring to buy into this risky category, and within a few years, the market for them had grown from nothing to more than $200 billion. This meant that when the Brady Bonds appeared in the late 1980s—the bonds that were created from the ashes of predominantly Latin American debt, and had a similar risk profile in quantitative if not qualitative terms—there were customers in situ willing to buy.

Brady Bonds, however, appealed to a much wider audience than simply the seat-of-your-pants, risk-taking, junk bond–buying investor. They came with a ready-made liquid secondary market on which they could be resold or bought; their redemption value was partially guaranteed by the United States; and their issue coincided with a relaxing of U.S. regulations governing the way banks accounted for their investments, allowing the banks greater flexibility to book losses and sell assets, and leaving them looking for new investments in which to put the freed capital. A large variety of institutional investors—mutual funds, pension funds, hedge funds, and insurance companies—soon entered the market, as well as small investors and commercial bankers. The demand for these bonds was so high that by the early to mid-1990s, many developing countries realized they could issue new bonds themselves and these would also be snapped up. And so, ignoring the crisis that borrowing had engendered in the 1980s, they did.

Bonds quickly overtook loans as the main way that most middle-income countries—in Latin America, Asia, the better-off parts of Africa, and, later, central and eastern Europe and the former Soviet

Union—raised money: today, bonds account for 60 percent of emerging-market debt, compared with only 13 percent in 1980. They are bonds that can be easily traded on a secondary market by the kinds of jumpy, nervous folks I interviewed, people who are often completely detached from the product that they sell and for whom trading is essentially a technical skill, divorced from the substance of the item traded, for whom bonds or bacon are all the same thing.

Of course, not everyone who buys developing-world debt buys it for recycling on the secondary market. Some investors, enjoying the yields and growth potential they offer—over the past five years emerging-market bonds have easily outperformed most equity markets, even taking into account the Russian, Turkish, and Argentinian crises—buy the bonds with the intention of staying in for some time. But, on the whole, the debt is repeatedly traded in the same way as shares or corporate bonds.

And what the traders try to do as always is buy low, sell high. Take a guess as to which way the market will move, and make sure you call it right. It doesn't matter whether or not you precipitate a crisis (as you will if a number of traders try to sell at once), as long as you aren't the one left holding the bag. "What happens is you sell Brazil because Russia looks cheaper, and then when Brazil looks like a better deal you sell Russia. You go in and out of a bond with no regard for what this does to a country," the former head of emerging-market trading at a major investment bank told me. Essentially, "it's a game of chicken." Or a game of musical chairs, the trick being to be in the right spot each time the music stops.

And the music frequently stops, because unlike the commercial bankers who lent to developing countries in the 1970s and early 1980s, and who often expected to hold on to their debt for years and years, most debt traders have no such expectations. As another trader told me with a wry smile, "The thing is, Noreena, capital has no soul."

Why the Bond Market Has Grown

Investors and traders are not the only ones who can make serious money from this new category of debt. Emerging-market bonds also present a nice business opportunity for the banks and securities firms that advise countries on the issuance of their bonds. Between 1992 and 2002, big securities firms made nearly $1 billion in fees from underwriting Argentine bonds alone, and not only do the banks that underwrite the issues earn significant fees, they also get to know key government officials in the issuer countries along the way, making contacts that put them ahead of other banks in the race for yet more lucrative business.

But emerging-market bonds aren't just appealing to the banks underwriting them or the traders buying and selling them. To those developing countries that can find buyers for their bonds—the world's neediest countries typically can't—borrowing money from the international capital market is perceived generally as a good thing. Why? First, developing countries typically need at least some external financing, perhaps not always as much as they think they need, but they generally do need some access to external funds. They are bad at mobilizing sufficient domestic resources to meet their spending needs. Increasing taxes is likely to be politically damaging (and increasingly hard to accomplish in the era of cross-border tax competition), as is selling off state assets. Although in some countries—India, for example—formalizing the black and informal economy has been seen as a way to raise revenue, these efforts have met with little success. Also, countries often believe that it will be cheaper to borrow abroad because dollar interest rates tend to be lower than domestic rates.

Compared with commercial loans, bonds are in many ways more attractive. Borrowing governments usually have much more free-dom in the way they spend the proceeds than they have with loans, bond covenants are less restrictive than loan covenants, the issuer doesn't need to perpetually fulfill conditions—like maintaining certain debt-to-export ratios—as long as interest is being paid. Fixed interest rates (when these are used) make bond repayments easier to plan for and, above a certain critical size of issuance (approximately $200 million), issuing bonds is simply more cost-effective.

Moreover, in times of crisis, commercial loan holders have in general been more troublesome than bondholders. In the Asian crisis in the 1990s, the commercial banks were much more disruptive than bondholders; indeed by refusing to coordinate their behavior they considerably exacerbated the situation. Typically, they drag their feet much more than bondholders when it comes to deciding how best to restructure loans—the commercial banks holding Latin American debts at the beginning of the 1980s, for example, took almost the whole decade to negotiate the restructuring process—while bondholders on the whole seem keener to reach resolution faster.

The Problems of Being Subject to Capital Markets

But like anything in life, there is a price to be paid for the relative ease and relative advantages of raising money on the bond markets. One of the main problem areas is that of currency fluctuation. In order to be of interest to foreign investors, bonds usually have to be denominated in a hard currency, which exposes the borrower to substantial currency risk. The reality of this danger was clearly brought home during the East Asian crisis of 1997–98 when effective debt burdens went shooting up to unmanageable levels as the currencies of Thailand, South Korea, Malaysia, Taiwan, Singapore, and the Philippines plummeted by as much as 50 percent against the dollar. The Indonesian rupiah fell by as much as 80 percent.

The absence of commercial bank, formal IMF, or World Bank strictures doesn't mean that the sovereign borrower is left to act unconstrained. Far from it. At best, the bond market is controlled by the amoral dictates of the "soulless" capital market and, at worst, by the positively immoral demands of the powerful players that shape it, which include, as we shall see, the IMF and World Bank. As James Carville, President Clinton's former campaign manager, has famously quipped: "I used to think if there was a reincarnation, I wanted to come back as the President or the Pope or a .400 baseball hitter. But now I want to come back as the bond market. You can intimidate everyone."

The main way in which the bond market "intimidates" is through the mechanism of interest rates. If it doesn't deem a country responsible or trustworthy, the interest it will demand will be extremely high. How the market determines "responsibility" and "trustworthiness" is the central element of this intimidation. Rates are derived essentially on the basis of two things—first, how well a country is perceived to be behaving, and second, the extent to which it is perceived as likely to default.

"Behaving" is, in this case, not about pledging allegiance to a particular flag. Here, a country is considered to be behaving if it conforms to the Wall Street and City traders' views of what a country should or should not do. This partly means not being too indebted in the first place, and having a healthy import-export ratio—but, most important, that the country be seen to be following the policies set by the World Bank and IMF. In effect, it has to adopt strict guidelines relating to fiscal discipline, balanced budgets, and low inflation, as well as adopt policies of privatization, deregulation, liberalization, and the reduction of trade barriers, or else risk market censure.

While countries that have a significant enough history of fiscal prudence at times can get away with some deviation from this strict path, most receive no leeway for short-term deviations from policy, whatever the problems or crisis they are trying to solve. If countries do seem to be "overspending" on social welfare programs, the market penalizes them. If their exports crash in price, their risk profile and interest rate rises. If natural disaster strikes, the yield demanded by the market rises almost instantaneously, dangerously impacting the country's ability to raise additional monies at the very time they can least afford to take on further financial commitments. At the slightest departure from conservative fiscal policy, at the slightest questioning of the orthodoxy, at moments of unexpected crisis, the markets are ready to rap a country's knuckles and heap punishment upon them in the form of higher, often crippling, interest rates. Not an increase of 1 or 2 percentage points, but sometimes as much as 15 percentage points in a matter of mere months. Imagine that, overnight, the interest you pay on your mortgage or your credit cards shot up by that amount. What would that mean for your budget, for your ability to provide for yourself or your family?

Of course, the market doesn't always penalize a country for not delivering on the orthodox economic front. The second criterion that the market uses to arrive at its judgment, "propensity to default," can sometimes override that. Soviet debt, for example, was viewed as having a negligible risk of default despite the fact that its economy could hardly have been said to have delivered on the mainstream economic orthodoxy. Tunisia, itself only a partial and reluctant subscriber to the neoliberal orthodoxy, can borrow at a mere 3 percent premium, the same rate at which Mexico typically borrows. In fact, all that matters to meet with approval on this count is either that the country in question has been seen to be of such geopolitical importance that whatever its internal policies, its relationship with the United States, the World Bank, and the IMF is such that it will be bailed out in times of crisis. This is the position the market took on Pakistani debt post-9/11, which moved from being traded at 60 cents on the dollar on September 10, 2001, to 105 cents on the dollar a year later, not because its economic situation had changed, but because it had become essential to American policy in the region.

Or the borrower government needs to be seen as "trustworthy," as far as its external stakeholders are concerned, that is. This means that the country doesn't have to be democratic, doesn't have to respect human rights or civil liberties, doesn't even have to be perceived as corruption-free. All that is necessary is for the lender to believe both that the borrowing government's commitment to repaying its debts is credible—the decision to repay is not necessarily connected with the *ability* to repay—and that it is unlikely that both the government will change *and* that any new government will fail to honor its predecessor's obligations. "In emerging markets," a leading analyst told me, "investors are always relieved when a strong figure comes into a country, especially after a period of chaos." Essentially, then, what investors are ideally looking for in the developing world is an investor-friendly dictator. Elected heads of state have to respond to the fluctuating and conflicting demands of their many different constituents.

Under President Vladimir Putin's authoritarian rule, therefore, Russian debt has, on the whole, seen its star rise precisely because Putin is perceived by the market as "strong and forceful." Tunisia enjoys its low-risk premium, despite its economic policies, because of its political stability—it is a constitutional dictatorship run by President Ben Ali since he took power in a bloodless coup in 1987. And while countless studies show that a history of armed conflict or political illegitimacy are not factors deemed important by the market, frequent changes in government *are* a highly significant predictor of default, and at least as important as any economic variable in determining perceived creditworthiness.

Brazil provides us with a good example of the opposite situation, a country being penalized by the market for "misbehaving" or being deemed a likely contender for default. In the run-up to its presidential elections in 2002, Brazil's economy seemed to be in tip-top shape: its economic fundamentals were stronger than the previous year, it was one of the world's top ten economies in terms of GDP, and it had stable political institutions and world-class companies. Nevertheless, as the former shoeshine boy Luis Inacio da Silva— "Lula"—rose up in the Brazilian polls, the yield the market demanded on Brazilian debt shot up in perfect tandem, from 7 percent in March 2002 to over 20 percent in September. Why? In large part, because analysts and traders had worked themselves up into a "the Russians are coming"–type frenzy: they were scared of Lula. "*Everyone* said Lula was a socialist," one emerging-markets trader related, "and if he were in power it would be a disaster." *Euromoney* magazine, an influential publication read by many investors, corroborated the dominant mood when it wrote in September 2002 that the market disapproved of this left-leaning politician's potentially "unfriendly" policies.

With forty-five million Brazilians living below the poverty line and Lula promising to wage war on hunger, analysts were terrified that he might not stick to Washington's rigid requirements. He might do something "rash," like increase budget expenditure, or decide that the $54 billion Brazil was paying out per year in debt service was just too much. Nor did the market like the fact that at the beginning of his campaign, Lula had pledged to suspend debt payments if elected (a statement that he spent the rest of his campaign trying to undo). The market "didn't believe that he would do the right thing under pressure," another trader told me.

It turned out that the market was, at that time at least, wrong. Indeed, Lula, after his election, not only stayed quite rigidly within budget but also kept to his later pledge and didn't default. As was to be expected, he was "rewarded" for this, at least by his external stakeholders. Citigroup's *Global Emerging Market Strategy Report* of July 2003 stated: "Our market benefited from notable improvements in fundamentals in a number of countries. The most important case was Brazil, where the outcome of the presidential election proved to be far more positive than many expected." Lula basically did as he was bid—not that surprising given that various influential emerging-market reports continued to make it very clear that if he did not maintain a tight macroeconomic policy designed to stabilize Brazil's debt after he was elected, he would be penalized with interest hikes he knew he could ill afford. When Brazil faced interest rates of 7 percent in March 2002, for example, the servicing cost of its debt was manageable—around 4 percent of GDP. When it rose to 24 percent at the height of anti-Lula paranoia, as Lula moved from below 30 percent to over 40 percent in the polls, the cost rose to over 15 percent of GDP, an amount that was more than half of all tax revenues, and which was way more than public spending on education and health combined. The rate fell back to 17 percent by December 2003 when Lula received more favorable international press, but this still imposed a significant burden on the economy.

Information Biases

Given the extent to which the market's determination of a country's eligibility impacts not only upon its investors' pockets but also on its people's day-to-day lives, it is essential to understand not only *why* but also *how* these judgments are arrived at by the individual traders and investors who make up the market.

While some banks and trading outfits do undertake primary research themselves—going off on their own fact-finding missions or hiring local "economic consultants" to help them determine the lay of the land—the two main sources of information, relied on by investors and borrowers alike, are the reports published by influential banks or securities firms' analysts and the ratings provided by rating agencies. Both are capable of distorting the way the market reads how "responsible" or "trustworthy" a country is.

Take the first, the proclamations of banks and securities firms' analysts. In the same way that, at the height of the 2000 tech bubble, Wall Street analysts had been talking up stocks so as to help their banks' corporate finance departments win contracts from companies for new share issues—Citigroup and Merrill Lynch were both heavily fined in 2002 for doing just that—the Chinese wall separating the research department from the underwriting department in investment banks for sovereign debt issues is similarly porous. This means that banks often both advise a country on a bond issue and also make supposedly independent recommendations that these bonds are worth buying, without having to disclose such a clear conflict of interest. The problem is exacerbated by the fact that bonuses are usually calculated for an emerging-market group as a whole, which means that it is to the analysts' clear advantage to help their banks sell the bonds they are responsible for "independently" analyzing.

Indeed, it is now clear that the lending frenzy to Argentina throughout the late 1990s and early 2000s was, to a large extent, driven by the bullish and influential proclamations of analysts from the very same firms that were underwriting Argentina's bond issues—firms that desperately needed to keep on pushing the Argentine bonds because financial crises in Asia and Russia in 1997 and 1998 had meant that if their clients didn't buy Argentine bonds, they probably wouldn't be buying anything. "It's a lot of self-censorship," said Federico Thomsen, former chief economist of the

Buenos Aires office of ING Barings. "It's like, if you have something good to say, you say it, but if you have something bad to say, just keep your mouth shut." Bad things like, say, the fact that former Argentine president Carlos Menem's reforms were clearly capricious, often incomplete, and sometimes illicit. Bad things like the fact that for a full year before the crisis hit, residents were withdrawing dollars from local banks at an accelerating rate, judging for the first time that their currency might be in trouble, and keeping their dollars at home in safes, creating the same effect as would capital flowing out of the country. Bad things like the fact that polls from 2001 onward were indicating that Argentine voters favored default. Even the increasing number of pro-default strikes and marches were underplayed. In 2000 and early 2001, when the recession was clearly biting and the marches proliferating, many of the analysts' reports, although less bullish than before, continued to predict that Argentina would muddle through.

And because the market works on the Greater Fool Theory— you're fine as long as there is someone out there stupid enough to buy the bonds from you—traders could afford to ignore the realities: after all, for a long time there appeared to be a limitless desire for Argentinian bonds. And the analysts' reports provided the traders with a great alibi: these bonds had the stamp of external approval, if things went wrong there was somewhere to pass the buck.

To be fair to the traders, almost everyone was ignoring the realities. As a senior trader told me: "'Ninety-seven, '98, '99 . . . we were just lending stupidly to Argentina. No one thought it could default, and there was always someone who would buy your bonds from you. The market was really liquid; it was really easy to sell on, to go on and on." "It was an orgy of lending," said one former Latin American bond trader of the late 1990s, "a bubble that seemed, like the Internet bubble, never likely to burst."

The analysts' bullishness played a critical role. Wall Street's continual optimism led to a perpetual inflow of money, in turn encouraging the Argentine government to issue more and more bonds as a way to service its debt. As Rogelio Frigerio, Argentine secretary of economic policy in 1998, said, "If you get the money so easily as we did, it's very tough to tell the politicians 'don't spend more, be prudent,' because the money was there and they knew it."

And so the market, aided and abetted by the analysts, made an astounding misjudgment: failing to anticipate the biggest sovereign default in history—$97 billion of public debt.

"The time has come to do our mea culpa," Hans Joerg Rudloff, chairman of the Executive Committee at Barclays Capital and godfather of the Eurobond market, said at a conference of bank and brokerage executives in London. "Argentina obviously stands as much as Enron [in showing that] things have been done and said by our industry which were realized at the time to be wrong, to be self-serving."

Thumbs Up

But it isn't just the $2-million-a-year analysts whose words determine how a country is perceived by the market. Their $200,000-a-year counterparts at organizations called rating agencies are, in many ways, even more influential. For in the same way that Michelin rates restaurants, or Ebert and Roeper rate movies, private rating agencies—primarily Moody's and Standard and Poor's, which between them cover 80 percent of the market—rate countries by assigning a letter to their name. This letter, paid for ironically by the borrower, is used by investors to help them determine not only how risky a country is, with an increasing percentage of investors only wanting higher-grade investments, but also whether or not it can even hold that country's debt at all. Most pension and mutual funds, for example, are not allowed to hold sub-investment-grade debt, debt rated below BBB–. The negligible participation of most low-income countries in the capital markets can be largely attributed to their failure to attain investment-grade ratings.

Essentially, the ratings agencies use the same calculations as the analysts to determine what letter to assign—they look at macroeconomic variables (for example, at the extent to which the country is following the economic orthodoxy) and the trustworthiness of the debtor. Moody's, for example, admitted that it downgraded Brazil's credit rating in the run-up to the presidential election because of Lula's poll ratings. And like the analysts, the rating agencies often misread the political dimensions of risk—the political factors that bear upon a country's ability or willingness to service its debt, the pressures a leader is under from his electorate when times are tough, and the impact of rising nationalist tendencies.

Indeed, ratings agencies often call things wrong, seriously wrong, and the consequences can be dire for both borrowers and lenders: dire for investors who get caught out if the rating agencies haven't downgraded a country fast enough, and dire for the borrowing country both if the agencies upgrade it too enthusiastically, as euphoric expectations will often stimulate excessive capital inflows, and if they downgrade it too keenly—as they are prone to do after they have got it wrong. Not only, for example, did the agencies not predict the Asian crisis of 1997, or indeed the Mexican so-called Tequila crisis a couple of years earlier, but also when they realized their mistake, they panicked, dropping the ratings of the countries concerned by four to five notches overnight.

And downgrades really matter. In the world of emerging markets, the stress that a downgrade can create can be too much to bear. When a country's debt is downgraded, its cost of (new) borrowing shoots up by, on average, 2 percentage points for each notch it falls. Pension and mutual funds that maintain a minimum debt rating below which they will not buy, immediately sell. Once investors smell blood in the water and see money pouring out of a country, they will all try to sell off their bonds. Domestic corporations from the country in question see their debt downgraded, since typically no corporate debt is rated higher than the sovereign debt of the country it hails from, meaning that they, too, now find it very hard to raise money, no matter how well run they may be, or however compelling their work.

The panic that a downgrade sparks is made significantly worse by the fact that the IMF, the World Bank, and the United States have traditionally been adamant that developing countries do not have any capital controls in place. This means that developing countries are neither able to stop "hot" speculative monies coming in, nor when money starts pouring out are they able to stop the outflow despite the significant evidence that those countries that have averted crises, such as Chile, are precisely those that were able to control the flow of money. Countries can see the price of their debt plummet and expected yields and cost of borrowing soar, simply because a herd of investors has decided to pull out.

Vultures

They can also face serious problems if a certain class of investor chooses at that moment to buy in. In the same way that European nations in the late nineteenth and early twentieth centuries used sovereign debt default as an excuse to invade foreign territory, a select group of rogue creditors, known as debt vultures, actively prey upon countries likely to default, buying up significant portions of their debt, and then storming in to demand that they repay their debts at 100 cents on the dollar. Debt vultures make huge gains if they are successful, because they have bought the debt at a significant discount on the secondary market, at a price that was arrived at under the assumption, of course, that the debt would never, ever, be redeemed at face value.

The New York–based Elliot Associates, for example, paid $11 million for Peruvian debt on the secondary market, then sued the Peruvian government for full payment plus capitalized interest, and astonishingly ended up with an award of $58 million—a $47 million profit. To them it was just good business, but to the children of Peru, it meant that schoolbooks, medicines, and clean water could no longer be provided. Another "debt vulture" is Kenneth Dart, the Cayman Islands–based heir to the Styrofoam cup fortune, who bought up $1.4 billion worth of Brazil's external debt at a 60 percent discount, refused to join in with the Brady restructuring plan agreed to by most of Brazil's creditors, and successfully fought to get his debt redeemed at face value. Dart recently sued Argentina for $700 million. Or the Leucadia Holding Company, which bought up

Nicaraguan debt in the secondary market of face value $26 million for only $1.14 million and received a judgment entitling it to collect $87 million from the country's government—one of the poorest in the world. Or the good-looking American in London, whose name I have promised not to reveal, who tells me from the back of his chauffeur-driven black Mercedes, that "I now own a country" in the South Pacific. "I bought 80 percent of its debt at a discount six months before the due date. The country didn't pay, and I'm now in the process of issuing a lien on all its international assets." Thanks to the actions of the vultures and to the delight of their attorneys, who take such cases on a contingency fee basis, at least a dozen of the world's poorest countries have faced or are facing similar legal challenges.

What the vultures do is not illegal—how they might be reined in is something that will be discussed in the concluding chapter. But what they do is at the extremes. Typical creditors take a cut on the profits they could realize when a country clearly cannot repay its debts, under the assumption that it is better to get something rather than nothing, and also because in many cases they have other interests in the country so do not want it to collapse. They are also concerned about safeguarding their own reputations and hope to engage in future business with the country in question. Debt vultures laugh in the face of such concerns, refuse to play ball, and instead exploit the situation for huge gain. "Scum" is what a major emerging-markets trader told me he thought of them for refusing to enter into rescheduling agreements, stopping other creditors from getting paid until their claims are resolved, and putting some of the world's poorest countries into the position of deciding to settle rather than become embroiled in costly legal battles.

"I feel bad when I think of poor people," my American in London tells me, but, echoing the trader I first met, concludes, "I can't save the world."

Yet again, the story of debt is the story of certain groups lining their pockets to the detriment of the masses. Yet again, we see debt as a tool that, despite the benefits it undoubtedly could engender if used wisely, instead all too often actively harms. The market discipline that the capital markets are supposed to bring, which in the fairy tale scenario ensures that governments do not go on unconstrained spending binges and use the debts for productive use, is on the whole just that: a fairy tale. For the most part, the workings of the market are so corrupted by special interests, biased or inaccurate information, and, of course, geopolitical distortions that private capital inflows can accelerate booms and exacerbate busts, and "good" countries can be penalized while the "profligate" are rewarded. As when Brazil faced the wrath of the market in 2002, not because it wasn't adopting sound policies, and not because it was struggling economically, but because its most popular presidential candidate didn't meet with market approval.

It is no wonder that to the traders and investors in developing-world debt it is all a big game—for that is precisely what it is, a game of smoke and mirrors, of illusions and deceit. No wonder that developing-world governments, recognizing this, often end up taking one of two paths—the "market-pleasing" path, in which they desperately try to do as the market bids, reflecting its wishes in their domestic policies, and prioritizing its desires above those of their domestic constituents, a strategy that as we will see can trigger social unrest. Or they take the "playing along too" path, in which the government issues bonds when they know they have no chance of ever redeeming them at face value, adding yet another layer to the pyramid in the knowledge that they will probably be long gone when it collapses.

Without sufficient safeguards in place, the bond market risks becoming the intermediary not only for the buying and selling of developing-country debt, but also for the trading of developing-world despair. But if it's misery we're interested in, then it is to the IMF and the World Bank that we must turn, for no two institutions have been blamed as much for developing-world suffering, or played such critical and ongoing roles in the story of debt.

6

Gray Men in Gray Suits

Imagine
your bank
manager said to you,
"I will lend to you, but
only if you jump up and
down on one spot 100
times, wear a haircloth
shirt, and suck my
dick."

Winter Blues

Winter in Russia is bleak and harsh. "Even the wolves have a hard time of it," said Maxim Gorky, the namesake of the city in which I spent most of my twenty-third year. Fresh out of Wharton, the American business school, I had been hired as a consultant by the International Finance Corporation (IFC), the sister organization of the World Bank, to help determine what advice they should give the Russian government on its economic reforms. Winter in Russia was something I came to understand very well.

I won't go into the details of what it was like living in Russia in the early 1990s—the jubilant triumph when I found a can opener at a supermarket; the endless weeks of eating nothing but buckwheat; the beauty of watching *Swan Lake* at the Bolshoi, surrounded by families with young children; the adventures I had and the characters I met when I hitched rides late at night after work, as there was no other way to get home; the loneliness, the excitement, the danger, and the new—but what I will go into is how I came to be increasingly disillusioned with what we were doing. And how the concerns I raised fell upon deaf ears.

Everything was changing in Russia just then. The birthmarked Mikhail Gorbachev had been usurped by the vodka-drinking Boris Yeltsin. Perestroika and glasnost were history. And I was there as part of a team taking orders from Washington, whose mission was to turn Russia into a market economy or, more precisely, into a new United States of America.

How naive this now seems, but back then it was supposed to be so easy. We would impose a few basic requirements on Russia— liberalize its prices, open its markets, privatize its state-owned enterprises—and, hey, presto, the U.S. of R.

Anyone who had spent any significant length of time in Russia— rather than just flying in for a couple of days at a time as was the habit of the Washington big shots—would first have quickly realized how unrealistic this was, and second, would have become increasingly concerned about the cost that these steps would impose. With the specific task of developing the Russian privatization program, I soon recognized both. It became obvious, through nights spent in conversation with Russian workers and managers against the backdrop of balalaika playing, that the country's traditions, culture, and history could not just be razed overnight—the "one size fits all" solution that we were trying to impose was not going to fit. Moreover, if Russia did do as it was told, if state-owned enterprises were privatized en masse as we were recommending, the social costs would be huge. What would happen, I asked my Washington bosses, when, under unbearable financial pressure, the factories I was spending time in had to lay off thousands of their employees? What would happen to the health care, the schools, the sanatoriums that these factories were providing—not just to their workers, but to the entire locality? And, I cautioned, shouldn't we be more careful about our recommendations, think more clearly about the consequences?

Nobody was listening. "This is about politics," I was explicitly told. "The whole point of the privatization process is to take state assets out of state hands so that the Communist Party never returns. If this means that it ends up in the hands of a few nonparty elites, so be it." "And what about the people?" I asked. "The market will sort them out."

But the market never did. Life expectancy fell by five years between 1990 and 1994, and suicide rates shot through the roof. As predicted, most of the country's assets ended up in the hands of a select few, people like Boris Berezhovsky, who lives richly off his gains in self-imposed exile in London, and Roman Abramovich, who, at the age of thirty-six, was able to buy Chelsea Football Club. But few have heard of the losers: Galina Raube, the Muscovite English professor who can no longer afford a basic basket of groceries; Marina Zasklavskaya, who fled with her family to Brighton Beach; Vasily Yeddokimov, the seventy-plus-year-old machinist in Voskresensk who only earns $47 a month, when he is paid, that is, to name but a few.

In the autumn of 1992, I left the IFC. The hubris of my bosses had finally got to me, and any lingering faith I had that we knew what we were doing had been firmly extinguished.

Yet at the time, I had no idea that I was but one of a series of IFC, World Bank, and IMF consultants and employees who had left or would leave with similar bitter feelings. Davison Budhoo, for example, resigned from the IMF in 1988 claiming that it had "knowingly created international credit problems for Trinidad and Tobago," claims backed up by a subsequent independent tribunal. Ravi Kanbur, the lead author of the World Bank's *World Development Report* on poverty, quit the Bank in 2000 in the late stages of authoring it after coming under immense pressure from the U.S. Treasury to tone down sections on the importance of social spending and redistributive tax policies in tackling global poverty. Or, most famously and most recently, Joseph Stiglitz, the Nobel Prize–winning economist and former chief economist of the World Bank who, after leaving the

Bank, launched a highly critical attack on the IMF in *Globalization and Its Discontents,* a lambasting that landed him not only on the *New York Times* bestseller list, but also prompted a particularly vitriolic and public ad hominem attack from the IMF. "Your ideas are at best highly controversial, at worst, snake oil," wrote Ken Rogoff, former economic counselor and director of the Research Department of the IMF, in an open letter to Stiglitz. Although I was a relatively junior insider questioning what on earth we were doing, it later transpired that others, much more senior, were questioning it, too.

But what are these two institutions, the World Bank and the IMF, that have engendered such strong and, at times, such public objections, even from their own employees? And what role do they play in our story of debt?

The Good Old Days

Let's go back in time again, to the summer of 1944, to a mountain resort in New Hampshire by the name of Bretton Woods, where a group of men are meeting—and I do mean men; in the photos of the meeting prominently displayed at World Bank headquarters, you see virtually no women in the gray-suited sea.

These are uneasy times. World War II continues to rage, and World War I and the global Great Depression of the 1930s are still living memories in the minds of these men. The aim of the meeting is threefold: how do we help a war-ravaged Europe rebuild herself?; what do we need to do to ensure that the world never again has to face a 1930s-type depression?; and how can we have full employment and expanding world trade at the same time?

While the attendees represented forty-four countries, two men took an early lead in the discussion: a Brit, John Maynard Keynes, the preeminent economist of his day; and an American, the lesser-known chief international economist of the U.S. Treasury, Harry Dexter White. In response to the first question, they made it clear that Europe needed access to funds and that the private capital markets could not be trusted to deliver. An institution was needed that could help a bombed-out Europe rebuild herself. And so, that summer at Bretton Woods, the International Bank for Reconstruction and Development was born—an institution that soon became known as the World Bank.

As far as the second and third questions went, Keynes and Dexter White both felt the Depression had occurred because countries had dealt with their balance of payment deficits (the fact that they were importing more than they were exporting) and their desire to safeguard employment in very destructive ways—essentially by putting up trade barriers so as to keep out imports, and by devaluing their currencies in an attempt to make their exports cheaper and earn the requisite foreign currency with which they could buy imports; both strategies leading to a beggar-thy-neighbor–type policy, a downward spiral with countries having to keep on devaluing their currencies and keep on hiking up trade barriers in order to compete. They proposed a two-step solution. First, the world needed to return to the gold standard—it had been abandoned in 1931 when Britain dropped it—so that fixed exchange rates could once more be put in place to prevent countries from devaluing their currency at will. Second, the management of balance of payment deficits needed to be radically rethought.

To that end, another new institution would be needed, an institution designed to preserve stability in international balance of payments. And it would do this in the following way. Countries experiencing a deficit, and therefore a shortage of foreign exchange, would be able to petition this new institution for a short-term loan with which they could buy the foreign currency they needed to purchase imports. This meant that they would not have to resort to the practices that had sparked the global depression of the 1930s. Once a country had got out of trouble, the idea was that it would repay the loan.

Keynes, however, differed from Dexter White in two essential ways. First, he felt that the onus of preserving the stability of the international financial system shouldn't fall only on deficit countries— surplus countries should also have to do something to address the disequilibrium and also be actively discouraged from running up a surplus in the first place. And, second, Keynes felt that the funds provided to the deficit country should have very few restrictions attached, including no time limits as to when they should be repaid. He envisaged this new institution as a bank where some people leave their savings and other people can get loans out of these savings. Dexter White, on the other hand, felt that not only should the burden of preserving global financial equilibrium fall on the deficit countries alone, but that any loans should only be temporary and be accompanied by demands for "adjustment"—a process in which deficit countries are forced to deflate and cut imports, so as to restore their balance of payments position. This difference of opinion was undoubtedly driven largely by the fact that, whereas Britain was, at the time, running a huge balance of payments deficit, the United States was running a large surplus.

Dexter Smith's vision was the one that won. Despite Keynes's considerable negotiating skills, the disparity in financial resources between the United States and Great Britain had always meant that American preferences would triumph. An institution was set up to manage balance of payment equilibrium and the fixed exchange rate system, and it was named the International Monetary Fund (IMF). According to its founding documents, this institution was to be a bank to which deficit countries could go to borrow short-term funds, but not one that would make demands on countries running up surpluses.

The Legacy

Initially, in the context of a First World devastated by war, the focus of both the Bretton Woods institutions was the developed world. This focus, however, quickly changed, most rapidly in the case of the World Bank, which almost immediately found itself redundant, given the United States' decision to launch the Marshall Plan in Europe.

In the face of the plan's massive $13.3 billion injection of aid, the

World Bank simply wasn't needed to make the loans to the region that had been anticipated. What was to be done? It needed a shift of focus, which it found by turning instead to the developing world. There it could make an impact. At first, it lent to large public infrastructure and development projects. In the late 1960s, under the presidency of Robert McNamara, poverty alleviation became its focus, and it also began to lend for education, health, and housing.

Some of the loans the World Bank made did address McNamara's poverty alleviation agenda—World Bank irrigation projects, for example, more than doubled the incomes of those farmers lucky enough to get water. Many others, however, were left high and, literally, dry. As Muhbub ul Haq, McNamara's right-hand man, said in 1981, "The bottom 20 percent of the population has remained largely outside the scope of our projects." And, in fact, less than 10 percent of the $77 billion worth of loans made during McNamara's reign went into water supply, health, family planning, education, or other programs that might have directly helped the poor. As was the case with the commercial banks or export credit agencies that we considered in previous chapters, a significant proportion of World Bank loans also ended up supporting environmentally or socially unsound projects, or ones that were obviously doomed to fail.

In 1981, for example, Brazil was lent $445 million by the World Bank for the PoloNoreste project—a 930-mile highway through the Amazon rain forest. While this was ostensibly to help create new rural settlements in order to reduce Brazil's overstretched urban centers, the project was ill-thought-out and ill-configured, prompted in large part by the Bank's mirroring of the commercial bank lenders of the time—an obsession with lending at all costs. In the words of a Bank employee, "The Bank money machine was looking for big projects in the late 1970s, there was a lot of pressure to lend; any argument for not lending was very unpopular; people's careers were being made or not made by the size of their lending." And the upshot? In the case of PoloNoreste—massive deforestation and destruction of native homelands. Six years later, World Bank president Barber Conable said, "It was a sobering example of an environmentally sound project gone wrong."

Through the 1990s, many loans continued to be ill-advised: the tension between the pressure to lend and the achievement of development goals persisted. A leaked internal memo acknowledged that the Bank at the end of the twentieth century was "driven by an ever growing list of mandates imposed on it through a variety of means . . . Bank President's favored subjects . . . board sentiments . . . public pressures, ideas generated by internal constituencies and even fads . . . No initiative that starts as a pilot is ever considered a failure because of a lack of any honest evaluation." Even when loans were evaluated—since the late 1980s formal Environmental Assessments have been undertaken of all Bank projects, for example—projects were rarely modified in the light of such analysis, frequently because by the time the assessments were ready it was too late to use them. And any environmental safeguards built into the project were rarely followed up on the ground once a project was approved. Not surprisingly, the World Bank's own evaluation of project performance in that decade showed that in the world's poorest regions, South Asia and Africa, between 60 and 70 percent of World Bank–funded projects had failed. While an internal evaluation of the Bank's decade-long forest strategy revealed that its policies in this area failed to help the poor, were inadequately monitored, and were directly responsible for driving deforestation. Not a great track record.

And as we've seen happen time and time again, many tyrannical rulers also ended up as major beneficiaries of the loans. The heinous military junta, for example, that ruled Argentina between 1976 and 1982 was a major beneficiary of the Bank's largesse. Apartheid South Africa borrowed a quarter of a billion dollars from the Bank between 1948 and 1966, making it one of the Bank's biggest clients at that time. The repressive regime of Colonel Mengistu Haile-Mariam of Ethiopia was lent more than $1 billion. In 1986, the year that the *Economist* declared Ethiopia's human rights record the worst in the world, Mengistu's government was lent more than $100 million by the Bank. Romania's despotic leader, Nicolae Ceauşescu, was another favored client.

Corrupt leaders were also favored borrowers. Indonesia was lent $30 billion by the World Bank during the Suharto reign, approximately one-third of which was stolen. Ferdinand Marcos's Philippines was lent $4 billion, and Abacha of Nigeria was also lent billions, monies that weren't spent on just shoes, effigies, and follies, but vast proportions of which ended up squirreled away in Swiss, German, U.K., and American bank accounts. In fact, so commonplace was this daylight robbery, that the World Bank coined its own term for it—"leakage." Recent World Bank audits reveal that, in many cases, as much as 60 to 70 percent of loans disappeared this way.

Corruption and tyranny simply didn't factor into the World Bank's lending decisions, especially if those being lent to were favorites of their major shareholders. All that mattered was that the loan would be paid back. After all, dictators are, from a banker's point of view, often better credit risks than democratically elected rulers. Moreover, they are often much better able to instigate and see through the unpopular reforms that the Bank usually prescribes than democratically elected governments that rely upon popular support.

While the Bank was lending willy-nilly in the developing world, the IMF also began to shift its focus away from the developed world, with similarly worrisome consequences. Until the 1970s, most of the $13 billion that the IMF lent to countries facing balance of payment deficits was primarily to countries in the developed world—the United Kingdom, for example, was the IMF's largest receiver of loans during the 1960s when it was experiencing significant balance of payments problems. But in the early 1970s this changed dramatically. Countries began losing confidence in the strength of the American economy and sold off their dollar reserves in favor of gold. The United States went off the gold standard once more, rather than risk losing its gold reserves. The postwar fixed exchange rate system, which was essentially pegged to the dollar, collapsed. And then, in 1973, as we know, the oil crisis hit, followed later by a global crash in commodity prices.

In the face of this triple whammy several developing countries ran up balance of payments deficits, especially the oil importers whose exports could not cover their import needs. If these were the countries that had the commercial banks knocking on their doors, it was to these that they now turned for loans. If they were countries of geopolitical importance, they went to their bilateral bankers. If, however, they found it impossible to obtain sufficient funds from private or bilateral sources to address their needs, they turned instead to the IMF.

The IMF loans came, however, at a significant political and economic cost. Zambia, for example, which first went to the IMF in 1973, was given, along with a loan, what soon became the IMF's standard to-do list. Raise your interest rates, depreciate your currency to reduce the demand for foreign goods, reduce your trade barriers, reduce your government expenditure: measures that fitted with what had become the IMF's prime obsession—the curing of balance of payment deficits by reducing inflation through a reduction of public spending, imports, and employment. It was a creed that, as so many of its beliefs, proved to be misguided—for even though it is true that no economy can succeed under conditions of hyperinflation, there is little evidence to suggest that pushing inflation to lower and lower levels generates benefits at all commensurate with the costs. Moreover, while the IMF's policies might have made sense in the case in which inflation was generated by high demand, they made no sense when the rise in inflation was generated by sudden and substantial increases in oil prices. In that case, a more efficient use of energy and investments to make the economy less vulnerable to oil shocks might have been a better solution.

The other major change that took place in the 1970s was that the IMF stopped providing temporary balance of payments support, the original mandate of the institution, and instead started to provide ongoing medium- and long-term financing. In the Zambian case, for example, six agreements with the IMF were struck between 1973 and 1986. An increasing number of developing countries with ongoing and seemingly intractable balance of payment difficulties repeatedly went to the IMF.

This increased lending meant that getting repaid became more and more of a priority for the institution. And in order for debtor countries to move into a position from which they could service and repay their IMF loans, not only did they have to follow the anti-inflation policies of the Fund listed above, they also had to boost their exports to generate the requisite foreign currency to repay their loans. Countries that had begun to industrialize were leaned upon to refocus on primary products, commodities that could be exported, so that they could earn the hard currency with which to pay back the monies. Poor countries were encouraged to switch agricultural production from foods that met domestic needs to cash crops suitable for export. This was advice that not only served to reinforce the dangerous dependency on raw material exports these countries already had, but also resulted in many countries losing the self-sufficiency they once had in feeding their own populations.

Revving Up

After the debt crisis of 1982, when countries hemorrhaging on debt service repayments also turned to them for help, the role of the World Bank and the IMF in providing loans to the developing world notched up a gear. The World Bank, which had hitherto only lent money for specific projects and had focused primarily on rural development and longer-term infrastructure investment, now joined the IMF in providing balance of payments loans to the whole host of new countries that came knocking on their door, now that commercial lending to the Third World had all but dried up.

This suited the World Bank and the IMF well for two reasons. First, as we saw in chapter 4, they feared that the commercial banks that had lent to the developing world during the petrodollar boom would collapse if these countries could not honor their debts, thereby jeopardizing not only the economic security of the United States (as it was from there that most of the banks hailed), but also the whole international financial system. More than glad to be called upon to do their bit in averting the collapse, they began doling out new loans with which countries could repay the mainly commercial old loans, a de facto bailing out of the private banks, completely disregarding the fact that they were also letting the irresponsible commercial lenders completely off the hook.

The second reason their new "savior status" suited the World Bank and the IMF so well was that they viewed lending as essential—it was after all their basic raison d'être. Staff in both these organizations were under extreme pressure to dole out loans: targets were set, and, if not met, promotion was at risk and jobs could even be lost. Such internal pressure to lend and keep lending goes some way to explaining why so many uneconomic or environmentally unsound projects were still being financed by the World Bank.

In fact, the international financial institutions were soon lending so much that in the 1980s they ousted the commercial banks from pole position in much of the developing world. Ghana, for example, received $200 million a year from the IMF between 1983 and 1986. Mozambique received a $45 million World Bank credit in 1985; Nigeria, $45 million that same year. Tanzania was given almost $200 million from the Fund and Bank in 1986.

And, the more the countries needed their money, the more stringent, questionable, and dogmatic the conditions attached to their loans became. New arrangements, known as "structural adjustment programs," a term that later became feared by many developing countries, were introduced by the World Bank and the IMF as a condition for providing loans. Although the key elements remained the same—devaluation, trade liberalization, and so forth—some new demands had been added. These included diktats to raise taxes, allow the prices of essential commodities and basic services to go up, abandon any dirigiste policies, curtail public expenditure, relax barriers to external capital flows, deregulate the labor market, cut public sector jobs, impose wage restraints, and sell off the states' "crown jewels." A never-ending, it sometimes seemed, list of detailed conditions. Some countries were aghast to find that their loans had as many as one hundred distinct conditions attached.

And these conditions had to be adhered to. For where the World Bank and the IMF differed from the cold war bilateral lenders, was that while the latter tended not to insist upon their economic policies being adopted by the borrower—they were more concerned about allegiance to flag or ideology—the World Bank and the IMF insisted upon the game being played by their rules. This was the era of Reagan and Thatcher, of extreme free-market policies, and a deep-rooted aversion to state intervention. It was the era of what had become known as the Washington Consensus. As Joseph Stiglitz has said, "There was within the World Bank [before he joined], the IMF and the U.S. Treasury a strong view that macrostability, privatization and liberalization were of the first order. Everything else was secondary."

One medicine, "structural adjustment," was prescribed for all the developing world by the IMF and World Bank "doctors," regardless of the particular ailment the country had.

"They used to come from Washington with ready-made models. They said, 'This is what we think is best for you. We know what development is. Implement it and you will be better off,'" recalls a former high-ranking official in the Senegalese Ministry of Finance. And there was no wavering allowed. As Lynda Chalker said in 1989, while minister for overseas development in the Thatcher government, "The countries must not be allowed to stop adjustment. Make no mistake—there is no alternative."

The consequences of these structural adjustment programs were, however, hardly as advertised.

Although it is true that, when the timing is right and social safety nets are in place, the kind of policies insisted upon by the Bretton Woods institutions can lead to positive outcomes; if these underlying conditions do not prevail, the converse is usually true. Indeed, rather than engendering growth or alleviating poverty—the stated goals of the IMF and World Bank respectively—growth declined and poverty and unemployment increased during this period of structural adjustment. In fact, detailed statistical analysis has revealed that IMF programs actively serve to reduce growth and exacerbate inequalities in income distribution, with several studies showing that the "single most consistent effect the IMF seems to have is its ability to redistribute income away from workers." In Latin America, for example, growth fell by 50 percent between the 1960–80 prestructural adjustment period and the 1980–2000 period when structural adjustment was the norm, a period during which the gap between rich and poor widened. In sub-Saharan Africa, the incomes of the poorest 20 percent fell by 2 percent a year between 1980 to 2000, the period when structural adjustment programs were the dominant policy instruments, while growth fell by 0.8 percent a year during this time, as compared with a rise of 2.3 percent per year between 1960 and 1975. The countries that did attain high rates of growth in that period—China, India, and Korea, for example—were precisely those that did not buy the World Bank's and IMF's lines, and instead followed more tailor-made models of development. Moreover, the currency devaluations and enforced price controls that the IMF and World Bank usually insisted upon as part of their structural adjustment package typically resulted in a decrease in effective household incomes, leaving the poor of many countries with even less expendable capital. In the countries in which privatization, deregulation, and a reduction in social spending were most extensive, the rich became richer at the expense of the poor.

While inequality was not viewed by most within the Bretton Woods institutions as a terrible ill in itself—it was seen as more important that the poor are made better off, whatever is going on with the rich—despite the negative impact inequality has on health, social capital, and society itself, negative growth was not something that either the IMF or the World Bank wished to admit might be their fault. "The countries in question never took the medicine as prescribed" was the IMF's standard response to this kind of evidence, claiming that they lacked the "political will" to implement Washington's austerity measures—not surprising when significant numbers were increasingly protesting these very dictates. But even the IMF's "star pupils," countries that could always be counted upon to dance to the IMF's tunes, often fared badly. Bolivia, for example, which between 1985 and 1986 underwent one of the most severe structural adjustment programs to date, and then continued to implement neoliberal reforms radically, comprehensively, and consistently, remains to this day the poorest country in South America and one of the poorest in the Western Hemisphere.

As Mark Malloch Brown, head of the UN Development Program, has said, "The poster children of the 1990s are among those who didn't do terribly well. There are structural restraints of development. Market reforms are not enough. You can't just liberalize, you need an interventionist strategy."

But an interventionist strategy didn't fit with the laissez-faire doctrine that the IMF and the World Bank had come to preach. This was because the same hypocrisy that we saw practiced by the rich countries in earlier chapters had become increasingly manifest within these institutions, too. So, for example, we saw both institutions tell developing countries to open up their markets, despite the fact that developed countries continued to maintain their own subsidies and tariffs, barriers to trade that cost the developing world hundreds of billions of dollars a year in lost trade. And also, despite the fact that most of today's successful developed countries used tariffs, subsidies, and other means to promote their industries in the earliest stages of development, and only started preaching free trade once they themselves had reached the top. Britain, for example, had been an aggressive user of protectionism since before 1846, and the United States was the most heavily protected economy in the world between the Civil War and World War II. The rich world owed much of its success to the very protectionist policies that were being denied to the developing world.

Why Just Sit There?

But if the conditions associated with the loans were this objectionable or unreasonable, you might reasonably be wondering why the poor countries didn't rise up, object, and demand different terms. Why did so much of the developing world allow the international financial institutions essentially to take control of their economic and monetary policy during the 1980s? Why did it allow them to interfere so much in important national debates?

Part of the reason lay in their lack of alternatives. By the time a country turned to the IMF for help, it had probably exhausted all its other options (no one else would lend it the "greenbacks" that typically at that point it desperately needed, a problem made more striking once the cold war had ended, and countries lost their geopolitical importance). And many of the poorest countries now needed the IMF's and World Bank's money just to survive.

Part of the reason was that the IMF was integral to the decisions on whether or not a country facing bilateral debt servicing difficulties could get that category of debt rescheduled: countries were eligible to enter restructuring or rescheduling negotiations at the Paris Club only if the IMF had agreed that the country could not repay its debt, and also if the debtor country had agreed to accept the IMF's conditions. While there were those cases, rare at that time, where there were commercial lenders potentially willing to buy a developing country's bonds, whether or not they actually did so, and the terms they demanded in return related to the country's exhibited willingness to take the IMF's conditions on.

Another factor was that the very members of the IMF and World Bank in whose interests it would, in theory at least, have been to confront the institutions' lending policies, countries of the developing world had very little voice within the institutions themselves. Because voting rights are related to the size of a country's GDP, low- and middle-income countries have less than 40 percent of the share of votes (the entirety of sub-Saharan Africa has only 4 percent) and control less than half the seats of their executive boards, despite the fact that the peoples of the developing world make up 84 percent of the world's population. G7 countries, on the other hand, account for over 40 percent of voting power, with the United States, a country with less than 5 percent of the world's population, the only country with an effective veto vote. The power asymmetry between the economically strong countries and the economically weak is thus institutionalized within both the IMF and the World Bank.

And, finally, why we saw so little dissent on the part of borrower countries during the 1980s was that within the countries that had little voice at the IMF and World Bank, it was *their* weak and voiceless who were disproportionately hurt by both the payment of the debt and the conditions associated with it, not the ruling elites. The Latin American peasants, for example, who, thanks to the austerity programs that accompanied structural adjustment, were forced to leave their communities to seek work; the women who "chose" to sell their bodies to ensure food on the table for their children, now that the state had been forced to choose between providing a safety net for its citizens and meeting IMF/World Bank strictures; the children who were no longer sent to school now that governments all over the developing world slashed budgets for social services and introduced user fees in health and education in order to meet IMF/World Bank demands that public expenditure be curtailed; the Filipino women who were "sold" by their government as mail-order brides, so as to generate foreign exchange with which to repay debt; the rural poor who, thanks to the tearing down of trade barriers and the liberalization and privatization of their economies, left the countryside to join the teeming slums—stories many of which we will come back to later on.

Those who bore the brunt of the conditions attached to IMF and World Bank debt were, once again, not only those who benefited least from it, but were also those whose complaints were least likely to be listened to. And as we will see, this came to generate a sense among the "losers" from debt that the state was not only sacrificing its own sovereignty in exchange for the loans it was taking, it was also selling them out—a realization that, as we will see in chapter 10, has far-reaching implications.

It wasn't that the IMF and World Bank did not realize the shortcomings of their policies. They were alerted to these quite early on. A G24 working group report of 1987, for example, whose members included four executive directors of the IMF and three executive directors of the World Bank, concluded that IMF-supported adjustment programs had led to a decline both in levels of output and rates of growth, and had increased unemployment and adversely affected income distribution in developing countries. The report went on to recommend that external adjustment "needs to be achieved by means that are consistent with other important objectives such as growth and income distribution."

But, despite these findings and such a clear recommendation, structural adjustment continued as the essential prerequisite for loans. By 1990, 378 structural adjustment loans had been extended to 71 debt-burdened developing countries, totaling some $118 billion in current U.S. dollars.

The noose around the neck of the developing world had just got even tighter.

The
Present

7

Stop Not Making Sense

> We
> had just got into
> power. It was 1994, just after
> the genocide. The streets of Kigali
> were littered with dead bodies. The
> previous regime had looted the coffers.
> There wasn't even a stapler or a typewriter
> left in ministerial offices. And so we went to
> the World Bank, that first week, and we said we
> desperately need some help. And you know
> what the World Bank said to us? Not until
> you have paid the $3 million interest on
> your outstanding debt.
> —*Senior Rwandan government official,*
> *Davos, January 2003*

The Parable of the Butterfly

There is an ancient Jewish parable that goes like this: A clever young man approaches a wise rabbi whose reputation for being able to answer every question is known across the land. Thinking he can get the better of the rabbi and catch him out, the young man comes with a butterfly cupped between his hands. "If you are so wise, O Rabbi," he says, "what's in my hand—a live butterfly or a dead one?" If the rabbi answers "alive," the young man thinks, he will clasp his hands together and crush the insect, while if the rabbi answers "dead" he will open his hands and release the butterfly. Either way, he will show the rabbi's failure to the world.

Without pausing for breath, and looking him straight in the eye, the rabbi replies, "The answer, my boy, is in your hands."

By the early 1990s, a partial answer to the worsening debt and development debacle was in the World Bank's and IMF's hands. Not only, as we have seen, were they responsible for a significant part of the debt owed, they also were responsible for insisting that in order to get any new loans or be eligible for any debt relief, developing countries adopt a host of policies that had been clearly shown not to work. Yet, instead of openly admitting these facts, and acting responsibly with this knowledge, the Bretton Woods institutions chose to play "dead butterfly–live butterfly," rather than face the truth, truly acknowledge responsibility for the disaster that was continuing to play out and change their policies.

There were some changes in rhetoric from the two institutions in the early 1990s—the Bank published the *World Development Report on Poverty* in 1990, remarkably, the first time that it publicly acknowledged that poverty alleviation should be factored into the design of structural adjustment programs, and claims were made that active participation by local policymakers and citizens would now be sought in planning and designing programs and policies— but, in 1994, many staff were still saying that the basic modus operandi remained the same.

Policies continued to be developed in Washington and parachuted in from above, policies that, far from helping, in fact exacerbated the situation they were supposed to be rectifying.

And alongside the discredited but unchanging policies came yet more loans, as the World Bank and the IMF opened up their coffers so that countries could repay old debts with even more new loans— the Bretton Woods institutions fearing that were they not to maintain the myth that loans were being repaid, their own credit ratings would be put at risk. While total debt owed by developing countries had already more than doubled between 1980 and 1990, by 1995 it had shot up by half as much again, with these two institutions accounting for a significant part of the hike—total developing-country debt owed to multilateral lending institutions rose from $61 billion in 1980 to $313 billion in 1994.

Developing countries, many of them unable to secure global capital in other ways, and with global commodity prices continuing to fall, had to do something about their ballooning debt burdens; they gratefully gobbled up these new loans. At the same time, they approached the Paris Club, cap in outstretched hand, to beg that their bilateral loans be rescheduled. The IMF and World Bank had made it clear that the rescheduling of *their* loans was not an option.

But even with repeated Paris Club reschedulings, the debt continued to grow. Outstanding debts to commercial creditors and non–Paris Club nations, many of which had been racked up years earlier by regimes long since gone, remained, now with World Bank and IMF loans added to them and increasing the strain. Worse still, the borrower countries often had little to show for the mountains of financial anxiety they had accumulated. All the debt had produced was, in fact, more debt. There was a debt overhang that stifled private investment, growth, and development, and took desperately needed resources away from cash-strapped government budgets. Tanzania, for example, spent $155 million on debt repayments during 1993 and 1994, twice what it invested in that period in providing safe drinking water—this despite the fact that fourteen million people, half its population at the time, lacked access to clean water.

Time to Change

In 1995, however, the mood changed. The G8, meeting in Halifax, formally recognized that Paris Club agreements were simply not solving the debt crisis. Many countries had by now gone back five or more times to reschedule their debts, and it was crystal clear that bilateral creditors could not remedy the situation themselves since the largest share of the debt of the world's poorest countries was now invariably owed to the World Bank and the IMF. Seeing that the external debt of a number of countries looked increasingly precarious, and fearing a 1980s-style debt crisis, the G8 demanded that "the Bretton Woods institutions develop a comprehensive approach to assist countries with multilateral debt problems through the flexible implementation of existing institutions and new mechanisms where necessary."

The new reformist president of the World Bank, James Wolfensohn, was open to this challenge. He had already realized that the situation could not continue, and that the multilateral institutions would also have to provide some debt relief. Nawal Kamel, a Canadian who headed up the international finance division in the Bank's research group, was charged with coming up with how the World Bank should address the issue of debt.

The program she came up with—a program in which the Bank and the Fund would provide debt relief to the world's poorest countries, without, most important, attaching any new structural adjustment–type conditions for so doing—was never adopted, however.

Stanley Fischer, first deputy managing director of the International Monetary Fund at the time, was furious at the prospect of any debt relief going to these countries at all, let alone in the way Kamel suggested. He thought it would be a dangerous signal to give, that it would open the doors to profligate economic policy, and create a "moral hazard" whereby countries believing that they would always be bailed out would again be encouraged to run up huge debts. His answer was that the Fund should instead provide the countries in question with yet more highly conditional loans. Loans, after all, enabled the Fund to maximize its own power in terms of budget size, staff, prestige, influence, and so forth. Without the ability to extend loans, this would be reduced significantly. The friction between the IMF and the World Bank soon grew into outright hostility.

But in 1996 two events occurred to help move things forward. First, the "God card" was played. Cardinal Basil Hume, the then de facto head of the Catholic Church in England and Wales and one of a growing number of people in the United Kingdom who were, by this time, actively championing the debt relief cause under the Jubilee banner, arranged a meeting with Michel Camdessus, the head of the IMF and a practicing Catholic. According to IMF insiders, when Mr. Camdessus agreed to accept the invitation from the cardinal, he told his staff that he would be embarrassed if the IMF were not seen to be participating in the debt relief program. The second event was an intervention by Lawrence Summers, at the time deputy secretary of the U.S. Treasury. He told Camdessus and Wolfensohn that their open squabbling had to stop.

In October 1996, the World Bank and IMF duly announced, amid major fanfare, the Heavily Indebted Poor Countries initiative (HIPC), a program that aimed "to reduce the external debt of eligible countries as part of a strategy to achieve debt sustainability."

The initiative was a significant departure from previous debt relief efforts. For the first time in their fifty-year history, a percentage of the World Bank's and the IMF's own loans were included for write-off—an essential concession, given that this category of debt had become the largest proportion of total external debt owing for many of the world's poorest countries.

But, although HIPC was undoubtedly an important turning point, and at least an acknowledgment by the Bank and the Fund that something had to be done, it was also seriously flawed. The structural adjustment conditions that Kamel had determined should not be attached to debt relief were reinstated by Camdessus. When asked why he was demanding seven years of adherence to structural adjustment policies (the final period was, in fact, six), Camdessus allegedly said, "Why not? It's a nice figure."

Also, the way debt sustainability was calculated—on the basis of the exports a country was generating, not on what it could reasonably afford to pay—didn't make sense. Overoptimistic growth projections were used to calculate the amounts of debt that should be canceled—projections that developing countries could never realistically meet. And the amount considered sustainable—a debt-to-exports ratio of 250 percent—meant that 40 percent of export revenues would have to be paid out in the form of debt payments; after World War II, the Allies capped the percentage of German export revenues used for debt repayments at 3.5 percent. Moreover, several countries that should have been eligible for the program, even under the World Bank's and IMF's narrow criteria, were not included. Nigeria, for example, disappeared off the list overnight, even though it clearly met the requirements that HIPC had laid out—perhaps the country's outstanding $28 billion debt was too overwhelming.

And the program was achingly slow: as of April 1998, only one country—Uganda—had graduated. By the end of 1998, sub-Saharan debt was now over three times greater than it had been in 1980, with the world's poorest countries still paying back more in debt service than they were receiving in aid.

More radical steps needed to be taken. In January 1999, influenced by the widespread popular support the pro–debt-cancellation Jubilee campaign by now enjoyed in Europe, and also by its increasingly high profile—the seventy-thousand-people-strong human chain linked around the G8 summit calling for the total eradication of poor countries' debt a few months earlier in Birmingham, made headline news all over the globe—German chancellor Gerhard Schroeder called for further alleviation of developing world debt. "Although the international community has made several attempts to make debt problems more bearable during the past few years," he wrote in the *Financial Times* in January 1999, "it is clear that without a radical debt reduction in many of the poorest countries there is no hope of bringing about a fresh start."

The tide seemed to be turning. Canadian prime minister Jean Chrétien was next to jump aboard, and the Nordic countries and the Netherlands were not far behind. Gordon Brown, the British chancellor of the exchequer, also started pushing hard for deeper, faster debt cancellation. "We must cut the debt, and cut it now," he said in an address to a Jubilee public meeting in St. Paul's Cathedral, London, in March 1999. This was despite the fact that Clare Short, the British secretary of state for international development at the time, did not favor blanket debt forgiveness. President Bill Clinton, getting wind of what the Europeans were after, threw the United States' hat into the ring. And at the June 1999 G8 summit in Cologne, against a backdrop of fifty thousand Jubilee protestors, a new international deal on debt cancellation was announced. It was the deal that Bono and Shriver would spend the next fifteen months working on, doing all they could to ensure that the United States honored its commitment.

The HIPC initiative would be expanded. More countries would now see more of their debt canceled. The thresholds used in the initial program to calculate the amount of debt to make a country eligible for cancellation would be lowered. The spurious six-year qualification period in which countries would have to jump through IMF conditionality hoops would be reduced. Poverty reduction would now become central to debt reduction, and civil society participation would be recognized officially in a new scheme under which debtor governments would have to consult widely with local churches, trade unions, NGOs, and parliaments on how to spend the proceeds from debt relief, in order either to qualify for full debt cancellation or to receive new World Bank and IMF loans. Furthermore, it was announced that $100 billion of debt relief would now be provided to the forty-two countries included in the HIPC group.

Although all of this fell well short of Jubilee's original objective— which was to write off *all* the unpayable debt for fifty-two countries (some $375 billion)—and that $100 billion figure included $55 billion of relief already agreed to under the original HIPC program, the announcement at Cologne at last seemed to offer many of the world's poorest countries a glimmer of hope. Perhaps they were finally on their way out of their debtors' prisons.

Promises, Promises

The optimism was misplaced.

The $100 billion in debt relief, so triumphantly promised at Cologne, never materialized; only a third has so far been delivered. In the spring of 2004, only ten of the twenty-four countries that should have fully passed through HIPC and received a substantial write-off in their stock of debt, had actually seen this take place. The U.S. commitment to provide 100 percent bilateral debt cancellation to thirty-three countries has not yet been realized. The same is true of most other major bilateral creditors who, back in 1999, made similar pledges.

And the new and revised Cologne HIPC program has turned out to be almost as flawed as its predecessor. The amount of debt that countries are eligible to have canceled continues to be measured in a way that reflects creditors' interests, not debtors' needs. Uganda, for example, the first country to make it through HIPC, still pays out roughly 12 percent of its government revenues to cover its outstanding debt. Zambia, a country with almost one million people affected by HIV/AIDS, is still spending 30 percent more on servicing its debt than it is on health care. As the adviser to the Rwandan president told me, "The IMF simply looks at the figures. For them we don't exist. We are just statistics."

Indeed, the total debt service for the world's poorest highly indebted countries—countries in which half their people live on less than $1 a day and one-third go hungry, in which one in every six children dies before the age of five and in which life expectancy has declined from fifty to forty-six years since 1990—increased rather than fell between 1998 and 2000. Millions of children continue to die every year because money that could be spent on preserving their health is still being spent on debt service. Millions of children are prevented from attending school because money that could be spent on their education is still being spent on repaying debt. Rather than being released from their debtors' jails, the world's poorest countries have, once again, seen the door slammed in their faces. So much for Cologne.

Nor has the revised HIPC process, thanks to a continuing use of inflated growth estimates to determine the amount of debt relief a country should receive, brought debts down to levels that even the IMF and World Bank would consider sustainable. Ethiopia, for example, was projected by HIPC to grow at 6 percent a year for the next decade, a record achieved in the past by only a few countries such as Singapore, Ireland, and South Korea, and almost three times the 2.1 percent per annum growth that Africa has experienced over the past two decades.

Similarly, given that external shocks to world commodity prices were not built in to World Bank and IMF calculations, and given that most of the countries on the list continue to rely on a small list of volatile and vulnerable export commodities, the export projections used to make the HIPC calculations were completely overstated. Uganda, for which coffee makes up the bulk of its exports, saw the price of coffee drop from $2,000 per metric ton to $300 in one year. HIPC calculations predicted that the price of coffee would basically remain stable. No wonder that Ugandan debt was again classed as unsustainable almost as soon as it had graduated from the HIPC program. And the miserly additional $1 billion that the G8 agreed to provide to those countries facing continued unsustainable debt burdens because of commodity price drops and lower than expected export prospects, still falls far short of what would be needed to make good the HIPC commitments, even taking into account the fact that recently many commodity prices have risen.

The World Bank and the IMF themselves admitted in April 2002 that their export projections had been grossly inaccurate, and that up to half the countries expected to reach completion points in the next few years would not achieve their HIPC debt sustainability targets. Today, World Bank officials concede that the initiative to cancel countries' debt was not implemented quickly enough. Yet despite these admissions, these two institutions, the major creditors of the world's poorest countries, refuse even to contemplate writing off any more of the debts owed *them* than they already have agreed to. Nor have they been pushing for a speeding-up of the process.

Add to the IMF's and World Bank's intransigence and their inept calculations the fact that countries still only become eligible for either bilateral or multilateral debt relief if they follow the World Bank's and IMF's discredited and fundamentally antidemocratic structural adjustment policies, and the situation looks even more bleak. The $100 billion of debt relief announced in 1999 requires countries to pass yet another set of tests, determined as usual by the IMF and the World Bank. Although the name "structural adjustment" has been exorcised and rebranded "poverty reduction and growth facilities" (PRGFs), Altria is still Philip Morris. PRGFs are essentially the same one-size-fits-all structural adjustment policies. Indeed, the IMF's own staff admits that the 1979 conditionality guidelines still remain essentially in place.

Charging for primary health care continues to be tacitly encouraged, despite the fact that this is proven to impact most on those already seriously disadvantaged. Governments are still told to cut their budgets, even though these include desperately needed monies to support social services and social infrastructure, expenses that the Bank and Fund now openly acknowledge as important. Poor countries are still required to open up their markets while rich countries continue to protect theirs.

Countries also continue to be told that they have to privatize their most cherished assets—or else. When the Zambian government refused—backed up by the democratically elected Zambian parliament—to privatize the Zambian National Bank in April 2003, for example, the IMF threatened to rescind its commitment to provide $1 billion of debt relief. Nicaragua was able to reach its HIPC decision point only if it agreed to the privatization of the country's national hydroelectric company, despite the fact that the Nicaraguan National Assembly had unanimously passed a law suspending all private concessions involving water use. Senegal, too, has been prevented from getting relief because of her failure to privatize the peanut industry. All this despite the fact that none of these countries has the capacity to regulate private industries sufficiently. And, as my Russian experience shows all too clearly, these fire sales typically end up with the state selling off its prized assets for . . . yup, you've got it . . . peanuts.

Eleven countries have experienced delays in receiving debt relief, not because they were found to be corrupt, not because they were abusing human rights, nor because their governments had yet to complete their consultations with civil society about how the funds should be used, but because they refused to meet all of the IMF's strict conditions—conditions that can easily pitch a government against its people. As Benjamin Mkapa, the Tanzanian president, said, "We are caught between a rock and a hard place in terms of managing IMF requirements and then dealing with the demands of our electorate."

Even the notoriously conservative *Wall Street Journal* wrote in a 1999 editorial that the IMF "is impoverishing people in a way that is morally indefensible and politically unsustainable." The IMF's own report on the Enhanced HIPC Initiative said: "Admittedly adjustment policies while beneficial in the long run may adversely affect certain segments of society in the short run." The Meltzer Commission's report in 2000 (headed by the conservative economist Alan Meltzer) concluded not only that the International Monetary Fund and World Bank were "largely failing in their mission to address world poverty and economic stability," but also that they should "forgive their loan claims held against the heavily indebted poor countries" and get out of the business of promoting economic growth, a call later echoed by the Council on Foreign Relations. But, despite the increasingly accepted evidence of the negative impact on growth, social and political stability, the environment, and poverty reduction, the IMF and the World Bank continue on their desperately damaging course. Poor countries continue to face a Kafkaesque nightmare—toe the IMF's discredited line or forsake any debt relief at all.

The Bretton Woods institutions also ignore the implications for national sovereignty of their insistence on adherence to *their* policies—in a recent seminar in Senegal, when the World Bank resident representative complained to the prime minister that some senior civil servants were not cooperating fully with the Bank, the prime minister was widely reported as cutting him off, saying, "Give me their names and they will be fired right away."

And what about the Bank's and Fund's pledges that the local community would be consulted on how to spend the proceeds of debt relief and that if it wasn't, the debtor government could expect neither full debt cancellation nor new World Bank or IMF loans? While in some cases this pledge has been delivered on and, as a consequence, civil society has been able to hold their governments to account, in many others—Bolivia, Mozambique, Bangladesh, to name a few—

civil society has remained either ignored or sidelined. In Nicaragua, the poverty reduction program was not even translated into Spanish, rendering it inaccessible to the majority of Nicaraguans. And the World Bank itself has admitted that even the Senegalese parliament wasn't fully involved in the Senegalese Poverty Reduction Strategy Paper.

Moreover, the bureaucracy associated with the preparation and subsequent monitoring of poverty reduction programs beggars belief. The World Bank's handbook advising countries on how to prepare their Poverty Reduction Strategy Papers runs to well over one thousand pages. The Tanzanian government had to write three thousand reports in 2002, and host endless World Bank and IMF missions, to monitor its poverty reduction progress—which for a cash- and capacity-strapped government is quite excessive, especially as the cost of the missions is taken off the amount of debt relief that they are provided with.

Rather than freeing up governments to serve the needs of the poor, the poverty reduction program, although undoubtedly well-intentioned, seems better designed to serve the needs, yet again, of World Bank and IMF bureaucrats.

Furthermore, the macroeconomic decisions remain the exclusive preserve of the IMF and the World Bank, with each individual nation's input limited to narrow budgeting discussions and efforts to gauge poverty levels. In several cases, civil society or parliamentary proposals for poverty reduction have been overridden by IMF economic austerity programs. And national policies that clearly impact on poverty reduction, such as those relating to the sequencing of the opening of markets and privatization, continue to be off-limits. At the same time, any possibility of the developing world having a greater voice in the Fund or Bank—and therefore more input into defining the rules of the game—continues to be extremely slim.

Although James Wolfensohn has, in recent times, attempted to take on that particular problem of expanding national representation in the World Bank, he has found himself running into American intransigence, which, as the United States is the IMF's and World Bank's major shareholder, almost always proves insurmountable. In a confidential memo written in June 2003, Carole Brookins, the U.S. executive director of the World Bank, wrote: "the shareholding principle underlying the distribution of voting rights in the Bank and the Fund . . . remains appropriate . . . giving population and other factors a weight in voting strength would create a radically different, less desirable and non-financial structure for the Bank . . . and would not receive broad support, including ours."

And What About the Rest?

There has also been almost no attempt to expand the list of countries included in the HIPC program. Despite the fact that findings show that economic malaise due to foreign indebtedness is not limited to the HIPC group, only two countries have been added to the HIPC list since 1998—Gambia and the Comoros. Countries like Bangladesh, Nigeria, and Pakistan, or newly poor countries like Ecuador, which do have high debt burdens but considerable foreign exchange earnings, are not included despite appallingly high levels of poverty or rampant health crises. Instead, such countries have to hope for ad hoc decisions in their favor.

Nigeria, for example, which now owes $34 billion, spent $2.9 billion servicing its debt in 2002, but only $350 million on the health care needs of its 120 million people, despite the fact that 12 percent of its population, the equivalent of the population of Florida, will be infected with HIV by 2010. Ecuador is spending $29 out of every $100 of her budget on repaying her debts—compare that with a total of only $13 per $100 to spend on both social welfare and education. This is while the number of Ecuadorians living in extreme poverty rose from 15 percent in 1995 to more than 34 percent in 1999 and has worsened ever since. Pakistan, with a GDP per capita of $1,860, is considered a middle-income country and thus ineligible for multilateral debt relief, despite the fact that its human development indicators reveal it to be at a lower level of development than many of the HIPCs. Peru is not granted debt relief either, despite the fact that in 2002 around 17.5 percent of the government budget was spent on servicing foreign debt, while just 17 percent and 9.3 percent were spent on health and education respectively—this in a country in which 54.8 percent of the population live in poverty.

No Cause for Jubilation

The promised Jubilee never took place. At the time of writing, the world's poorest countries owe $458 billion, and nineteen of the twenty-seven countries currently receiving some level of debt relief still sink more than 10 percent of government revenue into debt repayments. Four of the countries that have entered the HIPC initiative—Mali, Niger, Sierra Leone, and Zambia—have annual debt service payments due in 2003–2005 that will actually be higher than the debt service they paid in 1998–2003; five others—Ethiopia, Guinea-Bissau, Honduras, Nicaragua, and Uganda—will be paying almost as much in debt service as they were before they joined HIPC. Cameroon, Sierra Leone, and Mauritania continue to spend more than twice as much on debt as on education. And Iraq, the country the West was supposed to be delivering from evil, is still being asked to repay many of the debts racked up during Saddam Hussein's tyrannical reign.

In fact, progress on the developing-world debt front has been so negligible that, on a gloriously sunny, cotton-wool–clouds sort of day in May, a group of British members of Parliament gathered on College Green opposite the House of Lords to run a rather unusual race. Each contender would represent a debt-burdened country and be weighed down with sacks laden with appropriate amounts of debt. The aim was to reach the UN's millennium goal of halving global poverty by 2015. The obstacles? Hurdles of IMF and World Bank conditions.

So many MPs showed up, from all shades of the political spectrum, that four heats had to be run. In ill-tailored suits and shiny brogues, some balding, some portly, many red-faced with exertion; Julia Drown pregnant, in a bright pink suit, black hose and suspenders on view; Oona King brandishing a Nike swoosh, they crawled, writhed, and rolled, against the refrain of "Drop the debt," toward the finish line—Tory, Labour, Liberal Democrat alike.

With $2.6 billion in debt, Mali (Tony Colman) never made it over its hurdles. Zambia (Paul Burstow), with its $3.6 billion, faltered at hurdle number three. IMF and World Bank conditions finally stymied Bolivia (Stephen O'Brien) (as they did in real life—soon after the allegorical race, eighty people died in Bolivia in bloody protests against a new IMF austerity program, and its president, Gonzalo Sanchez de Lozada, resigned).

Yet the contestants continued to ham it up, for once united. As Caroline Spelman, the Conservative Shadow Minister of International Development at the time, said, "This is not a party political issue. This is about our responsibility to the rest of the world."

But, as we will see in the next few chapters of the book, addressing the issue of debt isn't only a matter of our responsibility to the *rest* of the world, it is about responsibility to our *own* world, too. By exacerbating poverty, eroding national self-worth, and promoting behavior on the part of states that is often to the detriment of society at large, debt has far-reaching consequences—consequences that directly impact on the air we breathe, the food we eat, the resources available to us, our health, and even our security. Debt equals danger, not only in the developing world, but in the developed, too.

But before we look at the more esoteric threats posed by debt, let's start with a much more straightforward scenario: what are the implications when a country simply refuses to honor its debts?

The
Threat

8

Can't Pay, Won't Pay

I . . .
place economy
among the first and
most important of
republican virtues, and
public debt as the greatest of
the dangers to be feared.
—*Thomas Jefferson, letter
to William Plumer,
July 21, 1816*

Do Cry for Me, Argentina

A young woman cancels her wedding because her dad, who was paying for it, sees his savings become nearly worthless overnight. An old man sees his monthly income collapse as the dividends he was relying upon to increase his meager pension suddenly dry up. A grandmother mourns that she cannot buy her granddaughter a present because her savings have disappeared. A divorcée is forced to put her apartment up for sale because she cannot afford to continue paying her mortgage now that her life savings have suddenly been wiped out. These are just some of the casualties of Argentina's sovereign debt default on $97 billion of outstanding debt in January 2002—the largest default in history.

But these weren't Argentinians. They were Italians: when Argentina defaulted, 15 percent of its outstanding foreign loans were in Italian hands. In 2001, just as sophisticated institutional investors were becoming wary of investing in Argentina, Italian banks were hard-selling Argentine bonds to their ordinary retail customers. "That's what kept Argentina going," said Tom White, former emerging-market bond manager at Metropolitan Life Insurance Company. "Those poor suckers didn't have a clue as to what they were buying."

The Italian bankers played on the historic and ethnic ties between the two countries, stressing the regular income stream that these bonds promised, while seriously underplaying the associated risks. "They told me [the bonds] were good, stable, guaranteed, and that since they were obligations they had to be paid back," said Felicia Mogliorini, who sank $135,000 of her life savings into Argentine bonds in March 2001. And their promises were believed. Italian bankers managed to sell approximately $15 billion of Argentine bonds to around four hundred thousand clients, many of whom were pensioners who had gambled their entire savings on this risky investment. When Argentina defaulted, so did the hopes and dreams of thousands of ordinary Italians.

Countries have defaulted on their debts in the past, of course—Argentina itself defaulted three times in the nineteenth century (its 1890 default causing a major panic in London, then the world's financial capital) and again in 1982 in the wake of the Mexican default; eighty-five governments have defaulted on commercial obligations since 1975. The impact can be very far-reaching. Quite how far-reaching is what this chapter will explore.

Do Worry

These particular defaults are defaults on commercial debts—debts owed to bankers, traders, bondholders, and investors usually by middle-income countries, the kind of debts that we focused on in chapters 4 and 5, and not defaults on IMF and World Bank debts. Those are a completely different kettle of fish—the consequences of defaulting on them are so dire for the borrowing country that we seldom see it take place.

And the primary question that needs answering is this. Is there reason to believe that we are soon going to see more defaults on commercial debt?

I believe that within the next five years, yes there is.

Why? Because indebtedness is rising in many emerging countries without the requisite conditions for this not to be problematic—a political consensus not to default, a favorable external environment, and the debts being used in productive ways to finance development and the building of export capacity. Increasingly, these conditions are unlikely to prevail.

As we have seen, rather than always being lent for productive use, monies continue to be both lent and borrowed in greedy, myopic, and delusional ways.

By greedy I mean those corrupt or self-seeking governments who use the borrowed money with no care for how the accumulated debt will be repaid. President Menem, the former Argentinian president, a compulsive overborrower, used much of his loans to line the pockets of those senators and governors who supported his quest for re-election. More recently, President Kuchma of Ukraine was reported to have financed a progovernment candidate during the 2004 presidential election campaign with a Eurobond issue. I also mean the avaricious investors who just keep on lending, focusing only on personal reward, heedless of the fact that often the only way the country can realistically pay off its debts is by effectively embarking on a pyramid scheme in which it will pay back only those higher up the pyramid if it manages to secure new loans.

Myopic? I am referring here to those governments who fail to see or actively disregard the long-term picture, borrowing monies so as not to have to make cost savings, exercise budgetary prudence, or seek out new ways to generate internal resources, although, to keep potential investors happy, they will often pay lip service to doing so.

I mean the ones who make populist or elite-serving spending decisions rather than investing in projects that will improve the economy over time, doing so because they know that when the debts are called in they will no longer be in office. This of course, is not exclusively a developing-world problem: George W. Bush with his deficit-generating tax-cutting policies is clearly in need of glasses too. In ten years' time, if the current trajectory continues, America's national debt will equal 51 percent of GDP, and interest payments will be costing the Fed $470 billion a year. And also from the developed world, the geopolitically motivated lenders who make their loans on the basis of a narrow understanding of self-interest with no care for the fact that in so doing they hamper the market's ability to read the situation accurately, meaning that borrowers and commercial lenders are not easily able to work out how much debt is too much. Were the IMF and the United States to disconnect their feeding tubes to Turkey, for example, the interest rates demanded on its bonds would in all likelihood shoot up and its debt would become unsustainable overnight.

And the delusional ones? I am thinking of those borrowers who are excessively optimistic about their debt-servicing capabilities, calculating them on the basis of best possible scenarios rather than more tempered and realistic ones, the projections often arrived at with the "help" of the IMF. Or those commercial lenders who continue to make sure the borrower blindly accepts the whole World Bank or IMF doctrine before they lend, despite the fact that many of these institutions' tenets are, as we have seen, plainly wrong—such as the demand to tighten fiscal policy even though the borrower is already in recession, a policy that then impairs its growth and consequently its ability to service its debt. This is the kind of advice the IMF gave Argentina in 2001, which, of course, is the opposite of what the rich world tends to do when it is in the economic dumps.

But the mere presence of the Three Horsemen of the Financial Apocalypse—Greed, Myopia, and Delusion—is not enough to lead me to predict a coming wave of defaults. They have been riding toward us for some time now, after all. What cements my prediction are the following.

The external environment they dominate is an especially volatile one. The War on Terror is not yet won—Code Orange alerts all too often, air marshals now flying on planes, Europe now a key target— which means that an all clear from a global recession is still impossible to give, with all the negative implications for the developing world's ability to export successfully and generate the requisite foreign exchange to service its debt that this brings.

Then there is the U.S. deficit, which, if Bush remains in power, is likely to continue to burgeon. What are the implications of this? There would almost certainly be a rise in U.S. interest rates, especially in the face of a relentless fall in the dollar—definitely a possible scenario. This means, as we have seen before, that the developing world's borrowing in dollars become significantly more expensive to service, and developing countries have to jack up the interest rates to levels they can ill afford on new bond issues so as to maintain their relative attractiveness as compared to dollar-denominated bonds.

And then, of course, there's the price of oil, which, in recent times, has already reached historic highs but still has the potential to edge up that bit more: the ramp-up of Iraqi production is likely to be slow; political turmoil may well continue to disrupt Venezuelan output; and OPEC may make good its threat to switch from the dollar to the euro as the way it values its oil—this would mean that any further devaluation of the dollar would jack up the price of OPEC oil. Although a hike in oil prices would be good for those developing countries that export it, for those that don't the consequences would be pretty bad.

Any of these factors is capable of providing the kind of external shocks that history teaches us affect a country's ability to honor prior obligations. Events like the Great Depression, World Wars I and II, the fall of the Berlin Wall, 9/11, and the war against Iraq all affected the yields demanded from borrowers. Which, in turn, affects a borrower country's ability to repay loans.

Add to this a host of other external factors. The continued subsidization of a whole range of products by developed countries renders many developing countries unable to compete in the very areas where they otherwise might have an advantage, thus damaging their ability to generate the requisite foreign exchange to service and repay their debts. This is a problem Europe faced in 1929 when high U.S. trade tariffs made it difficult for European nations to sell their goods to the United States, and led to countries beginning to default on their loans. There is also the consolidation of the global banking sector, which has resulted in reduced liquidity in the marketplace, thus raising the risk of huge amounts of money flowing out of a country at one time.

Then, of course, there is contagion, which although less marked than a few years back, still remains a real threat. In a world of global interconnectedness, in a world in which countries' debts have been commodified, a crisis in one place fast becomes another's crisis; a rise in interest rates in one country fast affects the yield another is asked to deliver. When one emerging market faces a crisis, investors pull out monies from others, particularly those viewed as similar, in an attempt to lower the risk profile of their overall portfolio, a reaction magnified once investors begin to move, as they always do, as a herd. The East Asian crisis of 1997 and the Russian default of 1998 had enormous global domino effects in Brazil, for example, which was forced to devalue the real as a consequence. This, in turn, affected Argentina as Brazil imported less from it. It also hurt Turkey. Infected countries have at the very least to raise their interest rates in response so as to attract foreign investment, thereby increasing their own debt service payments. At worst, these countries can find themselves on the brink of default as a result. Uruguay, in the wake of the default of its neighbor, Argentina, not only witnessed 33 percent of the deposits in its banks being withdrawn in the first six months of 2002—including the monies held in deposit at Uruguayan banks by Argentine residents—but also had to deal with a collapse of its tourist industry as Argentinians stopped vacationing there, as well as a collapse in exports to Argentina.

Finally, we are likely to see more defaults looming because more emerging-market populaces are increasingly likely to demand it from their politicians. Thanks to the freer flow of information, the man or woman in the street is now far more aware of where their money is going, and will not tolerate it being sent abroad instead of being used to address their needs at home. In the Argentinian case, for example, the public made clear that they would no longer tolerate the tax increases and government spending cuts that President de la Rua had instituted for the explicit purpose of repaying foreign debt. With the domestic situation deteriorating rapidly, the Argentinian people overwhelmingly registered their desire to default. Defaulting becomes an increasingly necessary, if still never entirely attractive, option when cash-strapped governments are faced with a choice between averting riots and feeding their starving masses, or paying off their creditors—a scenario that is only going to increase, given the growing gap between the haves and have-nots in many countries, and the increased public awareness of the fallibility of the IMF's advice. For how much longer will Lula be able to continue servicing his external debts, and follow IMF requirements, when unemployment is rising in all the main cities, poverty is growing, and economic performance continues to be lackluster?

Scalped

This is all disastrous news for the developed world.

First, because there is no organized bankruptcy procedure in place for sovereign default, as there would be for a company or individual who found themselves in similar circumstances, nor as yet are there widespread collective action clauses on emerging-market bonds that would prevent individual bondholders from vetoing restructuring proposals, attempts by creditors to recover their money, once default has been announced, are typically messy and drawn out, often stymied, as we have seen, by recalcitrant creditors such as the debt vultures. Even if agreement is reached, the amount of monies creditors can hope to recover is often very small. After Russia defaulted in 1998, for example, it had to pay its bondholders only 48 percent of what it owed. In early 2003, Argentina was offering those holding its bonds 25 cents on the dollar. "We're being scalped," a major investor in Argentina complained to me at the time. And write-downs of this kind affect all kinds of investors: pensioners, investment banks, insurance companies, and individuals alike—our Italian pensioners will never see very much of their investment returned.

Second, if it is commercial banks rather than bondholders who are among the main creditors, as was the case in the 1980s, one country's default can jeopardize the credibility of the entire financial system, as investors lose confidence in a whole "tainted" banking system. At the same time, the individual banks that have lent to the defaulter are left with the unenviable task of explaining to their shareholders where all their money has gone. JP Morgan Chase announced, for example, at the end of 2001, a loan loss provision against its $900 million outstanding loans to Argentina of $140 million. The share price of JP Morgan Chase fell dramatically.

Defaults are bad news for the developed world for a third reason—they are costly for business, not only for those who run them and own shares in them but for those who work for them too. Foreign companies operating in the crisis-stricken country suffer as they see their revenues collapse in the wake of the default. The French, Italian, and Spanish multinational telecommunication companies operating in Argentina saw their incomes fall by 82 percent in 2002. Major exporters to the defaulter also take a hit, as their old customers not only find it almost impossible to access credit lines to import goods now that their country has defaulted, but also typically suffer the consequences of a currency devaluation that makes the price of imports shoot up. The United States' record trade deficits in 1998 and 1999, for example, were partly due to reduced exports to Asia because of the Asian financial crisis. And lower exports usually mean fewer jobs at home—between 1998 and 2000, 513,000 U.S. jobs were lost in the manufacturing sector, again attributable in part to the Asian crisis.

The fourth reason why default is of such a concern for the developed world is that crises associated with a country's default, such as acute poverty and unemployment, increase the likelihood of people leaving their homes for better lives elsewhere—and the developed world is horribly ill-prepared to deal with this. We have seen the rise of right-wing xenophobic politicians in Europe: Joerg Haider in Austria, Jean-Marie Le Pen in France, and Christoph Blocher in

Switzerland, all of whom played the "immigrant card" to disturbingly good effect. Most worrisome, however, mainstream politicians are frequently now doing the same. In April 2002, the British home secretary David Blunkett expressed on BBC Radio 4's *Today* program his concern that some doctors' offices were being "swamped" by asylum-seekers (a term now commonly used to describe economic as well as political refugees). Language that an increasingly scaremongering media is also all too often using. "Our land is being *swamped* by a flood of fiddlers stretching our resources—and our patience—to breaking point," declared the British tabloid, the *Sun,* in March 2000. Quite.

But if defaults are costly to the developed world, so too are attempts to avert them. The cost of bailouts—the response of the world's rich countries to an imminent emerging-market default in those cases when it sees *its* interests (whether geopolitical or those of its domestic corporations) potentially threatened—is a cost that often falls directly on the shoulders of its taxpayers. Loans in these circumstances are seldom paid back in full. They also encourage a cycle of bad lending decisions, as investors, believing that they will be bailed out if their loans go sour and thereby escape serious losses, lend with little regard for what the monies are being spent on or whether the borrower can reasonably service the loan.

Moreover, like any other politically motivated lending decision, bailouts distort the market's ability to read the situation accurately, to make an accurate assessment of risk. The IMF, for example, gave huge loans to Russia in 1996 on the eve of Boris Yeltsin's reelection campaign purely to serve the geopolitical interests of major shareholders—Russia wasn't performing at all well on IMF or World Bank criteria at that point, and in 1998 it defaulted. When Indonesia was offered an extremely generous rescue package by the IMF in 1997, investors thought that Brazil would soon receive the same, and so there was a rush of investors willing to lend to Brazil, not because anything fundamental had changed but because investors were betting that the IMF would bail Brazil out too. Of course, such market distortions are themselves likely to lead to bad lending and borrowing decisions. Part of the reason for the overlending to Argentina was a mistaken belief on the part of investors that the IMF would always bail it out.

The Perspective of the Debtor

Clearly, overborrowing and overlending, whether it leads to crises, defaults, or bailouts, has deleterious consequences for the borrower too.

When a country defaults, the initial response of the international financial market is to freeze out the defaulter. Not only does this make it impossible for the country to get access to any new credit, but also almost impossible for any corporations within those countries to do so either, as corporate debt is typically rated no higher than the debt of the corporation's home country, no matter how well they may be run. The defaulter will face problems with importing goods, even critical ones such as life-saving drugs, as credit lines freeze and those selling into the country demand up-front cash payment. The most aggressive creditors may use the opportunity to attempt to seize government assets in lieu of payment. Some of the debt vultures I have spoken with have identified every hotel, apartment building, and property that the debtor country owns outside its own shores, and tell me that they would be more than ready to issue liens on them. Argentina already faces lawsuits from hundreds of bondholders seeking compensation for the government's decision to halt payments on its debt, some of which threaten to put at risk Argentine accounts and assets held abroad.

If a significant percentage of the sovereign debt is held by domestic investors—as is increasingly the case in many emerging markets—this creates other problems. The impact of having to write down a significant percentage of their outstanding loans, as would be the case in a default, could wipe out most of the capital of domestic financial institutions, making many insolvent and thus triggering a collapse of the domestic banking system. Such a scenario could play out in Brazil, for example, were it to default on its debt, given that it's Brazilian banks that hold almost 60 percent of the outstanding loans.

In a cruel irony, the act of default itself exacerbates the crisis that necessitated it in the first place. Ecuador suffered a severe recession in the wake of its default, as well as political unrest that included a short-lived military takeover. Eight months after its default, Argentina resembled Dickensian Britain. Living standards had dropped by 70 percent and GDP by 17 percent; 60 percent of the population had fallen below the poverty line—20 million people of whom 2.3 million were children were suffering from malnutrition, and unemployment was running at 30 percent. On the streets of Buenos Aires, *cartoneros* (cardboard collectors) rummaged through trash to salvage paper, glass, and cardboard to sell, while around its perimeter, three hundred thousand people lived off garbage dumps. Radio and TV announcers had become domestic servants, skilled engineers could be found selling handicrafts on the street, and those lucky enough to keep their former jobs had to put up with conditions that previously would have been unacceptable.

And the burden of economic crisis always falls disproportionately on the shoulders of women. There is considerable evidence, for example, that in the wake of a financial crisis there are increases in domestic prostitution, and also in the number of women leaving the country to work in sex industries abroad. (For it is women who in times of crisis lose their jobs first and, being the ones upon whom the family leans, embark upon such desperate measures.) There is also a rise in the numbers of women kidnapped and forced into prostitution.

In some cases, the negative impact of default can be relatively short-lived. Russia, for example, bounced back very quickly after its 1998 default, at least in terms of the way the markets viewed it, and by 2003 its debt was rated investment grade. Despite a horrific first twelve months after its default, Argentina seems to have been able to use the period to get back on its feet again, growing 7 percent in 2003, and looks likely to be able to attract speculative investors again very soon. Russia and Argentina are, however, the exceptions. In the majority of cases, the effect of default is a longer-lasting blow to the country's credit rating history. At worst, the country is unable to raise monies on the capital markets indefinitely, thereby finding itself in the kind of reality that sub-Saharan African countries, to whom almost no commercial creditors wish to lend at all, have lived in for many years. At best, the premium demanded by lenders remains raised for several years after default, creating a disincentive to borrow externally. Admittedly, this is not always such a terrible thing.

The resurgence of commercial emerging-market debt over the past fifteen years is more risky than is traditionally thought, and risky on a number of levels. It is risky not just for borrowers, but for lenders, too, because for them, within the context of a system that clouds market signals, it is very hard to distinguish when exactly a country is borrowing too much and therefore whether investors are likely to get their money back. It is risky because many of the conditions attached to IMF bailouts and loans end up impeding growth and exacerbating inequality, outcomes that ultimately accentuate the risk of default; and also because Argentina, the biggest sovereign defaulter in history, effectively used the fact it owed so much money to leverage extra-favorable terms from the IMF, gave its commercial creditors a ripe old run for their money, and, at the end of the day, probably benefited from its decision to default, although it is too early to be 100 percent certain. After a bumpy start, its economy is now recovering, its foreign exchange reserves have increased, inflation is falling, confidence about the future is rising, and industrial growth is up—making default seem a more appealing or at least viable strategy to select for other borrowers, despite its significant short-term costs.

It is also risky because, following the breakdown of trade talks in Cancun in September 2003 thanks to a coordinated stance on the part of twenty-two developing countries—the first time in decades that developing nations united to make clear that they were not prepared to accept the role that was established for them by the rich countries. "We should be taken seriously," said Lula, who led the developing world's charge—it is likely that we will see other coordinated acts of defiance, with a collective default now an increasingly possible scenario. There is an old adage worth remembering: if you owe a bank $1,000 you have a problem, if you owe them $1 million the problem is theirs, a scenario that, because of a lack of camaraderie, was never a real possibility in the 1980s. And it is risky because the tension between repaying debt and delivering on social justice is so visibly at the fore of political discourse—"We cannot pay the debt at the cost of sentencing Argentina to hunger and exclusion," said Argentinian president Nestor Kirchner in May 2003, when creditors were baying—making the balancing act between the demands of domestic constituents and creditors harder than ever, especially in those developing countries with left-leaning governments. And, finally, it is risky because there continue to be few ways of averting crises—capital controls, although gaining in favor along the political spectrum, are still not commonplace. Cost-effective mechanisms to hedge against commodity price fluctuations are available but countries rarely use them; and no orderly way of resolving the situation is as yet in place once a country has signaled clearly that it cannot cope. Nothing akin to a corporate, municipal, or individual bankruptcy procedure is available to a country. There is no mechanism in place that allows debtors to restructure their debts in an orderly and just fashion, and within which creditors can be assured that they will not have to bear protracted negotiation costs. With a real chance of big defaults looming, isn't it imperative this gets worked out?

It isn't that emerging markets shouldn't borrow or that lenders shouldn't lend to them—it is that the timing of when best to borrow and when best to lend needs to be much better appreciated; the nature and potential of debt and what it takes to service it needs to be much better understood. For without that appreciation, without that understanding, debt swiftly becomes a grenade—safe only until the pin has been pulled out, and bloodily destructive from then on. In much of the developing world, and in many emerging markets, this is precisely what has happened. Debt has become a grenade and the pin *has* been pulled out. How damaging and far-reaching is the explosion likely to be?

9

A Plague on Both Your Houses

> If
> developing countries
> scourged by disease do not
> develop, they cannot contribute to
> the broader global growth in which we
> have such a stake, at a time when more
> than 40 percent of our exports already go
> to developing countries. The national
> economic distress and political instability
> that inevitably accompany this . . . can
> cause greater damage to the global
> system as a whole.
> —Former U.S. secretary of the treasury
> Lawrence Summers

The Price of Soap

In 1991, a cholera epidemic ravaged Latin America. Within twelve months, it had spread from Peru to Ecuador to Colombia to Chile to the western tip of Brazil, affecting over four hundred thousand people and killing thousands. Debt was one of its major causes.

The first fatality was Cirila Poma, a sixty-year-old woman living on the outskirts of the Peruvian province of Chancay, some 50 miles from Lima. In common with three-quarters of the Peruvian population, Cirila lacked access to running water, forcing her to draw her drinking water from a small irrigation channel. This particular channel was also used for sewage disposal—and the sewage flowing into this creek had been contaminated by the cholera bacteria, probably from the waste of infected Chinese sailors from a freight ship that had recently docked in Chancay.

While countries with public health surveillance systems, crisis management structures, and a functioning water and sewage infrastructure can contain these sorts of health incidents (if they face them at all), countries that are poor and underdeveloped, where water and sanitation systems are inadequate and where health care is lacking or inefficient, simply cannot.

In 1991, Peru was such a country. Already poor, with 60 percent of its population living in extreme poverty, it was, at that time, navigating particularly treacherous economic straits. This was because its newly elected (and nowadays discredited) president Alberto Fujimori was attempting to remove Peru from the IMF's blacklist in order to become eligible for new loans. Only a few months before Cirila got sick, Fujimori had agreed, with immediate effect, not only to begin repaying his country's outstanding debts (many of which, as we saw in chapter 4, his predecessor Garcia had stopped paying), but also to allow the IMF to put Peru through a particularly harsh new structural adjustment program.

The impact of this decision was devastating. To paraphrase William Foege, former director of the Centers for Disease Control and Prevention in Atlanta, Georgia, structural adjustment programs typically worsen living conditions and improve the odds for emergent diseases. In Peru's case, living conditions worsened *so* significantly as a result of the IMF's adjustment program and the additional burden caused by the new debt, that the odds of a full-blown health crisis occurring rose dramatically.

And come it did, borne on the back of the cholera bacteria. Although it can appear with terrifying speed, cholera is actually a relatively easy disease to contain. Transmitted by food and water contaminated by infected human feces, outbreaks can be prevented simply by the washing of hands and the avoidance of untreated water. But the debt/structural adjustment duo was devastatingly effective at putting even these basic preventative measures out of reach of the Peruvian poor. The liberalization of prices, for example, one of the standard requirements of structural adjustment, meant in practice that the price of basic goods in Peru rose exponentially overnight. The impact of this on the poor was severe. Already reeling from rising unemployment and sinking wages—the other effects of structural adjustment—Peruvians awoke to find themselves unable to afford soap to wash their hands. At the same time, the price of potable water and the price of kerosene had shot through the roof, the latter jumping thirtyfold. Not only could they not wash their hands with soap and clean water, now the poor couldn't afford the means with which to cook or to boil water. The cholera bacteria was breeding freely, and there was nothing anyone could do to stop it.

If this wasn't problematic enough, President Fujimori, in order to meet his commitment to the IMF to repay outstanding debts, authorized a massive increase in the debt-servicing burden. Payments more than doubled from $60 million a month to over $150 million. The government, in order to be able to deal with this hike, slashed social and health expenditure even further (it was already pitifully low), deferred repairs to the sewage system and allowed preexisting social infrastructure to further deteriorate. No money was put aside for emergency health measure provisions. What could have been a contained health crisis became a full-fledged epidemic that swiftly spread across the region.

Within ten days of Cirila's death, incidents of cholera had been reported along the whole upper half of Peru's western coast. By the end of February 1991, 543 victims had been reported and by April 1, 140 people had died. By the end of the year, Peru's economy had collapsed as tourism withered, its regional trading partners were feeling the blow as Peru was no longer buying from them, and the disease had spread throughout Peru and into other countries in South, Central, and even North America. By January 1, 1992, the epidemic had affected hundreds of thousands of people and killed nearly 4,000—over five times as many as those who died from SARS in 2003.

Toxic Remedies

The Peruvian experience of cutting back on social expenditure in order to meet the requirements of the Bretton Woods institutions is a common response to IMF and World Bank demands. *Charging* for social services is another. In order to maintain health services in such economic conditions most governments begin to charge fees for their use. Again not good. Studies of developing-world countries show that when health care is not free, a significant proportion of people don't seek it out, that illnesses are left untreated and are more likely to become chronic.

Cutbacks in education budgets, or the policy of charging parents for their children's schooling—policies that are also sadly common-place—also negatively impact on health. Education is a key determinant of general health status. More particularly, health is affected by the level of education and the degree of literacy of girls (as it is women who are disproportionately responsible for a family's health care needs). Yet when parents, faced with school fees, have to choose between spending their money on sending their daughter or their son to learn, typically they choose the son.

The rural poor suffer adverse health effects from structural adjustment to an even greater degree, not only because they rarely see health workers in their localities, but also because they have often been driven out of their villages in search of employment, due in part to a waning market for the cash crops they have been "encouraged" to grow by the World Bank and IMF. While being mobile is not a health risk in and of itself, the situations encountered and behaviors engaged in while traveling have been shown to lead to an increase in vulnerability and an increased likelihood of disease, in particular HIV/AIDS. Urban shantytowns, teeming with economic refugees from the countryside, present a clear and significant health risk of their own.

Structural adjustment also demands the opening up of domestic markets, a demand that brings with it the possibility of even more detrimental effects. It is not that the opening up of markets is negative per se—of course it is not—but when countries with weak regulatory regimes open up their markets, the fact is that frequently they don't have the mechanisms in place to protect their citizens from the more rapacious elements of global capitalism. When, for example, developing countries were forced to open up their markets to Big Tobacco, smoking rates went up by 10 percent. An increase in bronchial disease, coronary problems, and cancer rates is hardly what many of the world's poorest countries need on top of all their other health problems, especially when deaths from coronary heart disease dwarf deaths from infectious diseases in all of the developing world apart from Africa.

But it's not just the conditions insisted upon by the World Bank, IMF, and other lenders in exchange for loans and promises of debt relief that help to foster and spread disease; it's the size of the inherited debt itself. In order to service the debt, the world's poorest countries, as we by now know, are forced to use up pitifully scarce resources.

And where do these come from? Government revenues. While for a country like the United States, the most indebted country in the world in absolute terms, the percentage of government budget spent on servicing debt is at present around a manageable 8.5 percent, in the world's most heavily indebted *poor* countries, as much as 50 percent of their revenues can be spent on servicing debt. Given that the countries in question are already significantly underspending in public and social service areas—for example, for most African countries the entire annual health budget is less than $10 a person versus $5,000 in the United States—and that just in order to combat AIDS and other serious infectious diseases it is estimated that annual health expenditure in low- and middle-income countries needs to increase from about $106 billion a year to $168 billion by 2007, the need to service the debt clearly makes what is already a bad situation even worse.

Diabetics in the developing world die because of a lack of insulin;

epileptics because of a lack of phenobarb, and many, many more from strokes and cardiovascular diseases, diseases that could be prevented through better access to cheap drugs such as aspirin and antihypertensives—drugs that cost just cents to buy. To make matters worse, these are diseases that, if untreated before the patient dies, can significantly increase the burden to the state. In some developing countries, 25 percent of the health budget is spent on the amputations, kidney failures, and incidents of blindness that are due to untreated diabetes. In rich countries, the squeezing of health budgets, though rarely desirable, usually doesn't have fatal consequences; in many of the world's poorest countries it can and does.

In Ethiopia, for example, where only 16 percent of women receive prenatal care, debt repayments total four times as much as public spending on health. In Niger, where fewer than 20 percent of young women are enrolled in schools, more is spent on debt repayments than on education and health care together. Tanzania spends $3.20 per person on health provision, a quarter of what the World Bank estimates is necessary to provide the most basic health care, but forks out $9 per person on debt service. In Africa as a whole, around thirty million people are living with HIV/AIDS, up to 70 percent of adults in many of its hospitals are suffering from AIDS-related illnesses, governments don't have the money to undertake effective educational campaigns to try to keep the epidemic under control, life expectancy is predicted to fall to levels not seen since the nineteenth century, forty million children will lose at least one parent to AIDS within the next decade, and only sixty thousand people are receiving any antiretroviral therapies (the treatment that in the West has revolutionized the life expectancy and quality of life of those with HIV). Nevertheless, Africa spends more on servicing its debt than it does on health and has had to cut its health expenditure to satisfy the IMF and World Bank criteria. No wonder Columbia academic Jeffrey Sachs, at the World Summit on Sustainable Development in 2002, urged participants, "Defend your people. It's untenable to be paying debt that could be used to fight the pandemic. It's imperative to channel those funds to AIDS, given this holocaust."

The Debt-Poverty Link

There is yet another relationship between servicing debt and an increase in ill health. As we saw in earlier chapters, by continuing to service debts that were not used to improve the economy or support productive areas, and by having to agree to macroeconomic policies at odds with growth and development, in many cases debt has exacerbated developing-world poverty, and poverty is the single most important determining factor of a nation's health.

The links between poverty and disease are well documented. Up to 70 percent of childhood cases of diarrheal disease, malaria, measles, and respiratory infections in the developing world—the big killers—are due to poverty-related malnutrition. People who live in extreme poverty, on less than $1 a day, as do approximately half the African subcontinent, are simply denied the basic prerequisites for good health. They can't afford to pay for "healthy" foods such as fresh vegetables and fruits that provide essential immune system–building nutrients and also help protect against chronic non-infectious diseases. They also lack the good sanitation, clean water, and housing that are essential for good health. They don't have the funds to buy necessary drugs, but even if they do, the drugs they need often don't exist as pharmaceutical companies do not invest in developing drugs that are specific to treating poor-world diseases—sleeping sickness, Chagas' disease, and the like—because they know that government subsidies will not be forthcoming to pay for them and that their target populations are clearly too poor to afford the medication. Mouanodji Mbaissourom, the lone cardiologist in N'Djamena, Chad, acknowledges that even if he writes a prescription for medicine to relieve hypertension, few of his patients will ever receive the medicine. "They often can't find the medicine in Chad and if they do they can't afford it," he has said. Furthermore, health care facilities for the poor are often dilapidated—one billion poor do not have access to primary health—and are inadequately stocked with basic medicines. In Burkina Faso, for example, nearly 20 percent of facilities do not have essential vaccines and in 24 percent of centers the refrigerators for storing the vaccines do not function.

And then there are the diseases that we can clearly link to poverty—cholera is one, HIV/AIDS is another. It's not just that poor populations are more vulnerable to HIV because poor women exacerbate its spread when forced to sell their bodies for food or school fees—as Mable Bande, a young Zambian prostitute who was abandoned in her teens when her parents died, said, "The only solution was to go onto the street, in the bars and disco houses to find money. I must find something to do to support me." It's not just that HIV spreads because young men, desperate to find work, travel far from home and, lonely, seek solace in the arms of sex workers or because developing-world governments have not effectively targeted the poor with their AIDS campaigns. It is because on a much more fundamental level, being poor makes one physically more vulnerable to HIV. Once one's immune system is seriously weakened by parasitic infections, malaria, tuberculosis, and an inadequate diet, one is significantly more vulnerable to infectious diseases including HIV/AIDS. And once the body has become coinfected, viremia, the level of HIV circulating in the bloodstream, increases. High viremia is associated with an increased risk of transmission. A deadly cycle.

In fact, the whole poverty-disease relationship, a relationship that debt has served so well to consolidate, can be thought of as a deadly cycle, reinforcing itself at every turn. High costs of medical care, an inability to earn money through work, the fact that illness in a breadwinner will undermine a poor household's ability to cope financially, the out-of-pocket payments for health services, all serve to make the poor even poorer and the sick even sicker. Poverty makes people sick, people become poorer because they are sick, and then sicker because they are poorer. It truly is a vicious circle.

As a fieldworker in Zambia observed:

> In the field you are often led into somebody's home. The first thing that hits you is that the patient will be on the floor. If that household was not poor before HIV/AIDS infected somebody, then by the end of the first few years, poverty will come to the household as all of their assets are sold off to pay for health care. Children have been taken out of school—daughters, particularly—to be-

come caregivers. Invariably, the person you have come to see will be on the floor without a blanket or pillow. If you look around the mud hut for food, you won't see it, and you won't smell people cooking. There is no food.

Add to this the fact that in many of the world's poorest countries doctors and nurses are leaving in droves, desperate to secure a decent life for themselves and aggressively sought by developed countries, and the situation looks even worse. Tens of thousands of African doctors and nurses are leaving their countries to work primarily in the United States and the United Kingdom: four thousand Kenyan nurses have left for the United States and the United Kingdom; approximately 60 percent of Ghanaian doctors trained in the 1980s have left the country; a few years ago Zambia had sixteen hundred doctors, now only four hundred are in practice; and there are more Sierra Leonean doctors practicing in Chicago than in Sierra Leone. And so it goes, the already meager wealth of developing countries slipping away ever faster to the rich. Western patients being treated by the developing world's carers, at precisely the time that they are so desperately needed at home.

Your Problem, My Problem

But developing-world disease exacerbated by developing-world debt isn't just a problem for the poor world. In the age of the airplane, it is fast becoming the problem of the rich world too. The speed and ease with which pathogens can cross borders and continents and therefore the risk of disease transmission between countries is greater today than ever before.

The spread of disease across national borders itself is hardly new. The Great Plague of London of 1665, which ended up killing about 20 percent of the population, arrived in England thanks to ships' rats, stowaways from South Asia, following the international trading routes of the fourteenth century. What makes the present situation different is the increased density and velocity of human travel, the increase in migration, the increase in illegal trafficking of people, the increase in tourism, the increase in international trade in food and biological products, and the rise in global warming, which means that dangerous insects are able to live and breed longer.

Dengue fever in Alabama, malaria sweeping through France, an Ebola outbreak in Berlin, a monkey pox epidemic in Tokyo, a cholera outbreak in Barcelona, a tuberculosis reappearance in the United Kingdom: no longer are these figments of a Hollywood screenwriter's imagination. Today they are a distinct possibility. In fact, all of these diseases have recently "crossed borders" from the developing to the industrialized world.

Medieval-sounding diseases—the plague, dengue fever, Rift Valley fever, Lassa fever, diseases with symptoms that range from bloody diarrhea and limb loss to disfiguring skin lesions—that are commonplace in developing countries, cannot be confined within national borders anymore when they are only a transcontinental flight away. One thousand new cases of malaria are now imported into the United Kingdom each year from countries in which the disease is endemic. In North America, malaria has reemerged in urban centers from California to Michigan, from New York City to Toronto. Tuberculosis, which for many decades was on the decline in the developed world, has been on the rise since the mid-1980s, thanks in part to its spread from South Asia and sub-Saharan Africa. Leishmaniasis, a disease caused by a parasite transmitted by the sandfly that attacks the spleen, liver, and bone marrow and which left untreated is fatal, has recently been appearing in Brazil and Turkey, places it was virtually unknown until only a few years ago. In the United States, 4,156 people were infected by the West Nile virus in 2002 alone. And we are now seeing subtypes of the AIDS virus previously found only in Africa appearing in the West. Each time one of these diseases rears its ugly head it is not only a public health worry, but also more fuel for right-wing, xenophobic rhetoric that claims that we can best fortify ourselves by keeping others out.

Poor, Dangerous, and Bankrupt

But it is not just the fact that the developed world might find itself overrun with developing-world diseases or xenophobic bigotry that should give it reason to concern itself with the poor world's sicknesses. A sicker developing world will mean a poorer, and more dangerous developed world.

Poorer? Yes. We already know that debt tends to be inimical to growth and development in the developing world. Disease, which debt burdens make worse, *also* stymies them both. A high prevalence of malaria, for example, has been shown to be associated with a 1 percent reduction in economic growth per year—the sick are of course less productive and more frequently absent than the healthy, while the negative impact upon economic growth is even more severe in those countries worst-afflicted with HIV/AIDS, the category into which most of our highly indebted countries fall. In those countries, an individual typically falls ill and dies at the very time in their life that they should be contributing most to both the national and household economies: in many African countries, more than a quarter of the potentially economically active population is now dead; by 2020, Mozambique will have lost one-fifth of its farmers to AIDS. As Nelson Mandela has said, "AIDS kills those on whom society relies to grow the crops, work in the mines and factories, run the schools and hospitals and govern countries."

But how do low rates of development and insufficient levels of growth in the developing world hurt those in the developed world? They affect the developed world because its multinational corporations can't sell enough of their products at home to continue to provide rising profits and dividends and thereby increase the tax base. This means they need to be able to sell their cola, their cars, their computers, their Cheez Whiz to places as yet unsaturated with their products—the developing world. And developing countries with low levels of growth and low rates of development do not ideal customers make.

A more dangerous world? That too. A high infant mortality rate is one of the main predictors of subsequent state collapse. A clear link exists between the prevalence of HIV/AIDS and security threats within the affected country. In partial democracies, the impact of AIDS has been found to be correlated strongly with state failure; there is the prospect of ethnic wars, genocides, disruptive regime transitions, and revolutionary wars all because of AIDS. But also there is a link between HIV/AIDS prevalence and *regional* security threats as wherever the virus reaches epidemic proportions it strikes disproportionately at the police, civil service, and military institutions that undergird national security. And a link with *international* security threats too as the consequences ripple outward from the nations under attack to their neighbors, trading partners, and allies, serving to destabilize what already at the beginning of a new millennium is a much more dangerous world.

And also a more morally bankrupt developed world. By permitting the sickness and death to continue in the developing world at rates that astound and shock, by not doing anything to avert this unfolding genocide when it so easily could, the rich world becomes complicit in the casualties and fatalities in the poor. It becomes as complicit as if it had mailed poisoned food packages to itself, as if it had stuck HIV-infected needles into its mothers and children. If the developed world were to put into sub-Saharan Africa, for example, the monies it needed to tackle the major infectious diseases and improve mother and child health, around $27 billion per year, almost half of which it could cover if its debts were canceled, the region would see millions of lives saved each year. There will never be enough rosaries that the developed world can say to absolve it of its blatant negligence toward the developing world's predicament.

The debt-disease nexus is shocking, immoral, dangerous, and most poignantly, unnecessary. People are dying every day in developing nations because of debt: babies, mothers, children, and teenagers are dying because the rich world is insisting upon a continual transfer of wealth and on a continual application of policies that have a detrimental health effect, especially on the poor. They are also dying because the poor world's governments are allowing the situation to continue by not joining forces to stop the pillage, and because their people are too sick and tired to do anything to shake their leaders out of their resignation or complacency. Global security is being threatened because countries weighed down with debt service payments and detrimental conditions for its relief are experiencing pandemics that are destabilizing and destructive.

There is no question that the additional funds that would be released by debt cancellation, and the gains engendered by the cessation of the old-style conditions that typically have been attached to debt relief, could stop people dying, give the sick the hope of longer, higher-quality lives, and also put the developing world on the road to economic recovery. Of course, the dividends would have to reach those who needed them, by no means a given anywhere in the world. The United States, for example, has trillion-dollar budgets, but 46 million of its people have no health insurance and very tenuous access to health care. Developing-world governments, too, have a history of underprioritizing the health of their own poor. And then, of course, there's the issue of whether the funds released would just go into additional military expenditure, already extremely high in developing-world countries. Western arms manufacturers would undoubtedly revel in this.

These are all extremely important issues, and I will address them in the final chapter. But in the meantime, in the hour or so it took you to read this chapter, nearly fifteen hundred poverty-stricken children died unnecessarily, and what are the governments of the West doing about all this? The answer is stark, and simple. They are neither channeling sufficient resources to countries that so desperately need them, nor appropriately seeking to ensure that the proceeds of any debt relief they are giving are suitably spent. Nor are they rethinking the conditions that go alongside debt cancellation so that they might actually foster development rather than thwart it. Instead, the world's richest governments are trying to kid themselves and placate others with debt relief programs that are completely inadequate and ill-thought-out, and promises of insubstantial amounts of aid. Only $2.1 billion has been raised so far for the Global Health Fund for AIDS, TB, and malaria, for example, the much-touted global initiative to tackle these diseases, which falls well short of the $7–10 billion-a-year target. And although President Bush's Emergency AIDS Plan for Africa, which promises to give $8.5 billion to fourteen countries over the next five years, sounds pretty generous, as we know, those countries typically pay more than that in debt service and repayment in one year alone. It's not the solution.

Once again the West is showing extreme shortsightedness. Once again it cannot just turn its back on the developing world's problems, turn its TV sets off, and pretend that this is the poor world's problem alone. It isn't. Disease, a manifestation of the dark side of debt, can fast become a developed-world problem, put its physical safety at risk, and hurt it in its pocket. The rich world's negligence also has the potential to corrupt its very soul.

There is still more. For developing-world debt has the potential to harm us in even more profound ways. The air we breathe, the food we eat, the species that surround us, our very sense of security, are all also in range of the debt grenade. It is to these we turn in the next chapter.

10

It's Not Just Osama

The
rising tide of the global
economy will create many
economic winners, but it will not lift all
boats. [It will] spawn conflicts at home and
abroad ensuring an ever-wider gap between
regional winners and losers than exists today.
[Globalization's] evolution will be rocky, marked by
chronic financial volatility and a widening economic
divide. Regions, countries and groups feeling left
behind will face deepening economic stagnation,
political instability and cultural alienation. They
will foster political, ethnic, ideological and
religious extremism, along with the violence
that often accompanies it.
—Central Intelligence Agency,
Global Trends 2015

The Berlusconi Wannabe

Today, Cem Uzan is one of Turkey's most notorious businessmen, but a few years ago he was thought of as one of its most successful. At the time, he was described as the country's blond-haired, blue-eyed boy, Turkey's Berlusconi in the making. This was a man who had, by his early thirties, successfully diversified his family's construction business into banking, media, and telecommunications, a man who, by the end of 2002, owned five national television stations, one of Turkey's leading newspapers, a clutch of utility companies, the country's second largest mobile phone network, and several banks.

Like Berlusconi, he had political aspirations. In August 2002, less than three months before the Turkish general election in November, Uzan founded a new political party, the Genc Party (the Young Party). The campaign he ran mixed balloons, pop music, and free food, with, you guessed it, a platform that was explicitly antidebt.

Two years before, at the height of its economic crisis, Turkey had been forced to go the IMF for help. Now in 2002, with his country struggling to service a crippling $31 billion loan and facing the consequences of the IMF's punishing economic austerity program, Uzan demanded that a moratorium be placed on Turkey's debt repayments. "Turkish people are starving to service that debt," Uzan said. "We don't need you, IMF!" roared the rallying cry.

Such rhetoric served him well. In only two and a half months, Uzan secured a highly respectable 7.3 percent of the vote. After the election the slim and suntanned Uzan took, if anything, an even more aggressive stance. "If I was in office I would get rid of the IMF," Uzan said in May 2003. A month later, he proclaimed that his first action if elected would be to expel the IMF. He refused to waver even when, later that year, the IMF agreed to reschedule a portion of Turkey's outstanding debt and the economy had begun to improve. In August 2003, his party was polling at around 17 percent.

Yet within only a few months of the election, Uzan and his family had been charged with embezzlement on a massive scale. His flagship banks were taken over by banking regulators, and all his companies and assets were seized, as administrators attempted to repay the banks' $7 billion liabilities. At the same time, Motorola and Nokia won a $4.2 billion judgment for fraud against Uzan, his family, and his companies in a New York court. Given that Uzan only began railing against foreign financial institutions the moment his creditors had begun to circle, and the threat of civil, regulatory, and criminal charges had begun to loom, his political rhetoric and aspirations can hardly be taken at face value. It can be no coincidence that, in Turkey, members of parliament have immunity from prosecution.

Indeed, despite the massive array of accusations levied against him in Turkey, Uzan remains a free man. Despite the Motorola and Nokia ruling; despite the fact that a U.K. judge has sentenced him to fifteen months in Pentonville Prison, and were he apprehended in the United Kingdom, he would go straight to jail; despite the fact that his father, brother and uncle, having been served with arrest warrants in Turkey, are now on the run and on Interpol's red bulletin, Uzan remains free. According to political analysts, the Turkish government cannot risk prosecuting him, for fear that such action would be seen as politically motivated. It cannot risk turning Uzan into a political martyr.

Given the $7 billion Uzan's banks owe, it is ironic that his antidebt platform, at the time of writing at least, has proved to be his savior. Although support for his political party has diminished, it continues to hover at around the same level it was in November 2002, before the fraud and embezzlement stories broke. Much of this support comes from those who suffer most under the debt and IMF burden: the young, the poor, the unemployed, and women.

Rhetoric of Debt and Conflation

We have seen in earlier chapters how debt servicing requirements and the conditions insisted upon to get loans or be eligible for debt relief have often been highly damaging for developing countries; how the net effect of conforming to the rich world's set of rules, and the net transfer of resources back to it, has often been greater inequality; rising levels of unemployment; increased social, health, and economic stresses; and the deterioration of the lives of those already on the margins. We have seen how debt has so often been a story of the rich made richer at the expense of the poor, of politically corrupt ruling classes grabbing what they can from their broken constituents, of enfeebled governments becoming push-me, pull-me asses so caught up in attempting to manage their various loan-masters that their constituents' needs are often ignored.

No wonder opposition politicians from Turkey to Bolivia to Thailand have successfully made political hay while the debt sun burned down, using it as a way both to explain their country's dire predicament and also to rally support.

This line of attack is frequently justifiable. But all too often politicians invoke debt only as an opportunistic way of gaining votes. They demonize lenders and institutions not because they honestly care about the horrendous damage being inflicted on their country, or because they have legitimate political reforms that are being thwarted by debt, but simply to rally nationalistic support or deflect attention from economic mismanagement or, as in Cem Uzan's case, from their own shortcomings.

Hitler fell into the first category, a politician who cynically used debt to fuel jingoistic sentiment. In his rise to power, he often used the debts Germany was obliged to meet under the Treaty of Versailles as a rhetorical tool with which to gain popular favor and fuel resentment against the nation's former foes, speaking of the "iniquities," "humiliation," "suffering," and "disgrace" the debt engendered. This was something John Maynard Keynes had so presciently anticipated when he wrote his impassioned outburst against the treaty. "Vengeance I dare predict," he wrote, "will not limp" if the victors insisted on impoverishing the vanquished. Robert Mugabe is a contemporary example of the second category, a politician who couples anti–IMF/World Bank rhetoric with accusations against commercial banks, to deflect attention from the failure of his own policies.

An even more damaging political trick is the cynical combination of antidebt, anti-IMF rhetoric with more general attacks against a demonized "other," be that the West, America, or something or someone closer to home. Robert Mugabe not only conflates anti–IMF/World Bank rhetoric with anticapitalist rhetoric, but also with antiwhite racism and even antihomosexual language—Tony Blair's "gay government" is one of his favorite targets. Amien Rais, the speaker of the Indonesian parliament, recently claimed that Indonesia could achieve recovery without the IMF, but this statement came coupled with more general vitriolic attacks against Western interests. Debt can fast become a vehicle for bigotry, intolerance, and more general anti-"other" talk.

This is an "other" that the indebted society is often willing to attack. Argentinian MP Alicia Castro, in a televised session of congress during the country's economic crisis of 2002, handed an American flag to the congress's leader and requested that those responsible for the country becoming "a mere secretariat of the IMF" replace the Argentine flag with the American one. This resonated strongly with an Argentine public that had become increasingly incapable of distinguishing its animosity toward the IMF from the animosity it felt toward the United States. So strong was the conflated and collective rage that when, at the end of November 2002, the opportunity arose to exhibit a Daniel Santoro painting of Eva Perón as Saint of the Poor decapitating Spruille Braden (the U.S. ambassador who clashed with General Perón in 1945), galleries fought over it.

Linking together antidebt, anti-IMF, anti–U.S., and anti-West rhetoric is not, however, the preserve only of gallery-playing politicians. Much more dangerously, the same language has been embraced by extremist groups like Al Qaeda. It has been reported that one way Osama bin Laden's terrorist network recruits is by denouncing "American financial institutions" (and by that read the IMF and World Bank, as well as commercial banks), depicting them as integral parts of the larger force that keeps corrupt governments in power, and as a significant cause of the dismal living conditions of his potential constituents. Similarly, American financial institutions have been cast as one of the common enemies around which sympathizers of the Palestinian and Iraqi causes, militants from Upper Egypt, Algeria, Pakistan, Chechnya, Sudan, Somalia, and the Philippines, the poor in the slums of Riyadh and the poor of Casablanca and Karachi should coalesce. Supporters of the recently revived Shining Path insurgency in Peru combine calls for the mobilization of masses of people to combat and defeat the oppressor" (i.e., the

United States) with references to the IMF and the World Bank as "financial tools of imperialism."

Debt's ugly progeny—poverty, inequality, and injustice—are also called upon to justify, and even legitimize, acts of the greatest violence. Only a few weeks after the World Trade Center was attacked, leading African commentator Michael Fortin wrote: "We have to recognize that this deplorable act of aggression may have been, at least in part, an act of revenge on the part of desperate and humiliated people, crushed by the weight of the economic oppression practiced by the peoples of the West." Fortin's language—"crushed," "oppression," "desperate," "humiliated"—is deliberately evocative. And it is manifestly clear that there is an audience with whom such words powerfully resonate.

For in today's global age of information, people are more conscious than ever of their relative state of deprivation. While part of the world enjoys double skinny lattes, wide-screen TVs, and Nike trainers as the norm, the bulk of humanity do not—*and they know it.* I will never forget Owens Wiwa (the brother of the late Nigerian activist Ken Saro-Wiwa, who was murdered by the Nigerian authorities for speaking out against their practices in Ogoniland) telling me what it was like growing up: "And then we got television. And we saw that other people had fancy apartments and drove expensive cars. And then we got angry."

It is impossible to ignore the size of this audience. There are now around 870 million "global desperados"—people living in slums in Karachi and Istanbul, in Indonesia, the Philippines, North and West Africa—whose lives are worse today than at any time over the past two decades, for a multiplicity of reasons, most of which can be traced back, at least in part, to national debt. Even if only a fraction of these people were to embrace the "let us risk everything for we have nothing" school of thought, we'd be talking about a hell of a lot of people. We don't need the majority of the poor and desperate to begin to think like this for it to become our collective problem. Just a few who are angry and desperate enough will do.

Militancy also provides employment. We've already seen young women forced into the sex industry in countries where debt burdens have caused unemployment rates among the poor to skyrocket. The appeal of a career in a local militia or extremist army for young, unemployed men in similarly debt-devastated or poverty-stricken environments—men educated for positions that no longer exist because of collapsing industrial sectors, men living either like sardines in teeming urban spaces or, alternatively, in deserted rural communities—cannot be overstated. Joining a militia or terrorist organization provides a job opportunity where otherwise there might not have been one: it was *unemployed* Hutu youth who joined the militia that committed the Rwandan 1994 genocide (unemployment shot up in Rwanda during the 1990s in the wake of IMF programs); the Shining Path movement of Peru has recently reappeared among the *jobless* of the high Andes and in the urban shantytowns of Lima (among the very people who were worst hit by their country's austerity programs); the unemployed of the *poorest* parts of Pakistan are proving ripe recruitment grounds for extremist groups looking for *jihadis*, or foot soldiers, to send to fight holy wars; while the militant Islamic movement of Uzbekistan is recruiting heavily among Uzbek youths who are unable to find alternative work. These jobs can often provide a significant income. A midlevel manager of one of Pakistan's militant groups, Lashkar-I-Taiba, the Army of the Pure, for example, earns 15,000 rupees a month, seven times what the average Pakistani makes. Often recruits' families are provided with a monthly income, too.

The amounts of money "career terrorists" or militiamen make by blowing themselves up or shooting each other is, of course, only one factor that leads young men to make such job choices. Historical grievances, ethnic persecution, territorial disputes, religious divides, and a desire to find a sense of belonging in a world in which community and identity are crumbling are all contributing factors, too. But it is the combination of the economic with these other factors that fuels the popularity of these young men. The recruiting pitch for a young man—and it is predominantly, though not exclusively, men we are talking about here—living in a country characterized by poverty, inequality, and absence of hope is not difficult to script: "By sacrificing your own life, you will be able to ensure your family and community a significantly better future." Alternatives that to us seem morally unacceptable can be seen, from a position of hopelessness, as not only worth contemplating but as inescapable.

Of course, most of the identifiable "brand-name terrorists," Osama bin Laden and some of the more recent suicide bombers from Palestine, are actually from privileged homes; and participants in Hezbollah's militant activities in the late 1980s and early 1990s tended to have a secondary education or higher. Indeed, most contemporary high-profile terrorists tend to be middle-class. Yet despite the fact that these militants may only have witnessed deprivation, rather than experienced it firsthand—it is an espoused desire to fight on behalf of a downtrodden mass that is the justification they use for their means, and is a significant basis of their popularity. Moreover, the foot soldiers that they recruit among the poor are essential for their success. By running guns, providing money-laundering opportunities, and creating safe havens, it is they who provide the supportive environment that the terrorists need.

Economic factors play a similarly critical role in the reasoning process behind many of the developing-world drug trade's "worker ants." The khat growers in Kenya, the coca farmers in Bolivia, and the dagga pickers in Mozambique just don't have viable alternatives: the prices of many legitimate agricultural commodities have collapsed. By growing illegal crops, they can ensure the survival of themselves or their families; if they rely upon growing legal crops or the charity of the state, they can't. The so-called drug mules, the Jamaican mothers, for example, who board planes to Heathrow and Newark, stomachs packed full of narcotics-filled condoms are in the vast majority of cases God-fearing, decent women whose lives never recovered from the time the Jamaican government acquiesced to IMF demands. This horrendously risky job is seen by them as their only chance for survival. The $1,500 they could earn from one successful trip would be enough to change their lives and their children's lives forever.

Desperation, insecurity, and a realization that one must fend for oneself, having been abandoned by the state, the leitmotifs of our story of debt are conditions that can, of course, lead the desperate to make choices that have ramifications for us all. Why, after all, should young men fear violent death in a holy war or young women death by cocaine overdose in an airplane toilet when they could die a violent, seemingly more pointless, death closer to home—whether that is a Bogotá favela or a *City of God*–like environment—where death rates due to violence or disease are already unacceptably high? Life is viewed differently in countries in which inequalities are great, and in which life is a Hobbesian nightmare—solitary, poor, nasty, brutish, and short.

Latter-day Saints

But debt doesn't only create opportunities for extremists and criminal factions to recruit the foot soldiers that provide the sea in which bigger fish can swim, to paraphrase Mao. We have already seen the extent to which developing-world debt has eroded the community fabric, how it has forced governments to cut funding for schools, hospitals, and social services. Imagine, then, what would happen if someone stepped forward who was willing to provide all of this in the state's stead. Regardless of whatever else his goody bag may contain, he will be perceived as a hero, a savior, a bearer of all things good.

We have seen this manifest itself in Latin America, where drug barons have garnered huge popular support in areas that the state has abandoned. Pablo Escobar, for example, the notorious Colombian drug lord, successfully courted Medellín's large disenfranchised population by providing them with access to electricity and water, and building them houses, soccer fields, basketball courts, and other sports facilities. In his hometown of Evingado, he underwrote the development of a local welfare system, built a housing development, and gave away one thousand houses to low-income residents. Carlos Lehder, another Colombian drug baron (now condemned to life-plus-135 years in a U.S. jail), was hailed by the local communities that he financed and supported as a *patroncito,* a word used to describe saints who perform miracles. Rafael Caro, a similarly feted Mexican drug lord, gained popular legitimacy by employing over thirty thousand people in his ranches, donating 100 million pesos for infrastructure construction to the village of Caborca in the state of Sonora, and building schools in places that the government had given up on.

Elsewhere we see extremist Islamic groups using the same strategy, observing the gaping void left by the state, and seizing the opportunity to step in as an alternative power source.

Take Pakistan, a country with very high levels of debt, no semblance of a welfare state, and a leadership intent on using scarce resources to fund military expenditure above all else—a country where 40 percent of the population live below the poverty line, 60 percent have no access to education, 50 percent have no access to basic health services, and government schools are sorely lacking in books, electricity, and teachers. An open invitation for radical Islam, which, through the founding of a network of madrassas—free religious schools that provide a strict Koranic education to boys who would not otherwise have had access to education at all—has not only been able to use the schools as a fertile recruiting ground, but also as a means to gaining more widespread popular support.

All faith-based organizations, whether in Louisiana or Lagos, Boston, Birmingham, or Bogotá, have their attendant problems in terms of agenda and accountability, and all are potentially susceptible to charges of indoctrination. Yet whatever they may be accused of, they don't use their influence to preach killing and jihad. One in six of Pakistan's thirty-nine thousand madrassas do, promulgating doctrines appropriate to the Crusades or the Spanish Inquisition. These are schools that offer only religious instruction and actively promote militancy, urging their barely literate students to fulfill their spiritual obligations by fighting against the Muslims of other sects in Pakistan, against the Hindus in Kashmir, or against the infidels of the West, especially an "imperialistic" United States. They provide an education capable of creating hundreds of thousands of Holy Warriors before their students even learn how to hold a gun.

In Pakistan, Darul Uloom Haqqania, a madrassa that counts most of the Taliban leadership among its alumni, receives over fifteen thousand applications from poor families every year for four hundred places. And the applications don't come just from Pakistan, but also from Sudan, Mali, Nigeria, Senegal, Yemen, Bangladesh, and Turkey (in some Pakistani madrassas up to 75 percent of students are from abroad). All these countries have, of course, this in common: they are places in which poverty is endemic, places in which mounting debt burdens are disproportionately shouldered by the poor. And the attraction of the madrassas is not surprising, because when the state doesn't provide education, health care, or social services, any alternative that does will be appealing. And not only do the madrassas educate children, they often feed, house, and clothe them too.

Thousands of madrassas are now appearing in Southeast Asia and sub-Saharan Africa, for example. Give me a child before the age of seven, said the Jesuit priest. How crazy the West is, doing nothing to stop the education of hundreds of thousands of the developing world's children by violent extremists.

But this assumption of social services by extremist forces is not only confined to the spread of madrassas. Other radical Islamic groups adopt similar strategies elsewhere. The Muslim Brotherhood in Egypt and Jordan, the FIS in Algeria, Hizb-al-Islah in Yemen and Hamas in Gaza, for example, all provide some combination of health, education, employment, and affordable housing to people in countries where the majority of people are poor, development has been highly uneven, and accelerated economic liberalization has increased social tensions and dislocations. In short, to places where the state is unable or unwilling to deliver social services. The Al-Rahid Trust, for example, one of the main organizations in America's "black book of terrorists," has set up shop in Afghanistan where, besides running training camps for the Taliban and separatists fighting in Kashmir, it also runs bakeries, sets up computer centers, provides clinics, and digs wells for drinking water. Often it is extremely difficult to distinguish between legitimate welfare providers and terrorist hothouses.

Of course, not *all* countries with collapsed welfare states and inadequate state education and health provision are in this position because of IMF or World Bank demands or unmanageable debt burdens. Moreover, not all are susceptible to extremist Islamic indoctrination or drug dealers' charms, to self-cast Robin Hoods in turbans or gold chains. For the former, there needs to be a significant Muslim population already in place, or a significant enclave, in order for extremist Islam to gain a foothold—we're not going to see Islamic extremists recruiting in the favelas of Rio, for example. For the latter, the geographical and weather conditions need to be right for the drugs to be grown in the first place. And there are some examples of *relatively* benign nonstate providers of social services. In recent years, for example, Christian missionaries have set up schools and clinics in Africa and Latin America. Shell, the multinational petroleum giant, spent $66.9 million on social investment programs in Nigeria in 2002 alone, over three times what the U.K. government provided in aid for the same year. But just mull this over. *All* of the world's most highly indebted poor countries are ones in which the state isn't delivering on social services, health, or education, and half of these *do have* majority Muslim populations. Most of the world's drug supply *is* grown in poor, often highly indebted countries where economic opportunities are scarce, law enforcement is weak, and officials can be bribed or eliminated. The danger of extremism or drug running taking hold in these weak environments is all too clear.

Failed States

And weak states can easily become failing or failed states. In fact, most of the failed or quasi-failed states one can think of— Afghanistan, Angola, Burundi, the DRC, Liberia, Sierra Leone, Sudan, Somalia, and Yemen—are severely indebted. Most were provided with loans during the cold war to support the superpowers' geopolitical and corporate interests, much of which money was spent on arms bought from the superpowers' own arms manufacturers. Most had rulers who were bankrolled by the West or the East and who sucked their countries dry—President Mobuto of Zaire, President Siaka Stevens of Sierra Leone, President Mohammed Siad Bare of Somalia, to name but three. Under IMF and World Bank austerity programs, most slashed health and education budgets, suffered from IMF/World Bank–imposed devaluations of their currencies, and experienced rising popular dissent as a consequence.

These states pose dangers not only to themselves and their neighbors but also to people across the globe. Immanuel Kant's words that "we are unavoidably side by side," written over two hundred years ago, ring truer today than ever before. For the ensuing random anarchic violence that results from the collapse of states sets off waves of domestic and transnational catastrophes such as refugee flows, epidemics of communicable disease, undernutrition, malnutrition, and rape that respect no borders and have far-reaching consequences, while attempts to contain the failing states come at a significant cost. The cost of attempting to keep the peace in Somalia with UN peacekeepers after it collapsed was $2 billion a year, for example, way more than anyone had ever put into that country in development aid—and by then it was of course far too late.

Moreover, failed states are safe havens for the very same terrorists and extremists who, we have seen, are already on the march. For it is in places where the apparatus of government has collapsed and the rule of law has given way to that of warlords where terrorists most easily find refuge and harbor—two of the men on the FBI's most wanted list, both involved with the East African bombings of 1998, were able to lie low for years in the Democratic Republic of Congo, before moving on to Liberia, a country where some of Osama bin Laden's most trusted lieutenants allegedly fled after the September 11 attacks and established a safe haven. It is in failed states that terrorists can supplement their financing opportunities—links between Al Qaeda, the Shia militant groups Hezbollah and Amal, and diamond dealers in Sierra Leone have been established. It is in failed states that terrorists train—the main training camps of Al

Qaeda were (and perhaps still are) in Afghanistan, and also in Sudan and Somalia. It is in conflict-ridden, and usually poor and debt-burdened countries that terrorism is able to breathe and breed.

The Air We Breathe . . .

There is yet more for us to fear. The burden that debt puts upon the developing world endangers us all in an even more fundamental way. It threatens the air we breathe, the food we eat, the survival of our species. It poses a threat to our very planet.

The world's fish stocks are facing collapse, great apes are facing extinction, toxic shrimps are being found in many waters. Sugar maple yields are falling, ocean levels are rising, coral reefs, rain forests and mangrove wetlands are disappearing. Insurance loss claims in America due to natural disasters are already spiraling out of control (claims between 1990 and 2000 were equal to those of the previous thirty years combined) and costs of global warming are expected to reach $300 billion a year in coming decades. All this and much more can be linked to debt.

How so? First, in order to generate the requisite foreign exchange they need to service their debts, developing countries tend to exploit whatever natural resources they have. The more debts they have, the more they exploit. Clear links can be made, for example, between levels of debt and rates of deforestation. And deforestation is a key driver of global warming—25 percent of global greenhouse gas emissions are due to changes in land use, principally deforestation, most of which is taking place in the developing world—and global warming is a key driver of climate change.

At the same time, the opening up of forests and woodlands to industrial logging companies, a move increasingly favored in order to meet the privatization requirements of the IMF, itself creates serious problems. Since industrial loggers have moved in, hordes of people have been drawn to the hitherto inaccessible forests of Central and West Africa in search of work. In order to survive, these people are killing off pigs, elephants, chimpanzees, and gorillas at an unprecedented rate. If today's rates of slaughter persist, not only will indigenous forest people no longer have a secure source of food, these species will be extinct within the next twenty years.

Second, countries devastated by debt simply cannot afford to act in an environmentally responsible way. They can't afford to replant their forests if they raze them, so the world loses its carbon sinks; they can't afford to put money into environmental preservation schemes when they are facing more immediate problems—health crises, unemployment, social unrest, etc. And so environmental degradation persists. There has been a 50 percent reduction in funds for environmental preservation in the Amazon, for example, since the 1980s, when structural adjustment programs were first put in place. And even if a country does have environmental protection legislation, it cannot afford to enforce it—the Democratic Republic of Congo has some of the most sophisticated environmental protections in the world but cannot find the money to pay the policemen to administer it. In the Philippines, where the government sold off all official vehicles in order to meet IMF-imposed budgetary constraints, you have the bizarre situation of forestry officials being forced to beg rides from the very loggers they are supposed to be controlling! The upshot? More exploitation, more environmental risk.

Third, the pressure of servicing debt in poverty-stricken countries inspires short-termist behavior. The world's poorest countries—Ghana, Gambia, Honduras, Nicaragua—are selling off their fishing rights, for example, to fleets from the world's richest, in part to repay their debts. Never mind the fact that these rich countries have already overfished their own seas, and are clearly hell-bent on exporting their overfishing practices to new waters. Never mind that, as a consequence, the developing countries are seeing the livelihoods of their own local fishing communities being destroyed, unable to compete with big commercial fleets. And never mind the fact that if developing-world countries continue to sell off their fishing rights at the current rates, the world's entire fish stock will collapse. And this isn't scaremongering. In the past fifty years, the world's mechanized fishing fleets have already managed to wipe out nine-tenths of the world's biggest and most economically important species of fish, including swordfish, cod, halibut, and tuna. Just think what could happen if such fleets are able to trawl unregulated in developing-world waters.

Fourth, loans are very often provided for clearly environmentally damaging projects. Remember the PoloNoreste Project in Brazil, the 930-mile road built through the Amazon, financed by the World Bank in order to create new rural settlements and ease urban congestion—which resulted in widespread deforestation, the dislocation of indigenous peoples, and the loss of many endangered species. More recently, we have seen mangrove wetlands, the saltwater equivalents of the rain forests, being destroyed in Thailand, Indonesia, Ecuador, Bangladesh, Nigeria, Ghana, Malawi, and elsewhere as World Bank–financed shrimp farms are built on these sites—shrimp farms are now the primary cause of mangrove and wetland destruction in the tropics. Hundreds of millions of dollars are being lent by the World Bank for projects which, on top of contributing to global warming, not only are proving incapable of generating the foreign exchange they were supposed to create (which should, of course, have been obvious: with so many countries being lent money to set up such farms all at the same time, there was an immediate global glut of shrimps, and their price plummeted), but are also threatening local food security: in Asia, for example, over half the shrimp farms that were set up are, because of the glut, now abandoned, which has led to a significant drop in the availability of food, as land formerly used for crop growing now lies fallow. Having been salinated for the shrimps to flourish, it is now unsuitable for other use. Furthermore, the products are all too often toxic, as shrimp growers pump their products with chemicals so as to maximize yields. Thai, Pakistani, Vietnamese, and Indonesian prawns have all been found to contain traces of the cancer-causing antibiotic nitrofuran, and in 2002 several of Britain's leading food retailers were asked by the Food Standards Authority to withdraw various Asian prawns from their shelves, because they contained not only this illegal chemical but also pesticides deemed dangerous by the World Health Organization.

Export credit agencies are also guilty in this environmentally unsound lending equation. They are responsible, as we have seen, for financing most dams and thermal power plants in developing countries and several have done serious damage. The Rihand mega–power plant in India, for example, financed by export credits provided by Western governments so that their big corporations—in this case NEI and GEC—could profit, had to be cooled with water from the Rihand Lake, thus raising the lake's temperature and changing the ecology; the power plant was also fed with coal from the Singrauli strip mine, one of the last habitats for the Bengal tiger. While U.S. export credit agencies OPIC and Ex-Im are currently in litigation, charged with having provided over $32 billion in loans and insurance over the past ten years for the building of oil fields and coal-fired power projects in developing countries. Loans that it is claimed by the cities of Boulder and Oakland—which in conjunction with Friends of the Earth and Greenpeace have brought the case to bear—will lead directly to climate change, and as a result will diminish U.S. drinking water supplies, increase the risk of salt water contamination in groundwater aquifers, overwhelm sewage systems, and aggravate respiratory illnesses. In the case of Oakland, climate change *already* puts its airport at risk: given that it was built on a former wetland at about ten feet above sea level, it is now susceptible to flooding from the extreme tides that accompany global warming.

And remember, the United States' export credit agencies are more environmentally sound than almost all of their counterparts!

Of course, blaming the developing world for the destruction of the developed world's environment is in some ways pretty rich. If anything, the developed world owes an ecological debt to the developing world: carbon dioxide emissions from the rich world currently far exceed those from the poor. The commitment of the 1992 UN Framework Convention on Climate Change, under which developed countries were supposed to reduce emissions, remains largely unfulfilled. Both America and Russia have refused to ratify the Kyoto Protocol. And frighteningly little change is expected on the emissions front, especially given that the United States alone accounts for 21 percent of total world emissions and that the Bush administration is hell-bent on downplaying the impact on global warming.

But by lending money for projects it knows are environmentally unsound, and by making poor countries deprioritize the environment and sell off their natural resources in order to meet IMF conditions, the rich world once again shoots itself in the foot. Once again, this is a case not of developed-world myopia, but of developed-world blindness.

The security threat we face if we continue to ravage our environment at current rates is going to make even Osama bin Laden look pretty tame. In a recent report, the Pentagon announced that global warming is now a greater threat than terrorism. The latest scientific research predicts that water, dry land, and energy resources will become increasingly scarce and increasingly fought over within our lifetime. And that civil wars and regional conflicts will grow as tens of millions of people displaced by floods, droughts, cyclones, and rising sea levels will pour across borders and huddled refugee camps, leaving disease, misery, and anger in their wake. Millions are likely to starve as climate changes take hold; ill-configured World Bank–funded monoculture projects, and the depletion of the oceans are likely to cause the collapse of food production in countries that already have severely undernourished populations. Those who survive will find sustenance in their rage. Disease could spread, as rising temperatures are anticipated to lead to increased incidences of insect-borne illnesses such as malaria and dengue fever, illnesses against which our borders no longer provide barriers. Species after species are projected to become extinct—already 24 percent of mammals are threatened with extinction thanks to logging, forest clearing, and overfishing practices: an extraordinary rate of extinction even compared with the ice ages. With each death, the number of possible medical cures drops, and our fragile and complex ecosystem will be further irreversibly damaged.

The Cree Indians warn that "after the last tree has been cut down; after the last river has been poisoned; after the last fish has been caught, only then will you find that money cannot be eaten." We are approaching that last tree, last river, last fish.

The debt threat is real and it faces us now. Countries weighed down by unmanageable debt burdens are already sicker, poorer, more economically unstable, more politically volatile, more fractured than they would otherwise be. Their environments are more ravaged. Confidence in their leaders is already increasingly weakened as more and more people ask whether it is to them or their bankers that their loyalties lie.

And in this ever globalizing world of ours what is "theirs" fast becomes "ours," *their* sicknesses become *our* sicknesses, *their* despair *our* despair, *their* damage *our* damage; their dysfunctionality, the dysfunctionality of us all. We will never be able to build walls high enough to keep angry beggar armies out. No amount of "shock" or "awe" will be sufficient to dispel the ever growing hordes of the disgruntled and disenfranchised. Paper surgical masks will be unable to protect us from the spread of diseases that respect no borders. No number of herbicide-spraying sorties will stop poor, dispossessed farmers from growing drugs. *Our* environment will be irrevocably damaged by the environmentally damaging decisions taken by others many thousands of miles away. *Our* economies threatened, by the game of chicken that Wall Street and the leaders of the developing world so often play.

Debt, the rallying point for disaffection, the drain on resources that exacerbates poverty, the symptom of a poor understanding of our long-term national interests, is playing a pivotal role in putting our collective security at risk. Yet despite this, the developed world continues to lend unwisely, continues to demand that the developing world repay its outstanding loans. Despite this, the debt threat is at best underplayed and at worst completely ignored. The spiral of disillusion, poverty, environmental degradation, violence, crises, and despair that it engenders is one that could be averted. *How* is what the final chapter will explore.

The
Blueprint

11

Truth, Reconciliation, and Regeneration

Five
years ago, I came to
protest outside the G8 in
Birmingham to call for debt cancellation.
In Zambia we have had enough debt relief to
repaint our hospitals and schools but not enough
to pay for doctors and teachers. I'm here to
celebrate what we have achieved and to remind people
that a lot more still needs to be done.
—*Mulima Akapelwa, head of the Economic Justice Unit of Zambia's*
Catholic Commission for Justice, Development and Peace in Zambia,
upon her return to Birmingham, England, May 13, 2003

We are all sorry when we are found out. The
question is what lesson have we learned? The
question is, what are we going to do now that
we are sorry?
—*Issacs accepting Lurie's apology in*
J. M. Coetzee's novel Disgrace

Truth

Sometimes in life one has to admit that things just aren't working. This is one of those times.

The manner in which we deal with the debt of developing countries has come a long way since the Latin American debt crisis of the early 1980s. But it hasn't come far enough. And it's manifestly failing debtors and creditors alike.

Despite the promises made in Cologne, the world's poorest countries have yet to see any meaningful reduction in their debt burden—only 12 percent of their debt has been canceled thus far. Sub-Saharan Africa continues to pay out over $10 billion a year to creditors, despite the fact that it is getting poorer and sicker by the day. Iraq, the most visible casualty of bad lending practices, has been offered a debt cancellation program by its creditors. But the program is one that, to paraphrase Iraqi Islamic Party politician Dr. Hajim Al Hassan, demands that the Iraqi people continue to pay for the knives that were used by Saddam to slaughter them. The system is failing and increasingly chaotic, with no systematic processes in place to resolve debt crises, and limited means to prevent them occurring in the first place: Argentina's protracted and bitter negotiations with its creditors are likely to set the tone for the foreseeable future.

We simply have to start from the beginning. We have to remind ourselves of *why* developing countries got into debt in the first place, and of just how destructive the consequences are, for all of us. And then the hard work starts. Collectively, we need to come up with a new way forward, a way forward that exposes the truth about debt, reconciles the interests of all parties in an equitable fashion, and, most important, offers the prospect of regeneration—and reconciliation—for all.

To accomplish this we will have to accept this fundamental principle—that there are some debts that should never have to be repaid, some debts that are so clearly illegitimate or unpayable that countries should never be asked to honor them. It is a matter of justice, not mercy or charity.

But be forewarned. Negotiating the minefield of what a country should or shouldn't repay and defining terms such as "illegitimate" is very complex stuff, both conceptually *and* politically, and it takes us into difficult, alien terrain. It is crucial that we navigate this terrain though, for only by thinking these issues through clearly and critically will we be able to fairly evaluate creditor and debtor claims, and overcome the threat of debt in a just and equitable way.

Let's begin with the concept of illegitimacy. The definition I propose is this, that sovereign debts should be deemed illegitimate if three conditions simultaneously hold:

1. **The regime that borrowed the monies lacked democratic consent.**
2. **The monies were used in ways that were inimical to the interests of the population.**
3. **The lender knew that monies would be used in such a way.**

Domestic law helps us establish a legal basis for the first condition. In basic contract law, contracts are valid only if the parties entering into the contract had the capacity or authority to do so. An individual is not liable for contracts entered into by third parties without their knowledge and without the authority to do so; similarly, corporations are able to escape liability for contracts that their CEO or other officers enter into if it can be shown that the CEO or officers did not have the necessary authority.

While there is no rational reason that this same notion of "agency" should not also be applied to contracts that sovereign states enter into, this is rarely the case. International law tends to assume that, just by merit of being in power, the ruling party has the authority to enter into contracts on behalf of its citizens regardless of how that regime came to power, how it exercises its power, and the extent to which it is supported or opposed by the population it rules.

This assumption needs to be set aside. It stems from an increasingly outmoded concept of what constitutes sovereignty and, increasingly, international human rights law is beginning to recognize that the legitimacy of a state, and therefore its ability to enter into contracts on behalf of its people, is not a given. Democratic consent, it realizes, is an important precondition, and although there will be cases in which consent is less clear than in others, most would agree that a dictatorial regime that maintained its position through fear and oppression, for example, could rarely be seen as having the democratic consent of its population.

But even if democratic consent is demonstrably absent, should this be enough of a reason by itself to nullify all contracts entered into by a regime? No.

Why not? Because it is possible for a regime operating without such consent to borrow money and use it in the interests of the people. In such an instance, it would be unfair to hold that the loan should not be repaid merely because the regime failed to demonstrate a mandate from its people. We don't, after all, want to create a situation where a future democratic China, for example, could repudiate its $170 billion of debt, purely on the grounds that the government of the day was not elected.

Which means another criterion must be added in order to establish whether or not a loan is legitimate.

This is condition number 2, that the monies borrowed were not used in the interests of the people, and that the debtor nation failed to benefit from the loans. There are a number of legal precedents of loan contracts having been deemed null and void on the basis of conditions 1 and 2 both having been met. In 1867, the Mexican government under President Juarez repudiated the entire debt that the Habsburg emperor Maximilian had contracted between 1863 and 1867, arguing that the debts had been used "to maintain the usurper in his place against the legitimate authority" and to suppress violently any uprisings. In 1898, when it was effectively overseeing the island, the United States used similar reasoning to justify repudiating Cuba's debts to Spain, claiming that Cuba did not owe these monies to its former colonizer, because the debts had been imposed on the people of Cuba without their consent (in this case by the force of arms) and had not been incurred for the benefit of the people of Cuba, but for the government of Spain. While in 2000, the Argentinian judge Dr. Jorge Ballestero ruled that Argentina's foreign debt raised by its former military dictatorship was illegal, fraudulent, and therefore illegitimate as it not only had been contracted by a dictatorship but it had not been used for the interests and needs of the state.

But perhaps we need to qualify this second condition too? Let's go back to our bank manager (who's been lying low for a while). Imagine on this occasion that she lent you some monies under the belief that you would use them for a particular purpose, to buy a new car say, and that in establishing whether or not to lend you the money she displayed due diligence, asked you how you would spend the monies, looked at your prior spending patterns, established that the amount borrowed is what you would need to buy a car, and therefore lent in good faith. If you didn't buy a car, however, but used the money to buy a kilo of cocaine to set yourself up as a drug dealer, the bank could not be held responsible for your actions. In other words, if the bank manager had no reasonable way of knowing that you would use the monies in such a way, she would still be entitled to recover her loan.

Which means that yes, once again, we do need to qualify our definition of legitimacy. Debts should be deemed illegitimate only when: (a) the regime lent to lacked a popular mandate, (b) the monies lent were not used in the interests of the state as a whole, and (c) condition number 3—the lender *knew* that this would be so.

Sometimes such knowledge is easy to obtain. The cases where a lender, while ostensibly lending to a country simply transferred the funds to a dictator's foreign bank account, for example, are clear cut. As are cases similar to that of the Royal Bank of Canada's lending monies to Costa Rica in 1918, knowing full well that this money was to be used by its retiring President Federico Tinoco for his personal support once he had flown into exile. At other times, the story is less obvious. We can, for example, imagine a situation in which a loan was given to a developing country for a specific purpose—to bring electricity to villages, or to set up an immunization program—but was siphoned off by the government, and used either for odious purposes or simply embezzled. We can also imagine cases where the loans were used properly, but as a consequence freed up resources that the state then used inappropriately. In General Sani Abacha's

Nigeria, for example, many of the loans given were not stolen, but were actually used to run the government while state revenues from other sources (taxes and oil) were stolen. In such cases, it is less straightforward to claim that the lender knew that he was lending inappropriately. Less straightforward, perhaps, but still quite possible. If the regime to which the monies were being lent was known typically to use funds in ways that were inimical to the interests of its people—if for example a pattern had already been set by the borrower for dissipating common pool funds—a strong case could be made against the lender, to the effect that, based on previous history, the lender should have known that any loans made would have made the nation worse off as a consequence.

When the British government, for example, lent £3 billion to Nigeria during the eras of Abacha and General Ibrahim Babangida, it should have presumed that those notoriously brazen and kleptocratic military regimes would misspend the funds, either directly or indirectly. When the World Bank lent to the Suharto regime in Indonesia, it should have known that a significant tranche would be stolen (in fact, $10 billion of a $30 billion loan ended up being embezzled)—after all, its own records show that it knew all too well how endemic corruption was at the time. When Western governments lent $3 billion to Zaire in the late 1970s and early 1980s, they should have presumed that it would be misspent. After all, the IMF's own man in the country, Edwin Blumenthal, had resigned in protest at corruption so grave and endemic that there was "no chance that Zaire's creditors [would] ever recover their loans." And the list keeps going. When the IMF lent to South Africa in 1976 just months after the Soweto uprising, it should have presumed that by so doing it was helping to prop up a regime known to be cruelly suppressing dissent and perpetrating crimes against humanity. This also applies to the commercial banks who lent to that regime. In fact, in 1982 two lawyers with the First National Bank of Chicago warned in an article that loans made to South Africa might be deemed illegitimate (the term they used was "odious") and therefore not chargeable to a successor regime.

But lending to a violent regime in circumstances where it is reasonable to expect that the monies would be put to immoral use, not only serves to render the loan illegitimate; it also serves to render the creditor complicit in abuses committed as a result of the loan. If I asked my bank manager to lend me money to hire a hit man, for example, and the hit man went out and killed someone, the bank manager would not just have forfeited the loan, he would also be considered to have aided and abetted me in carrying out the crime.

Again, this is a principle that international law already recognizes. In 1820, for example, the U.S. Congress determined that not only were the direct perpetrators of the slave trade to be held subject to the death penalty, but so too were those who built, fitted out, and equipped vessels used for the transportation of slaves, along with those who loaded the ships.

The Nuremberg Tribunal upheld this important principle 130 years later when it held:

> Those who execute the plan do not avoid responsibility by showing that they acted under the direction of the man who conceived it . . . He had to have the cooperation of statesmen, military leaders, diplomats and businessmen. When they, with the knowledge of his aims gave him their cooperation, they made themselves parties to the plan he had initiated. They are not to be deemed innocent . . . if they knew what they were doing.

It is this kind of reasoning that forms the basis of the current class action suit before the U.S. courts by 168 South Africans who claim that they suffered various crimes against humanity at the hands of the apartheid regime and now seek to recover damages from the companies that, in propping up the regime, were vicariously liable for its crimes. Eight banks, namely Barclays National Bank, Citigroup, Commerzbank, Credit Suisse, Deutsche Bank, Dresdner Bank, JP Morgan, and UBS AAG, are named among the corporations sued. Cited as evidence for this is a statement by apartheid South African prime minister John Vorster that "each bank loan, each new investment is another brick in the wall of our continued existence."

The case for deeming certain debts illegitimate is not only strong and compelling; it is a matter of justice and reason. The need is painfully clear: over the past thirty years as much as 60 percent of loans made were committed by creditors to countries whose governments at the time were corrupt or whose people were in chains. Even now, for example, the Japanese government continues to make low-cost loans available to the repressive government of Myanmar. It is essential that the conditions of debt be completely recast.

Rights

But illegitimacy is not the *only* basis upon which a country should be forgiven its debts. The following, I would argue, also constitute grounds for debt forgiveness: If, as a consequence of having to pay its debts, a country is unable to guarantee its citizens subsistence levels of food, water, clothing, and shelter and basic health care and education; if, in order to service its debts, it is forced to destroy and degrade the environment; or if, by merit of its massive debt burden, it is deemed ineligible for much-needed aid. Why? Because such situations actively render a debtor state unable to guarantee the most basic rights of its people, rights that every human rights declaration since World War II has sought to protect. Insistence on debt repayment also makes citizens and governments in the rich world complicit in the ongoing misery, poverty, and deprivation of the poor.

The principle that creditors' rights should not be allowed to override fundamental human rights is, of course, the same principle that underlies contemporary religious calls to cancel debts. Remember how Bono would invoke the biblical concept of Jubilee in his dealing with Helms and Callahan. It also provided the spiritual and intellectual foundation for debt cancellation in ancient Athens and Babylon. "If a man owe a debt and the storm god inundate his field and carry away the produce, or if, through lack of water grain has not grown in the field, in that year he shall not make any return of grain to the creditor, he shall alter his contract-tablet and he shall not pay the interest for that year," the king of Babylon proclaimed in the Code of Hammurabi, circa 1780 B.C.

It is also the underlying basis for the protection afforded by law to debtors in most contemporary legal systems. While debtors' prisons were a sad fact of life in Dickensian Britain and, before that, people were known, literally, to sell themselves into serfdom in order to discharge their debts, today's domestic bankruptcy proceedings typically protect insolvent individuals from being stripped of everything. Their last vestiges of hope and dignity—their tools of trade, an income that allows them a reasonable standard of living, and the roof over their head—remain untouched.

The same principle holds at a larger civic level. In the United States, citizens of municipalities—whether a school district, a city, or a county—are afforded similar protection when the municipality faces financial difficulty. If they are unable to service their debt, municipalities are required neither to raise taxes nor to liquidate their assets in order to repay creditors. Moreover, their ability to deliver public services and provide essential social safety nets is "fenced off" from the creditors. Indeed, the very goal of a chapter 9 bankruptcy procedure (the chapter of the U.S. bankruptcy code that deals with municipalities) is to ensure that, given the vital public services the municipality provides, it is able to continue functioning.

But what holds on a national level once again fails to translate onto the world stage: when a country finds itself bankrupt, its citizens are not typically afforded a similar level of protection (the cancellation of Germany's debts in 1953 and Indonesia's in 1971 are notable exceptions). Although we have ostensibly come a long way since 1876 when the British and French responded to Egypt's financial difficulties by taking over the country's finances and diverting more than half of its revenues to service its debts, or since 1902 when Italian, German, and British warships blocked and shelled Venezuelan seaports because that country refused to pay the money it owed them, citizens of insolvent countries continue to suffer in not dissimilar ways. This is either because to service their debts their governments have to eat into often desperately needed social expenditure budgets, or because default imposes very high costs of its own.

This injustice remains for one simple reason: the principle that countries should not have to service those debts that disable them from meeting the fundamental needs of their citizens has not formally been taken up at the international level. Remember how the World Bank and IMF calculate how much debt a country is eligible to have canceled. The calculation is based on how much foreign exchange a country is expected to generate, and is thus believed to be capable of paying back. The country's ability both to pay the debt *and* to safeguard its people's human rights is not even taken into consideration, which is why those few countries that have received some debt relief are still having to service debts at the expense of the security and dignity of their citizens. Hungry people are dying every day in low-income parts of the world, because the rich world is forcing their governments to repay their debts, because the rich world continues to try to squeeze blood from a stone.

For reasons of equity and justice, but also for reasons of collective self-interest—we saw all too clearly in the previous few chapters the consequences for all of us of states unable to safeguard their citizens and their environments, the window this opens for extremist organizations, and the despair and civil unrest this can fuel—the world's poorest countries must not be forced to repay debts that, in order to be serviced, will make the lives of their citizens unconscionably desperate.

Witness the lip service politicians now pay to developing-world poverty. Africa is a "scar upon the conscience of the world," says Tony Blair. "Our commitment to human dignity" is being "challenged by persistent poverty and raging disease," says George W. Bush. Developed countries have made many column inches of their signing up for the UN's Millennium Development Goals—goals that pledge, among other things, that every country in the world will have free primary education, and that the number of people living in poverty, suffering from hunger, and without access to potable water will be halved, all by 2015.

Such pledges are worthy, but if they are not to be viewed by the developing world as empty promises, the international community will have to put its money where its mouth is. And quickly. Everyone is agreed that for these goals to be met, significant new resources are urgently needed. Yet sadly, if not unpredictably, most of those who signed up to the pledges so rapidly, have failed to match that speed with a corresponding amount of aid, most failing to deliver on the 0.7 percent of GDP they all agreed to commit. The United States, for example, is still spending only one-tenth of 1 percent of its GDP on aid, Japan even less. And the United States seems likely to squeeze its development aid budget even more in order to offset its military expenditure and reconstruction effort in Iraq. Nor have the Europeans or Americans desisted from their subsidizing of farmers and agricultural conglomerates—cows are subsidized in the European Union to the tune of $2.20 a day, while over a billion people live on less than that! Unless countries receive enough debt relief to free up resources to address their citizens' basic needs—which, yes, for most of the world's poorest countries, would mean at the minimum an effective cancellation of *all* debt—there is no chance in hell that the Millennium Development Goals will be met.

Reconciliation

But even assuming that the will behind the rhetoric does harden, how can we determine which debts are illegitimate and which unpayable, and therefore not to be repaid? What kind of process would enable us to do so? And what political realities would need to be overcome in order for it to become operational?

As far as the process goes, there is no need to reinvent the wheel. The parallel with domestic bankruptcy, particularly municipal bankruptcies in the United States, provides us with a good basis on which to design a mechanism for determining which sovereign debts are unpayable or illegitimate, and how debtors and creditors should be treated as a result.

It has a long and distinguished history. Since Adam Smith gave a favorable nod to international bankruptcies in his 1776 *Wealth of*

Nations, a coterie of eminent economists has supported the creation of such a process. Contemporary supporters include two Nobel Prize–winning economists—Joseph Stiglitz and Lawrence Klein—Jeffrey Sachs, now the head of the Earth Institute at Columbia University, and Austrian academic Kunibert Raffer. The idea of some sort of international process to ensure that debtor nations are accorded the right to start anew has been mooted in different ways by politicians from all sides of the political spectrum: Republican Jim Leach, the former chairman of the House Banking and Financial Services Committee in Washington; Gordon Brown, the British Labor Party chancellor of the exchequer; and Kofi Annan; the secretary-general of the United Nations, as well as the Jubilee network and various Southern NGOs. Even the IMF has mooted a proposal in this vein—the "Sovereign Debt Restructuring Mechanism" (SDRM)—with Anne Krueger, the deputy director of the IMF, very publicly arguing for such a process.

Of course, this wouldn't be international politics without some dissent, and the various proposals do differ along important lines about who should rule on the debts—a single judge? judges? arbitrators?—and who should pick whom to rule. There is also argument over which category of debts to include—the IMF proposal, for example, deems that only commercial debts (bonds and loans), and not multi- nor bilateral debts should be considered, the World Bank and IMF arguing that if they were forced to cancel the debts owed them, their credit ratings would collapse and they would then be unable to help needy countries, an argument that is at best exaggerated and at worst just nonsense. But if the process is to be able to deliver on both the illegitimacy and unpayability fronts, and also have relevance for the world's poorest countries, most of whose debts are owed to official lenders, *all* categories of debts would have to be eligible. There is also the question whether an international bankruptcy court is needed, or whether we should be considering arbitration panels instead—when Germany's debts were canceled in 1953, likewise Indonesia's eighteen years afterward, ad hoc arbitration tribunals were used. I lean toward arbitration because this is an accepted mechanism for balancing interests of all sides. Although it is not used for loan disputes, it is already an accepted procedure for dealing with international trade disputes, as well as difficulties in fulfilling contractual obligations not only between similar parties but also between private and public bodies, corporations, and sovereign states. Other questions still to be resolved include how a new supranational body would be accorded compulsory jurisdiction, what role civil society should play in the process, and what process there should be, if any, for appeal.

Of more significance is the fact that some of the proposals ignore the issue of legitimacy altogether. This is simply not a valid option. Nevertheless, I fully accept that there will be difficulties. In some cases, arbitrators may have difficulty in determining the extent to which the new regime has actually broken with the past (important to establish so that loathsome regimes cannot get their own illegitimate debts canceled); in ruling upon whether or not a lender knew it was lending to an illegitimate regime; on whether monies were used in the interest of the people; and also on whether or not a regime had an effective democratic mandate. Which is why, to save time, a ruling on the payability of debt should take place first. I also fully appreciate the corporate lobbying efforts that will attempt to thwart such a legitimacy procedure. But if all parties are to be accorded a real opportunity to move on and lay the past to rest, a ruling on the legitimacy of the debts will have to be an integral part of the process (in domestic bankruptcy procedures any loans that have no legal standing are immediately discounted, after all), as will decisions, where relevant, on whether or not reparations are due. And citizens of the debtor country must be granted full opportunity to give evidence before the arbitration panel, too.

In order, however, that rulings on legitimacy do not deter investors from future lending to developing countries, fearing that were they to do so they would be likely once again to face an arbitration panel where debts could be called illegitimate anew, a country should be allowed to have its illegitimate debts ruled upon only up until a predetermined cutoff date. From that point hence, the only debts to be ruled illegitimate should be those where a regime has been deemed odious in advance. (The UN Security Council essentially already does this in the context of trade sanctions.) And lenders would be prewarned that lending to such odious regimes will not be protected by law.

There are crucial differences among the various proposals. Nevertheless, what must be underlined is that the basic underlying principles of *all* the proposals from civil society, the IMF, and governments of differing political shades are essentially the same—that the costs of debt crises and debt restructuring must be mitigated, and that the debtor should be offered the opportunity to make a fresh start—the original Jubilee call.

The importance of this unanimity on principle cannot be overstressed.

But if there is such fundamental shared support for the designing of a new way to deal with sovereign debts based upon domestic bankruptcy procedures and such essential agreement on matters of principle, why do insiders say that the one proposal that was actually gaining momentum—the IMF's—is completely dead in the water?

There are four main reasons. First, commercial and investment banks don't want it to happen. If it did, not only would they see some of their existing debts written down, they would also see the value of any relevant bonds that they or their clients were holding slashed. Their opposition has been completely unambiguous. An alliance of banks including Citigroup, JP Morgan Chase, UBS, and Deutsche Bank responded to the IMF's SDRM proposal with a statement to the effect that the plan was unworkable in *any* form. "No changes in any specific aspect of the plan" would alter their "serious concern about the proposal," the banks said. And they wield immense political clout.

Second, despite Treasury Secretary Paul O'Neill's support for a bankruptcy-type procedure while he was still in office, no one within the Bush administration has got behind the idea since O'Neill's abrupt resignation in December 2002. This is not surprising, given that all variants of this plan would entail the United States handing over the de facto control it enjoys through the World Bank and the

IMF to a neutral authority. Multilateralism, as we all know, has not been high up on the Bush administration's agenda.

Third, because while many poorer countries have registered support for a mediation- or bankruptcy-type procedure, some important middle-income countries such as Mexico and South Africa have actively come out against it. Those countries are terrified that were they to join any process that ruled on legitimacy or unpayability of debts, they would be penalized with negative credit ratings, be hit with higher interest rates should they issue new bonds, and see a drying-up of investment flows to their country. They fear that even the mere existence of such a process would result in a downturn in investment.

And fourth, because the grassroots pressure to do something on this front, the uncomfortable environment that typically must be created by civil society before politicians or businesspeople do respond hasn't as yet been created. The twenty-four million people who signed the petition in support of canceling debts that was presented in Cologne to the world's leaders in the summer of 1999, have not as yet coalesced around the second wave of activism that debt now demands.

None of these reasons can be allowed to prevail.

The problems are not as large as they may seem at first glance. While it makes sense for the private sector to be concerned—a bankruptcy-type procedure, ruling on both legitimacy and unpayability of debts, *would* result in commercial banks and bondholders taking a hit—there is no reason to believe that ultimately the process would necessarily be any more costly for creditors than the alternative ad hoc, unanticipated and messy defaults, repeated appeals for restructuring and threats of retroactive rulings on legitimacy à la tobacco companies) hanging over them. It may well end up less costly. Furthermore, it is far from clear that such a process would encourage countries to fabricate or exaggerate claims of unpayable debt. The market would hammer any country that did so with punitive interest rate hikes and it would be easy to establish the facts.

In any case, it would be reasonably straightforward to come up with ways to mitigate commercial banks' losses—a bank's debts could be bought by international donors, amnesty could be granted—and similar ways of compensating bondholders could also be found. Should we want to, that is. Remember that the banks have had it pretty good for a very long time, in many cases making back several times the original loan in interest payments, while the discount at which bondholders bought their debt would have factored in the possibility that they might never see the debt redeemed. Only if the expected impact on the financial sector was deemed potentially so great that it could trigger an international or domestic financial crisis, should any efforts be spent considering ways of mitigating commercial banks' losses at all.

As far as middle-income countries such as Mexico or South Africa are concerned, they first need to be advised that, while it is impossible to determine with certainty what the market's response would be, historical cases of orderly debt relief show that in the majority of cases orderly debt relief procedures neither increase interest rates nor reduce inflows of funds. In fact, in some cases the converse has been true. When Poland canceled its debts in the early 1990s, not only was it not penalized by the market, it was actively rewarded—its credit rating soared and its credit terms significantly improved. Understandably—it had less debt. What counts in terms of future reputation is not whether when a country honestly can't pay its debts it tries to see them canceled, but whether the country is honest, has reasonable economic policies, and is seeking a fair settlement. However, given that despite the historical precedents complete assurance as to what will happen if a country decides to embark upon bankruptcy cannot be provided, it should also be made clear to these countries that the decision to embark on this path should be left to the discretion of individual countries. This will enable them to undertake their own cost-benefit analyses to determine whether the risks were, on balance, worth taking—remembering that this process would allow them to be relieved, not only of unpayable debts, but also of any illegitimate ones. If a government did not decide to use such a mechanism, however, it would have to be ready to explain its reasoning to its people. And I would hope that its citizens, in such cases, would demand a full explanation.

The Bush administration's lack of support for such a process, without O'Neill, is a far more serious issue. At the time of writing, George W. Bush is still in office, and, without his administration's support, any mechanism for establishing illegitimacy or unpayability would fail, not only because the United States is a major creditor and extremely influential at the IMF and World Bank, but also because the proposal would probably need an international treaty to give it force of law, which the U.S. Congress would need to ratify.

But here we have one of those rare nexuses, where self-interest meets collective interest. Just imagine the political capital that the United States could enjoy in the developing world (and also Europe) were it to support a neutral mechanism for resolving debt crises—an olive branch to multilateralism and international law; political capital that is much needed in the wake of the fallout over the war on Iraq. And because debt cancellation has proven not to be a partisan issue—it is an issue that finds staunch support among Democrats and Republicans—I am hopeful that whoever is in power in the United States in 2005 will, with enough of a "nudge," find the political will to do what is right despite the vested interests of commercial creditors and help to move this process along.

Which brings to the role civil society must play in all of this—in the developed and developing world. For some this will involve taking up the debt cause for the second time; for others it will be a new experience. Either way, its importance cannot be overstressed. The millions who signed the debt petition, the seventy thousand people who surrounded the G8 summit in Birmingham in 1998, the churches that played such an important role in getting debt on the international agenda, the students who wore "Drop the Debt" T-shirts, the activists in Uganda, Nigeria, and the Philippines who have passionately championed debt relief, need to be mobilized once more.

The debt burden that continues to weigh down much of the developing world is a symptom of the failure of development to date. A failure that is partly attributable to bad government in developing countries, but also to the serious errors of judgment of developed-world governments and corporations. The developing world will never be able to move on unless the past is unveiled, names named and those deserving of it shamed, the asymmetric weight given to creditor interests redressed, and resources freed up so that mothers can secure medical care for their children, daughters are able to go to school, and young men are not tempted by drug lords and extremist organizations. The developed world will never be able to sleep soundly at night until a line is drawn in the sand once and for all.

And the amazing thing is that it wouldn't cost that much to free countries from their yoke of debt. If *none* of the entire $170 billion worth of debt of sub-Saharan Africa were to be collected, for example, this would only cost creditors, once debts had been written down, approximately $24 billion, by one calculation. While this is not a trivial sum, it *is* within our reach. It represents, after all, the cost of only sixteen stealth bombers. The issue is not one of available resources, but of how we choose to use them.

However, and we need to be very clear on this, although a process for determining illegitimacy and unpayability of debts will deliver in terms of truth and, potentially, in terms of reconciliation too, it will not necessarily deliver in meaningful material ways. For even if countries do see their debt burden diminish as a consequence, the process does not guarantee that monies saved will ever reach those who most need them—the poor, the sick, the uneducated, and the unemployed—or even the environment. A bankruptcy-type procedure to rule on matters of justice and equity is necessary, that is clear. But it is not sufficient.

Regeneration

Again, let's get real here—many developing-world governments don't have a very good track record at using the resources they do have at their disposal to address the needs of their poor, needy, and sick. In fact, one of the main complaints of many developing-country activists is that their own governments are blind to the needs of their own people. Pakistan spends approximately 5 percent of its GDP on defense but only 3 percent on education and 0.8 percent on health. This in a country in which, if you recall, poverty is endemic and extremist religious organizations are playing an increasingly necessary social welfare role. President Obasanjo of oil-rich Nigeria spent $330 million in 2000 on building a new national stadium in Abuja, a figure that was more than that year's combined health and education budgets—notwithstanding the fact that Nigeria already had a national stadium in Lagos, and nine other modern stadiums across the country, which had been renovated and used for FIFA's World Youth Championship in 1999. Nowadays, part of that country's current budget is dedicated to launching a satellite; this in a country that has little or no power supply! Yet in terms of illegitimacy and unpayability both of these countries would be eligible for debt relief under my scheme as it currently stands. While the people of Bolivia—one of the first recipients of debt relief—have already seen their government make a U-turn on its commitment to use $670 million of the monies it obtained during debt relief negotiations to finance its poverty reduction strategy, public health and education, putting the monies into its general coffers instead.

If debts are canceled on grounds of illegitimacy and unpayability, without ensuring in advance that the monies freed up will be used for development, the danger is, not only that they may be squandered or won't reach those who need them, but that the funds so released might serve to prop up undesirable regimes. That the money might not only end up "down a rathole"—you remember former U.S. congressman Sonny Callahan's objection to debt relief I am sure—but actually serve to feed the rat. This means that if the bankruptcy process is to provide a real opportunity for citizens of the afflicted country to make a fresh start, we will have to come up with a way of ensuring that new monies go to those who most need them. We must ensure that debt relief becomes a meaningful and constructive development tool.

What this doesn't mean, however—*and let me be very clear on this*—is that we stall the bankruptcy process and withhold debt relief until a government is deemed to have sufficiently stepped up to the plate. That is basically the international community's current strategy, with regard not only to debt relief but also to aid. For nowadays most donors determine whether a country should get debt relief or new aid on the basis of whether it meets "good governance" requirements—if it doesn't, it has to wait. And we've seen how "good governance" more often than not ends up being defined as a country conforming to a very narrow range of neoliberal macroeconomic policies, rather than being a measure of a country's commitment to human rights, democratic values, or transparency.

But even if good governance was measured that way, there just isn't the time to wait for countries to demonstrate meaningful improvements on these fronts before debt relief is given. As Jose Pedro de Marias Jr. recently said at the World Bank/IMF meetings on behalf of a group of twenty African countries, "Even with the best of commitment from country authorities, strengthening institutional capacity to enforce good governance takes time." Too many millions are dying, too many being lured to join extremist organizations, too many becoming angry and resentful, for us to be able to wait for a country to get a perfect scorecard on governance before providing it with debt relief. By not relieving debts, we allow poverty to deepen, and poverty not only engenders corruption, it makes good governance extremely hard to achieve. It is rising living standards that tend to prompt calls for cleaner government, not stagnant or falling ones.

We need to stop countries from having to repay illegitimate and unpayable debts as soon as possible, and then make sure that the monies thereby saved do go to where they are most needed.

But how to do this? As the saying goes, if the mountain won't go to Mohammed, Mohammed must go to the mountain. We must create legally established "islands" of good governance—let us call them National Regeneration Trusts—into which the flows deemed as a result of the bankruptcy process not to have to be paid back to creditors must be channeled instead. These Trusts would effectively earmark debt savings to meet development goals. And only a minority of trustees should be government appointees. Money would thereby be protected from abuses or from being squandered to make disbursements that complement rather than supplant existing development programs.

Before you decry me as imperialist or neocolonialist, let me quickly qualify my proposal. First, the trustees must be majority nationals, with the only nonnationals appointed from United Nations bodies such as UNICEF or the World Health Organization, trustees whose expertise and experience on the ground will be invaluable. Second, the accounts of the Trust must be easily accessible to the public, so that everyone can know how much money is in it, track how it is being spent, and hold trustees, if necessary, to account. Third, putting monies into the Trust must be the only condition for a country to be eligible to participate in the process. There will be no more structural-adjustment-type conditions. The *only* condition for the debt to be relieved must be that the monies saved actually do serve to meet the needs of the sick, uneducated, and poor (both directly and, for example, through investments in infrastructure) and the environment, and are not siphoned off into foreign bank accounts, or to fund white elephant projects or civil wars. Fourth, in order that a country doesn't end up having to take money out of its budget to make payments into the Trust (which would, of course, defeat the Trust's development goals), the international donor community will have to pledge to continue financing these flows to the extent that it previously was. And this time these pledges would have to be met, not be just more empty promises. At the same time, the rich world must provide incentives to developing-country governments so that they do not slash social expenditure on development by the amount of money that goes into the Trust. Additional aid could perhaps be contingent upon them maintaining levels of social expenditure at prior (inflation-adjusted) levels and a kicker be built in if expenditure in these areas goes up. It could be left to the arbitration panel to determine, if necessary, the extent to which a debtor government has the capacity to pledge to the Trust, and the extent to which the international community must provide the shortfall. Fifth and finally, at such a time that a country is recognized as democratic and reaches a predetermined level of human development, measured in such terms as numbers of children attending school, infant mortality rates, and so forth—the Millennium Development Goals would be an appropriate benchmark to use—the Trust should be wound up, international donors should no longer be asked to finance debt repayment flows, and any remaining debt stock still to be canceled should simply be written off. The eventual aim of the National Regeneration Trusts should be their disappearance.

Countries that at the point of arbitration already meet the human development and democracy conditions, like, for example, Brazil or Argentina, would not be subjected to the Trust mechanism at all, but would simply see their illegitimate and unpayable debts immediately canceled.

Why will these Trusts be more likely to deliver to the poor, vulnerable, and needy than governments in places of low human development and weak governance structures? Three reasons. First, they will be run predominately by civil society—it is from there that the predominance of trustees will be elected—and civil society is significantly less likely to be beholden to domestic elites than ruling politicians. Second, any concern over the motivation or independence of the civil society trustees, or over the government meeting its obligation to transfer funds into the Trust, would be addressed by the fact that debt would be effectively canceled in installments (rather than be canceled all at once) with debt payments transformed into annual cash flows into the Trust rather than paid to creditors. This would mean that if, upon being audited (as the Trust would be on a regular basis), a Trust was found not to be fulfilling its mandate, flows could be frozen until such a time as it was deemed to be capable of functioning in the way intended—either with new trustees on board, or a renewed commitment of the government to the process, if it had been the obstacle. And third, an international arbitral body, separate from the Trust itself, would judge the spending of the money and seek to legally hold both the Trust and the country to account. In this way, funds would be protected in a way that has not been done before.

There are, of course, some countries such as Mugabe's Zimbabwe or Myanmar where the level of confidence in government is so low that the conditions for the Trust are likely to be absent. And others, where finding suitable trustees from civil society will present a formidable challenge. However, in the majority of cases this is not the case. Moreover, a strong financial incentive exists to keep to the terms of the Trust—a failure to do so could lead to the international community dissolving it and requiring the country to resume hard currency repayments (resources transferred into the Trust are, of course, in domestic currency).

This proposal *is* radical, I admit, but it is not completely unprecedented. For while an autonomous trust into which debt relief flows has never yet been established (nor, incidentally, are there any such trusts into which grants can be put), and the mechanisms I propose to govern the National Regeneration Trusts are novel too, we do have examples of trusts or quasi-trusts having been established for not dissimilar development goals. There are also now several conservation trusts operating throughout the developing world—in Bhutan, in Madagascar, in the Philippines, in Belize, and elsewhere—with environmental protection mandates. And a few trusts have been set up to deal with revenues arising from oil exploitation in the developed and developing world alike. Alaska distributes oil earnings to its citizens through a trust fund mechanism; Chad has recently set up a trust vehicle to deal with oil revenues from the Chad-Cameroon Petroleum Development project (although, in that case, the Chadian government used part of its "signing bonus" to buy weapons!). Iraq had a trust fund in the 1950s to which part of its oil revenues were directed and whose disbursements were decided by Iraqi and foreign overseers. And the idea of an Oil Revenue Permanent Trust Fund has recently been mooted as a way of safeguarding revenues for the Iraqi people now that the war is over—an idea that has gathered support from Iraqis across the political and religious spectrum. Lessons can be drawn from each of these existing models to help us refine the National Regeneration Trust concept even more.

Moreover, developing-world government support for the concept looks likely to be forthcoming. Several of the countries that have so far received debt relief under the HIPC initiative have al-

ready transferred significant amounts of their savings into social spending—Mozambique has used some of the monies saved to introduce a free immunization program; user fees for education have been abolished in Uganda, Malawi, Tanzania, and in rural Benin; and projections for increases in health and education spending in several countries that have received debt relief look encouraging. The formalizing of such a process is therefore not a big stretch of the imagination. Uganda even has a Poverty Action Fund, into which the government now puts most of its debt savings.

And the Trust concept is one that has been recognized in most of the developing world for a very long time. Muslim jurists in the seventh, eighth, and ninth centuries developed the concept of a *waqf*, a legal institution that would provide an endowment of a public nature. Latin America has the concept of a *fideicomiso*. Southeast Asia the concept of a *yayasan*. The idea of safeguarding assets is one that is embedded in almost all cultures.

Looking to the Future

But even if this great step is taken and the past resolved, we will still need to plan for the future. To avoid the debt threat reappearing in another few years, and developing countries ending up back in despair, new principles for borrowers and lenders will have to be adopted, on top of the bankruptcy procedure and the National Regeneration Trusts.

Let me suggest just five.

First, instead of borrowing so much, those developing-world governments that can, need to make improved efforts to mobilize domestic resources—through better tax collection in those countries where the tax base can reasonably bear it; through spending more frugally on nonessential matters (over the long run, prudent fiscal management will provide more sustainable social policies); by attracting back monies that have flown out, but also through generating new resources themselves. Remittances from Latin American and Caribbean overseas workers, for example, are currently worth

$38 billion a year. If they are securitized—pooled, turned into a bond, and then sold to investors—as Banco do Brasil has recently done, these can present an excellent new revenue stream. The cost of borrowing externally is, as we have seen, often inordinately high, both in financial terms and in terms of what it means for sovereignty. Developing-world governments need thus to see external borrowing as a last, not a first resort.

Second, all classes of lenders need to be mandated to make transparency of borrowing a condition of the issuing of loans, in the same way that several oil companies are now committing to "publish what they pay." The secrecy of debt—with loans negotiated in back rooms between governments and creditors—must be no more. Developing-world governments also need to be much more open with their public about what they are borrowing and why.

Third, developing countries that borrow in the international capital markets must be allowed to control capital in- and outflows. The experience gained in the late 1990s from the wave of emerging market crises teaches us how turbulent and dangerous capital markets can be for developing countries. And developing-world borrowers must provide incentives for financial investors to keep their monies in for longer terms, perhaps through taxing incoming foreign capital at a rate that declines the longer the capital remains in the host country. Such ex ante measures are to be preferred to ex post controls.

Fourth, there must be a complete overhaul of the West's export credit agencies so as to ensure that rich countries stop lending so carelessly, stop providing loans to developing-world governments to buy arms, and stop financing environmentally unsound and overpriced projects. Rich governments must also stop lending to countries when they obviously will not be able to pay the monies back or when no credible plans for how the monies will be repaid have been presented. Government agencies that do not adhere to these principles need to be held publicly and, where possible, legally to account. And the rich world also needs to consider its own borrowing. The United States' increasing debt burden, for example, has all the ingredients of a future debt crisis in the making.

Fifth and finally, the IMF's and World Bank's role in the story of debt must be completely recast. The immunity of the IMF and World Bank needs to be waived. Where professional negligence or lack of due diligence in lending can be proven, a claimant, whether a village, an individual or a nation, must be able to hold the institutions liable in the same way that a bank can be held liable by law. Also, internal procedures need to be drastically improved so that when officers lend in ways that contravene their own institutions' charters, as they so often do, they are held firmly to account. And, crucially, the IMF and World Bank must cease their dogged insistence on the blanket meeting of structural adjustment–type conditions once and for all.

I have laid out an agenda for how to overcome the debt threat and for how to move on, but of course solving problems of poverty, inequality, disease, and insecurity is not just a matter of canceling debts and lending better in the future.

If we are serious about attempting to safeguard our collective lives and ensuring that we can all sleep safely at night; if we are serious about attempting to ensure our children and grandchildren do have a planet to play in, and that a child, wherever he or she is born, is entitled to the prospect of a decent life, then we will need to do more than just lend better and more wisely, do more than just cancel illegitimate and unpayable debts. To breach the gap between need and resources in those countries that, even with all their debts canceled, would still not have enough money for health or education or to meet the needs of their poor, the rich world will need, given the urgency of the situation, to reach deep into its pockets and give much more—in the form of grants. Not in the way it has in the past: grants were, of course, as susceptible to political hijack as loans. But either through the Trust mechanism, in those cases in which it is deemed necessary to safeguard aid flows, or, otherwise, in a way that is closely aligned to the spirit of the Trust. That aims to get money more directly to those that most need it and to provide a foundation for a country to be able to attract long-term investment and growth. The rich world will also need to curb its desire to protect its own industries if the poor world is to be given a chance to earn its own way out of misery and be able to generate wealth for itself. For, if the developing world is truly to be able to regenerate, it is debt relief, aid, and trade that are the Holy Trinity.

The challenge will be how to ensure that those in the rich world who find their own lives tough—the elderly, the poor, the unemployed, the sick, or even those just struggling to keep their mortgage payments going and send their kids to school—do not bear the financial brunt. So rather than diverting resources for aid or paying for debt relief from government budgets that could instead be spent on social expenditure or domestic welfare needs, or raising funds in the form of new across-the-board income taxes, the money will have to be found elsewhere.

Cuts in military expenditure (for the price of four stealth bombers, 155 million children can be sent to school for a year); windfall taxes on the debt vultures' extraordinary profits; active measures to help expedite the repatriation of corrupt dictators' stolen funds (billions of pillaged dollars are just sitting in offshore accounts), made more possible today than ever before given the post-9/11 trend toward repealing bank secrecy laws and rolling back banker-customer confidentiality; the securitizing of migrant workers' income taxes so as to create a "development bond," and global pollution taxes on energy companies (with monies collected earmarked for environmental purposes) are all measures that would raise billions of dollars and would not fall on everyone's shoulders alike. There are also innovative financing schemes that the British chancellor of the exchequer, Gordon Brown; George Soros; and Joseph Stiglitz have all recently proposed. Gordon Brown's International Financing Facility, for example, which securitizes rich countries' future aid pledges, could raise an extra $50 billion a year at no additional cost to taxpayers.

And, in order that the cessation of subsidies on Western products, so critical for the developing world's success, does not destroy communities and heartlands in the West, measures must be taken to create new jobs and provide new opportunities for those there who in the short term could, as a result, lose out. Free trade must also be fair. Hardly beyond the wit of human ingenuity.

• • •

A better, safer, more just, and more equitable world for all of us *is* possible. By addressing the injustices of the past, confronting the realities of the present, and charting the right course for the future we can get there. It won't come for free, but we can apply principles of justice and equity to determine who should carry the cost. Nor will it be easy. There are various elites who will wish to retain the status quo, whose interests will need to be overridden. And it isn't just going to happen. Our political leaders will first have to be convinced that this is what their constituents want. Opinion has to be massively mobilized.

But indifference and apathy to the developing world's plight are no longer viable options. The dangers of allowing the fissures between the rich and the poor world to continue to widen are increasingly obvious to us all. The proposal I have laid out is a *blueprint* for a new way forward. Discuss it. Refine it. Improve upon it. But don't ignore it. You can't afford to.

Notes

Chapter Two

25 " 'it threatens the independence . . . ' ": Cited in G. García Márquez, *The General in His Labyrinth,* Vintage, 2003.

25 "Atal Behari Vajpayee announced": "No More Aid Please," *Economist,* June 19, 2003.

25 "India was no longer willing": "Delusion of Grandeur," *The Hindu Business Line,* June 30, 2003.

26 "their greatest threat": Ironically, Soviet archives have recently revealed that Stalin, rather than being hell-bent on expansionism, was in fact feeling vulnerable and apprehensive.

26 "The Bay of Pigs fiasco": Although talk of an "Alliance for Progress" had been outlined by Kennedy only a month before.

26 " 'To those people in the huts . . . ' ": Cited in D. Porter, *U.S. Economic Foreign Aid: A Case Study of the United States Agency for International Development,* Garland Publishing, New York, 1990, pp. 12–13.

27 " 'Less than a month ago . . . ' ": See "Public Papers of the Presidents: John F. Kennedy"; Herbert Feis, *Foreign Aid and Foreign Policy,* Delta, 1966.

27 "Latin America's external debt": F. J. Hinkelammert, *La Deuda Externa de América Latina,* Departamento de Investigaciones Económicas, San José, 1988.

27 "Among loans made by the Bank": See, for example, Bartram S. Brown, *The United States and the Politicization of the World Bank: Issues of International Law and Policy,* Kegan Paul International, London, 1992; see also Miles Kahler, "The United States and the International Monetary Fund: Declining Influence or Declining Interest?' in *The United States and Multilateral Institutions: Patterns of Changing Instrumentality and Influence* (eds. Karen A. Mingst and Margaret R. Karns), Unwin Hyman, Boston, 1990.

28 "$1.6 billion": In 1985 yuan.

28 "securing influence in Africa": In its pursuit of that goal, the Soviet Union

provided Africa with $900 million in economic aid, and the Chinese provided $350 million between 1954 and 1967, both mostly in the form of loans.

29   " 'US-AID should be used . . . ' ": "Memorandum from Ulric Haynes of the National Security Council Staff to Robert W. Komer of the National Security Council Staff," May 18, 1965, Johnson Library, National Security File, Haynes Files, CHRONO (Haynes). Secret.

30   "Today the people of the Democratic Republic of Congo": According to the Decision Point document for Democratic Republic of Congo as of 2003.

30   "Gross national income per capita is $90": As of 2002 (latest year available) World Development Indicators, World Bank.

30   "came from Arab states": Controversy remains over whether money from Gulf countries was lent or given. Also, it is hard to come up with an exact figure of monies lent, although we do know that financiers are claiming repayment of between $120–130 billion, including interest.

30   "Iraqgate-BNL": See, for example, "CIA Found Italian Tie to Atlanta Bank's Sales to Iraq," *Washington Post,* November 1, 1992; *Banca Nazionale del Lavoro,* Institute for Science and International Security, Washington, D.C.

31   "Ngo Dinh Diem": *Encyclopedia of the Cold War,* Facts on File, 1994; *A Dictionary of 20th Century World Biography,* Oxford University Press, 1992.

31   " 'Shit, Diem's the only boy . . . ' ": Stanley Karnow, *Vietnam: A History,* Penguin Books, 1997, p. 214.

32   "Grants weren't available": Ferraro Vincent and Melissa Roserer, "Global Debt and Third World Development," in *World Security in Challenges for a New Century* (eds. Michael Klare and Daniel Thomas), St. Martin's Press, New York, 1994.

33   "things changed": See, for example, Harold James, "From Grandmotherliness to Governance: The Evolution of IMF Conditionality," *Finance and Development,* December 1998.

33   "Loans were called in overnight": Demba Moussa Dembele, former high-ranking Senegalese official, verifies this in conversation with the author in London, 2003, as do Anne Boschini and Anders Olofsgard in "Foreign Aid: An Instrument for Fighting Poverty or Communism?" Paper presented at European Economic Association, August 2002.

33   "repayment of outstanding loans": Much confusion arose over what was actually owed: many of their cold war credits had been denominated in "transferable rubles," a currency that never actually existed, and so had no clear exchange rate.

34   "saw its U.S. backing disappear": Cohen in Robert Bottome, *In the*

Shadow of the Debt: Emerging Issues in Latin America, Twentieth Century Fund Press, New York, 1992.

34   " 'The Cold War's demise . . . ' ": To support the thesis that aid was used throughout the cold war as an instrument for the donor country's own military security, see, for example, Anne Boschini and Anders Olofsgard, "Foreign Aid: An Instrument for Fighting Poverty or Communism?" paper presented at European Economic Association, August 2002.

35   " 'relieve potential balance of payments needs . . . ' ": White House Budget Document, March 2003.

35   " 'Bob Rubin . . . ' ": Bill Clinton in conversation with Ernesto Zedillo at Davos, Jan./Feb. 2002.

35   "competing for diplomatic recognition in Africa": For example, Guinea-Bissau and the Central African Republic both switched recognition from Taipei to Beijing in 1997 when Taiwan turned down their respective loan requests of $90 million and $120 million, and Beijing agreed to pay in its stead. P. Liu, "Cross-Strait Scramble for Africa: A Hidden Agenda in China-Africa Cooperation Forum," *Harvard Asia Quarterly,* Spring 2001.

36   "looking to shore up support": This was a period when we saw many unsavory examples of the United States "lobbying" the three African members of the UN Security Council, all of which were heavily dependent on aid and investment from the United States.

37   "The U.S. Treasury did not even consider": Soren Ambrose, "Multilateral Debt," in *50 Years Is Enough,* Alliance for Global Justice, 1999.

37   "The United States decided": See, for example, "U.S. May Cut Aid Over Court Immunity," *Washington Post,* July 1, 2003; "Colombia Accepts a U.S. Deal on Exemptions in Rights Cases," *New York Times,* September 19, 2003.

37   "When Yemen, for example, voted": The vote took place on November 29, 1990.

38   "Finland and the Netherlands spring to mind": Sir John Vereker, the former permanent secretary, Department for International Development, suggests these in an e-mail correspondence with the author, 2004. But bear in mind that even these countries have still often provided loans to serve the interests of their domestic corporations through their export credit agencies, as the following chapter will reveal.

38   "The altruism is missing": Even the acclaimed Marshall Plan, the early U.S. foreign aid program, which pumped some $13 billion–plus into the European economy between 1948 and 1951 (mainly in the form of outright grants), as recent scholarship based on U.S. archival documents reveals, was essentially a defensive measure to combat the supposedly aggressive Soviet designs in Europe—especially France and Italy. So, although pub-

licly U.S. secretary of state George Marshall claimed that his plan was not directed "against any country or doctrine, but against hunger, poverty, desperation and chaos," privately he knew better. In February 1947, in a White House meeting with select congressmen, Marshall persuasively argued in favor of extending aid to Europe in order to address the growing communist influence in Greece, Turkey, and elsewhere. Draft Notes explaining why the United States should grant financial aid to Greece and Turkey, February 27, 1947, Truman Library Archive Online; M. Leffer, *Preponderance of Power: National Security, The Truman Administration and the Cold War,* Stanford University Press, Stanford CA, 1992; M. Hogan, *The Marshall Plan: America, Britain and the Reconstruction of Western Europe 1947–52,* Cambridge University Press, Cambridge, 1987.

Chapter Three

42   "The British government even continued": "How $1 Billion Was Lost When Thatcher Propped Up Saddam," *Guardian,* February 28, 2003.

42   " 'The State Department has exerted . . . ' ": H. C. Clark, interoffice memo to J. A. Condoux, "Subject: I/J Pipeline Development," February 29, 1984.

43   "Around 95 percent of the debt": Nicholas Hildyard and Susan Hawley, "The Environmental Audit Committee Inquiry Export Credits Guarantee Department and Sustainable Development Memorandum," May 19, 2003, www.thecornerhouse,org.uk.

43   "While 65 percent": OECD Annual Estimates of Total External Debt.

43   "Much like a department store": Aaron Goldzimer provides this analogy in Aaron Goldzimer, "Worse Than the World Bank? Export Credit Agencies—the Secret Engine of Globalization," *Backgrounder,* Winter 2003, vol. 9, no. 1.

43   "the $26 billion–plus": This figure includes interest owed. Based on Paris Club figures, as of July 2003, the total owed to these countries was $12.8 billion excluding interest. The Paris Club says that the interest is roughly equal to the principal, so $26 billion is roughly correct.

43   "international military manufacturers": Although it is impossible to state categorically how much of the Western export credit debt went directly for weapons, it is generally believed to be very high. The former Polish finance minister, Marek Belka, for example, suggested at the IMF summit in Dubai in September 2003 that the military component might be as high as 90 percent of the debt. What is certain is that Saddam's military spending had to have been supported by loans, as military expenditure was far greater than the revenues ($120 billion military spending between 1981

and 1985 versus $48.4 billion in oil earnings); hence every cent of credit for any goods would have freed up money for Saddam to use on the military.

43   "told to repay this debt": At the time of writing, it looks likely that Paris Club countries will announce a considerable write-off of Iraqi debt, but no admission of the illegitimacy of the debt has been acknowledged. It is also unknown whether non–Paris Club members will similarly write off any of their debts owed, and the host of conditions attached to the write-off as later chapters will show are likely to harm the Iraqi economy more than bolster it.

43   "some facts": See, for example, Bruce Rich, "Exporting Destruction," *Environmental Forum,* September 1, 2000.

44   "export credit debts": Horst Kohler, "Reforming the International Financial System," *The Berne Union 2001 Yearbook,* February 2001.

45   "Gabon, Nigeria, and Algeria": Eurodad.

45   " 'You see, before . . . ' ": Quoted in Killing Secrets, *ECGD: The Export Credit Guarantee Department,* Killing Secrets, 1998, kill secrets @msn.com.

45   "especially beautiful": Conversation with former HSBC employee involved in export credit arrangements, June 2003.

46   " 'The Export Import Bank . . . ' ": Wayne Leslie, "A Guardian of Jobs or a Reverse Robin Hood," *New York Times,* September 1, 2002.

46   "ECAs provide exporters with incentives": Aaron Goldzimer, "Worse Than the World Bank? Export Credit Agencies—The Secret Engine of Globalization," *Backgrounder,* Winter 2003, vol. 9, no. 1.

46   "many ECAs have suffered huge losses": E-mail correspondence with Sir John Vereker, former permanent secretary, Department for International Development.

47   "cut more than three hundred thousand jobs": According to the Department of Labor, *BusinessWeek Online,* August 12, 2002, and *Seattle Times,* June 12, 2003; see also Michael Borrus, "Exploiters of Regionalization: The Asian Production Networks of U.S. Electronics Firm," in *International Production Networks in Asia: Rivalry or Riches?* (eds. Michael Borrus, Dieter Ernst, and Stephen Haggard), Brunner-Routledge, 2000.

47   "more than 60 percent": Calculated from Export-Import Bank of the United States Fiscal Year 2001, "Loans and Long Term Guarantees," Annual Report 2001, pp. 24–30.

47   "A former employee of HSBC": Conversation with former employee of HSBC, June 2003.

48   "convicted in a Lesotho court": "Firm Guilty of Lesotho Bribery," *Guardian,* June 19, 2003.

48   " 'smacked of mark up practices . . . ' ": "Foreign Funded Power Projects Marked Up," PLN, *Jakarta Post,* October 17, 2000.

48   "This reflects similar findings": Dieter Frisch, "Export Credit Insurance and the Fight Against International Corruption," *Transparency International Working Paper,* February 26, 1999.

48   " 'close to complicity . . . ' ": From Dieter Frisch, "Export Credit Insurance and the Fight Against International Corruption," *Transparency International Working Paper,* February 26, 1999, www.transparency.org/working_papers/frisch/dfrisch.html.

49   "Empirical study after empirical study": See, for example, Paulo Mauro, "Corruption and Growth," *The Quarterly Journal of Economics,* vol. 110, no. 3, August 1995, pp. 681–712; or Andrei Shleifer and Robert Vishny, "Corruption," *The Quarterly Journal of Economics,* vol. 109, 1993, pp. 599–617, for links between corruption and declining levels of investment.

49   "requires companies to state": See also OECD Guidelines for ECAs, www.oecd.org/ech/act/xcred-en.htm; Michael H. Wiehen, "OECD Working Paper on Export Credits and Export Guarantees," *Transparency International Working Paper,* 2000.

49   "insufficient and unenforceable": See Susan Hawley, "The Questions Taxpayers Must Ask," *Observer,* February 2, 2003.

49   " 'None of the ECAs . . . ' ": Presentation to the ECGD by Michael Wiehen, Member of the Board, Transparency International, April 23, 2003.

50   "the Bataan Nuclear Power Plant": Ex-Im made the construction of Bataan possible with its authorization of a direct project loan of $227.2 million and guarantees of an additional $367.2 million. The bank also guaranteed the sale of bonds by a foreign public corporation to American investors to secure additional funding of the plant so as to meet the shortfall that commercial banks were unwilling to shoulder. See Aaron Goldzimer, "Worse Than the World Bank? Export Credit Agencies—The Secret Engine of Globalization," *Backgrounder,* vol. 9, no. 1, Winter 2003.

50   "costing the Philippines $170,000 a day": See, for example, Maristela de la Cruz-Cardenas, "ECAs and Debt: A Look into the Philippine Power Industry and the Debt Crisis," Freedom from Debt Coalition, pp. 2–3.

51   "nuclear power plants": Bruce Rich raises the point in "Exporting Destruction," in *Environmental Forum,* September 1, 2000, that the French, Canadian, German, and U.S. ECAs are effectively keeping their countries' nuclear power construction industries on life support by enabling them to export plants to the developing world at a time that an appetite for building them at home has been slight.

51   "The Three Gorges Dam project": See, for example, Elaine Kurtenback, "Water Begins to Back Up Behind China Dam," AP, June 7, 2003; Aaron Goldzimer, "Worse Than the World Bank? Export Credit Agencies—The Secret Engine of Globalization," *Backgrounder*, vol. 9, no. 1, Winter 2003; Probe International, "Three Gorges Dam Project," www.probe international.org.

51   "oil, gas, and coal projects": Note that from a climate point of view gas is clearly preferable.

52   "currently being taken to court": "Two Western Cities Join Suit to Fight Global Warming," *New York Times*, December 24, 2002.

52   "intervention by British chancellor of the exchequer": "U.K. Extends Arms Sales Ban to 63 Countries," Reuters, January 11, 1999; Larry Elliot, "Brown Attempts to Stop Aid and Debt Relief Being Used for Military Spending," *Guardian*, January 12, 2000.

52   "a third of France's export credits": Bruce Rich, "Exporting Destruction," *Environmental Forum*, September 1, 2000.

52   "loans to the Indonesian authorities": "Submission by the Campaign Against the Arms Trade," in response to the Export Credits Guarantees Department review of its mission, www.caat.org.uk/information/publications/government/ecgd-submission-1099.php.

52   "Aceh province": "Indonesia Uses UK Hawks in Aceh Offensive," *Guardian*, May 20, 2003.

53   "When students protested": Bruce Rich, "Exporting Destruction," *Environmental Forum*, September 1, 2000.

54   "the Protocol does not require emissions limits": Aaron Goldzimer, "Worse Than the World Bank? Export Credit Agencies—The Secret Engine of Globalization," *Backgrounder*, vol. 9, no. 1, Winter 2003.

54   "subsidize its exporters": There is a WTO carve-out for OECD export credits—a special exemption for rich-country export credits written right into the WTO agreement.

Chapter Four

58   "Eurodollar syndicated loans": Luis De Sebastian, *La Deuda Externa de América Latina y la Banca Internacional*, UCA Ediciones, San Salvador, 1987.

58   "Commercial lending to Africa": IMF World Economic Outlook, 1980.

58   "35 percent of regional debt": Nicolas Van de Walle, *African Economies and the Politics of Permanent Crisis, 1979–1999*, Cambridge University Press, 2001.

60 " 'The banks were hot to get in . . . ' ": J. Roddick, *The Dance of the Millions: Latin America and the Debt Crisis,* Latin American Bureau, London, 1988, p. 29.

60 "a beacon for poorer countries": W. A. Darity, *The Loan Pushers: The Role of Commercial Banks in the International Debt Crisis,* Ballinger, Cambridge, 1988.

60 "huge relief to be offered these loans": Stabilizing oil prices would have been a better option, but that was a nonstarter. Recycling by OPEC would have been second best—this had been promised but not implemented, oil revenues were used to fund the weapons trade instead. Third best would have been higher levels of aid. OECD countries didn't deliver, partly because they themselves were confronted with a higher import bill. So borrowing from commercial banks was in many cases fourth best, but the only alternative.

61 " 'I remember how the bankers . . . ' ": Conversation in Davos, 2003, with former Colombian finance minister; see also Susan George, *A Fate Worse Than Debt,* Penguin, London, 1988.

62 "the external debt of Argentina": See S. Griffith Jones and O. Sunkel, *Debt and Development in Latin America,* Oxford University Press, 1986; J. Schatan, *El Saqueo de América Latina,* Lom Ediciones, Santiago, 1998, p. 51.

62 "Similar scenarios played themselves out": See, for example, Nancy Birdsall and John Williamson, *Delivering on Debt Relief: From IMF Gold to a New Aid Architecture,* Institute for International Economics, Washington DC, 2002.

63 "In Togo": Susan George, *A Fate Worse Than Debt,* Penguin, London, 1988.

63 "the vast majority of which was commercial": J. Roddick in *The Dance of the Millions: Latin America and the Debt Crisis,* Latin American Bureau, London, 1988, notes that in 1978 when the total debt of Latin America was $21.8 billion, public money accounted for only 7.3 percent of it, while private money, mainly private banks, was responsible for the remaining 92.7 percent.

63 "A loan is said to have been granted": Luis De Sebastian, *La Deuda Externa de América Latina y la Banca Internacional,* UCA Ediciones, San Salvador, 1987, quoting R. W. Lombardi, *Debt Trap,* Praeger Publishers, New York, 1985.

63 " 'I am far from alone . . . ' ": J. Roddick, *The Dance of the Millions: Latin America and the Debt Crisis,* Latin American Bureau, London, 1988, quoting S. C. Gwynne, "Adventures in the Loan Trade," *Harper's,* vol. 267, no. 1600.

64   "Salomon Brothers' report": "U.S. Multinational Banking: Current and Perspective Strategies," Salomon Brothers, 1976.

64   "had *quintupled* their earnings": R. W. Lombardi, *Debt Trap,* Praeger Publishers, New York, 1985.

64   " 'It was the greatest transfer of wealth . . . ' ": Interview between Anthony Sampson and Walter Wriston, June 13, 1980, *Money Lenders,* Viking, 1983.

64   " 'We reject the view . . . ' ": International Banking Operations, Hearings before the Subcommittee on Financial Institutions of the House Committee on Banking, Finance and Urban Affairs, 1977.

65   " 'Banks who lend too much . . . ' ": This quotation is ascribed to a New York banker by Al Wojniloewr, chief economist for First Boston, on the basis of conversations between the two of them, in Mark Hulbert, "The Causes and Risks of Excessive Foreign Lending," *Policy Analysis,* no. 23, April 20, 1983.

65   "had gone through several cycles": Usually in tandem with boom and bust periods in the West. See, for example, C. Marichal, *A Century of Debt Crises in Latin America: From Independence to the Great Depression, 1820–1930,* Princeton University Press, Princeton, NJ, 1989.

66   "Itaipu Dam project": S. Branford, and B. Kucinski, *The Debt Squads: The U.S., the Banks and Latin America,* Zed Books, London, 1988.

67   "Capital flew out of the region": Alexander Theberge, "The Latin American Debt Crisis of the 1980s and Its Historical Precursors," Columbia University working paper, April 8, 1999.

67   "Lopez Portillo": See, for example, J. M. Mora, *Esto nos dio Lopez Portillo,* Anaya, Mexico City, 1982.

67   "Herzog had been turned down": J. Augustin, *Tragicomedia Mexicana 2: La Vida en Mexico de 1970 a 1982,* Planeta, Mexico City, 1992.

67   "whatever assets creditors might have attempted to seize": Although there are cases where creditors have attempted to seize the assets of a defaulting country (see, for example, William Cline in *International Debt: Systematic Risk and Policy Perspective,* 1984), and in July 2000, a Russian tall ship, the *Sedov,* was impounded by order of a French court in Brest harbor for fifty hours with 15 schoolchildren and 100 students on board, as well as a crew of 61 from Murmansk, at the request of the Swiss firm Noga, which was seeking $60 million apparently owed to it from oil for food business deals with Moscow dating back to 1991, the hope of Western courts upholding such actions is slim (in the Noga case a judgment from a French court ended the seizure). See, for example, Anatole Kaletsky in *Costs of Default,* Priority Press Publications, 1985. Kaletsky also raises the point that seizures would rarely be enough to meet the size of the sum owed.

68   "The *Economist* expressed its fears": Cited in J. M. Mora, *Esto nos dio Lopez Portillo,* Anaya, Mexico City, 1982, p. 127.

68   "an emergency loan": Paul Cammack, David Pool, and William Tordoff, *Third World Politics,* Macmillan, 1988.

69   "allowed to act in concert": Correspondence with Ajit Singh, November 2003. Also J. Augustin, *Tragicomedia Mexicana 2: La Vida en Mexico de 1970 a 1982,* Planeta, Mexico City, 1992.

69   "Strong-arm tactics were employed": B. J. Cohen, "U.S. Debt Policy in Latin America: The Melody Lingers On," in R. Bottome, et al., *In the Shadow of the Debt: Emerging Issues in Latin America,* The Twentieth Century Fund Press, New York, 1992, pp. 153–73, 162.

69   "fast became counterproductive": See B. J. Cohen, "U.S. Debt Policy in Latin America: The Melody Lingers On," in R. Bottome, et al., *In the Shadow of the Debt: Emerging Issues in Latin America,* The Twentieth Century Fund Press, New York, 1992, pp. 153–72. Anne Krueger refers to: "The low growth–high service debt trap" in A. O. Krueger, "Debt, Capital Flows and LDC Growth," in *American Economic Review,* vol. 77, no. 2, 1987.

69   " 'This debt is not only unpayable . . . ' ": P. O'Brien, "The Debt Cannot Be Paid: Castro and the Latin American Debt," *Bulletin of Latin American Research,* vol. 5, no. 1, 1986; Fidel Castro, "This Debt Is Not Only Unpayable but Also Uncollectible," address in the 4th Congress of the Latin American Federation of Journalists, July 7, 1985.

69   "But most of the governments": Paul Volcker and Toyoo Gyohten, *Changing Fortunes,* Times Books, 1992; Paul Cammack, David Pool, and William Tordoff, *Third World Politics,* Macmillan, 1988.

70   "obligations from Latin America": Luis De Sebastian, *La Deuda Externa de América Latina y la Banca Internacional,* UCA Ediciones, San Salvador, 1987.

70   "Nearly two-thirds of this": H. Lever and C. Huhne, *Debt and Danger: The World Financial Crisis,* Penguin, 1985, pp. 26–27.

71   "Latin America had been hemorrhaging": "Since 1982, the Mexican labour force has grown by more than 4 million people, but from 1981–4 not a single job was created," according to the 1986 World Bank Report on Poverty in Latin America. "Unemployment doubled in Chile during the crisis, and tripled in Bolivia. . . . Cuts in health spending, 1980–4: Argentina—13.9%, Chile—23.8%, Bolivia—77.7%," in J. Roddick, *The Dance of the Millions: Latin America and the Debt Crisis,* Latin American Bureau, London, pp. 85, 89, and 98.

71   "the ruling elites anticipated": See Robert R. Kaufman, *The Politics of the Debt in Argentina, Brazil and Mexico,* University of California, Berkeley, 1988.

72   "developing countries accepted the path": For some, the path laid out by the Bretton Woods institutions was entirely welcomed. President de La Madrid, the Mexican president at that time, was a strong advocate of the neoliberal agenda these institutions preached. See, for example, Robert R. Kaufman, *The Politics of the Debt in Argentina, Brazil and Mexico,* University of California, Berkeley, 1988.

72   "underwritten by the U.S. Treasury": M. Chamberlain, "The Brady Plan: The First Ten Years and Beyond," *Latin Finance,* 2000, pp. 60–63.

72   "made it even easier": There had been a market in existence for banks that had wanted to sell existing loans before all this, but it was very illiquid and very small.

72   "more than $170 billion worth of Brady Bonds": See, for example, William Miles, "Securitization, Liquidity and the Brady Plan," *The North American Journal of Finance and Economics,* 1999.

72   "developing countries soon issued other bonds": Trading volume grew from $1.5 billion per annum in 1985 to $200 billion in 1995.

Chapter Five

75   "To give an illustrative example": "King of the Castle," *New York Post,* July 15, 2003.

75   "high-risk bonds": The benchmark against which all risk is gauged is the "risk free" rate, the U.S. Treasury Bond rate—considered zero risk because the probability of a U.S. government default is considered zero, although this assumption is questionable.

76   "junk bonds": While junk bonds had been around for decades, it was not until Milken recognized the market's potential that they became popular.

76   "high-net-worth individuals": Junk bonds were particularly appealing to high-net-worth individuals who paid capital gains tax on bond appreciation rather than income tax as was the case with stocks, and who were able to offset capital losses against other income as well as carry it forward.

77   "bonds account for 60 percent": *Global Development Finance 2003,* World Bank.

77   "essentially a technical skill": E-mail exchange with Caitlin Zaloom, NYU, July 11, 2003.

77   "all the same thing": This is not the case, though, with those who trade the most risky "sub-investment"–grade bonds; these traders, if they are to be successful, do need to come to grips with the essence of the country, and do have to understand what it is they are trading as risk of default is much more real.

77   "easily outperformed most equity markets": The JP Morgan EMBI Composite Index showed an annual return of 5.9 percent over the past five years—Argentina, however, was dropped from it after its January 2002 default.

77   "the debt is repeatedly traded": Trading of the largest emerging-market countries' debt totals in the billions of dollars daily.

77   "a game of musical chairs": It is this constantly changing supply and demand for a bond that makes its value constantly change too.

78   "nearly $1 billion in fees": Paul Blustein, *Washington Post*, August 3, 2003.

78   "ahead of other banks in the race": Also, many banks, burnt in the early 1980s, would rather themselves lend through the bond market than provide loans. By so doing, they don't have to deal with regulatory reserve requirements and monitoring costs and can diversify their risk in a way that they could not through syndicated loans when they carried significant proportions of the loan risk on their balance sheets, meaning that they stood to lose large sums of money in the event of any emerging-market loan default.

78   "much more freedom": This is not to say that there is no regard for how the monies will be spent. In recent years there have been growing numbers of investors demanding to know how the money will be used.

79   "refusing to coordinate their behavior": Professor Ajit Singh, in e-mail correspondence, November 5, 2003, suggests that it was essentially a prisoner's dilemma–type situation in which "if all leading banks had cooperated, there may not have been a crisis at all. The reason they did not cooperate was that each one, considering the situation in only its own terms, wanted to get out and not be left holding the debts."

79   "hard currency": Usually, but not always, CSFB and Deutsche Bank were the biggest buyers of Russian ruble–denominated debt (GKOs) in the 1990s.

79   "currency risk": The derivatives market does offer an opportunity to get around the currency exposure risk in theory, but there are no liquid derivative markets for most developing-country currencies, especially those of the smaller and poorer countries. Also, given the higher volatility of developing-country currencies, even for those countries where there is a relatively liquid market, the derivatives that could be used for hedging are very expensive.

79   "East Asian crisis": *Global Development Finance 2003*, World Bank.

79   " 'I used to think . . . ' ": Cited in Dani Rodrik, "Why Financial Markets Misbehave," in *Real World Economic Outlook* (ed. Ann Pettifor), Palgrave Macmillan, 2003.

81   "because it had become essential to American policy": Another factor

that played a part was the substantial capital repatriations by expat Pakistanis afraid of having their bank deposits frozen.

81   "commitment to repaying its debts is credible": Michael Tomz, "Voter Sophistication and Domestic Preferences Regarding Debt Default," *Stanford Working Paper,* March 2004.

81   "not necessarily connected with the *ability* to repay": Jeremy Bulow and Kenneth Rogoff, "A Constant Recontracting Model of Sovereign Debt," *Journal of Political Economy,* vol. 97, no. 1, pp. 155–78, University of Chicago, 1989. Also whether residents are confident enough to keep their money in local banks is often an important signal for international investors.

82   "Putin's authoritarian rule": Although, around the time of Kholokovsky's incarceration, we did see a dip as the market began to question whether its and Putin's interests were in fact aligned, www.bradynet.com/bbs/em/100354-0.html.

82   "armed conflict or political illegitimacy are not factors deemed important": Thomas L. Brewer and Pietra Rivoli, "Politics and Perceived Country Credit Worthiness in International Banking," *Journal of Money, Credit and Banking,* 1990.

82   "frequent changes in government *are* a highly significant predictor": J. T. Citron and G. Nickelsburg, "Country Risk and Political Instability," *Journal of Developmental Economics,* 1987, vol. 25, pp. 385–92. There can, however, be a sour reaction if the dictator is perceived to have overstayed his welcome, as was the case at the end of both terms of Peru's President Fujimori.

82   "as important as any economic variable": Thomas L. Brewer and Pietra Rivoli, "Politics and Perceived Country Credit Worthiness in International Banking," *Journal of Money, Credit and Banking,* 1990.

82   "one of the world's top ten economies": 2003 GDP (Gross Domestic Product) Rankings put Brazil as the tenth largest economy in the world with an economy of $1.34 trillion behind the United States, China, Japan, India, Germany, France, the United Kingdom, Italy, and Russia.

82   "potentially 'unfriendly' policies": *Euromoney,* September 2002.

83   "the $54 billion Brazil was paying out": Brazil paid $54 billion in debt service in 2001, of which $37 billion was principal repayment and, more important, $17 billion was interest. *Global Development Finance 2003,* World Bank.

83   "When it rose to 24 percent": Dani–Rodrik, "Why Financial Markets Misbehave," in *Real World Economic Outlook* (ed. Ann Pettifor), Palgrave Macmillan, 2003.

84   "were both heavily fined": (www.forbes.com/home/2002/10/24/cx_aw_1024fine.html.)

84   "lending frenzy to Argentina": More than $40 billion lent between 1990 and 2000, *Global Development Finance 2003,* World Bank.

84   " 'It's a lot of self-censorship' ": Paul Blustein, *Washington Post,* August 2003.

85   "Carlos Menem's reforms": Jane Marcus-Delgado, "Corruption, Governability and Trust: The Case of Argentina," American Political Science Association Meetings, Boston, August 29, 2002.

85   "polls from 2001 on": Michael Tomz, 'Voter Sophistication and Domestic Preferences Regarding Debt Default," *Stanford Working Paper,* March 2004.

85   "analysts' reports": Paul Blustein, *Washington Post,* August 2003.

85   " 'If you get the money . . . ' ": Cited in Paul Blustein, *Washington Post,* March 8, 2003.

87   "Brazil's credit rating": "Will Brazil Default?" *Latin News—*Economy and Business, July 29, 2002.

87   "often misread the political dimensions of risk": It's not that they don't have local offices in the country—they do; it is that they often seem unable to glean the full impact of what is happening on the ground.

87   " 'Tequila' crisis": 1994–95.

87   "downgrades really matter": Graciela Kaminsky and Sergio Schmukler, "Emerging Markets Instability: Do Sovereign Ratings Affect Country Risk and Stock Returns?," paper provided by the World Bank in its series "Working Papers—Domestic Finance. Saving, Financial Systems, Stock Markets," no. 2678, September 2001, (http://ideas.repec.org/p/wop/wobadc/2678.html.)

87   "when a country's debt is downgraded": Helmut Reisen and Julia von Maltzan, "Boom and Bust and Sovereign Ratings," *International Finance,* vol. 2, no. 2, 1999, pp. 273–93.

87   "Once investors smell blood": G. Ferri, L. Liu, and J. Stiglitz, "The Procyclical Role of Rating Agencies: Evidence from the East Asian Crisis," *Economic Notes,* vol. 28, 1999, pp. 335–55; "Characteristics and Appraisal of Major Rating Agencies," Japan Center for International Finance, January 2000.

87   "debt downgraded": G. Ferri, L. Liu, and J. Stiglitz, "The Procyclical Role of Rating Agencies: Evidence from the East Asian Crisis," *Economic Notes,* vol. 28, 1999, pp. 335–55, argue that the rating agencies themselves perpetuate a downward spiral.

87   "capital controls": The IMF has a new view about capital controls, as of autumn 2003, which is that if they do not produce economic distortions and a country has the administrative capacity to manage them, there is nothing to complain about. Also, countries should not relax capital con-

trols if they don't have the capacity to ensure that institutions do not abuse their new privileges.

88   "Debt vultures": The collective action clauses that many are calling for would serve to keep vulture predators away from sovereign bonds as they will "bind in" all creditors to participate in the rescheduling terms agreed upon by a critical mass of bondholders—e-mail correspondence with Richard Segal, November 6, 2003.

88   "Kenneth Dart": At the time of writing, Dart was granted judgment in his favor, although it is not yet clear whether he will collect.

89   "Scum": Interestingly, this same trader's bank is increasingly involved, as are many other investment banks, in essentially doing the same thing with emerging-market corporate debt, especially in Asia. This business, known as "nonperforming loans business," works like this: the banks buy up the loans at a fraction of the cost and then, to quote a senior banker at the same bank, "break people's kneecaps to get the money back."

90   "is on the whole just that": There are a few examples of small countries, such as Bulgaria, that bond markets have rewarded for good fiscal performance.

90   "corrupted by special interests": See Dani Rodrik, "Why Financial Markets Misbehave," in *Real World Economic Outlook* (ed. Ann Pettifor), Palgrave Macmillan, 2003.

Chapter Six

91   " 'Even the wolves have a hard time of it' ": Maxim Gorky, "Chums," translation taken from www.biblomania.com.

91   "my twenty-third year": By then, Gorky had already been renamed Nizhniy Novgorod.

93   "suicide rates": Suicide rates rose from 26.4 per 100,000 in 1990 to 42.1 per 100,000 in 1994, www.cdi.org/russia/johnson/7257-3.cfm.

93   "the losers": See, for example, "Russian Factories, Prey of Bankers, Rust Away," *New York Times*, August 10, 1998.

93   "Davison Budhoo": Davison Budhoo, *Enough Is Enough. Open Letter of Resignation from the Staff of the IMF*, New Horizons Press, New York, 1990.

93   "Ravi Kanbur": *Guardian*, September 13, 2000.

94   " 'Your ideas are at best . . . ' ": This quotation can be found in "An Open Letter to Joseph Stiglitz" by Kenneth Rogoff, July 2002. A footnote to that letter explains that it was "used as opening remarks at a June 28 dis-

cussion of Mr. Stiglitz's book at the World Bank, organized by the World Bank's Infoshop," www.imf.org/external/np/vc/2002/070202.htm. The remarks were first delivered at a discussion of Stiglitz's book at the World Bank on June 28, 2002. See previous note.

96   "American preferences would triumph": Miles Kahler, "The United States and the International Monetary Fund: Declining Influence or Declining Interest?" in *The United States and Multilateral Institutions: Patterns of Changing Instrumentality and Influence* (eds. Karen A. Mingst and Margaret R. Karns), Unwin Hyman, Boston, 1990.

96   "$13.3 billion injection of aid": The Marshall Foundation quotes total expenditure from 1948 to 1952 as $13,325.8 million ($13.3 billion), www .marshallfoundation.org/about_gcm/marshall_plan.htm expenditures.

97   "World Bank irrigation projects": Joseph Stiglitz, *Globalization and Its Discontents,* W. W. Norton & Company, 2003.

97   " 'The bottom 20 percent . . . ' ": Cited in Catherine Caufield, *Masters of Illusion: The World Bank and the Poverty of Nations,* Henry Holt & Co., 1997.

97   " 'The Bank money machine . . . ' ": Cited in Robert Wade, "Greening the Bank: The Struggle Over the Environment, 1970–1995," in *World Bank: Its First Half Century: vol. 2, Perspectives* (eds. Devesh Kapur, John Lewis, and Richard Webb), Brookings Institution, Washington DC, 1997, ch. 13.

98   "ill-advised": Findings of the Bank's own review of its lending portfolio—the 1992 Wapenhans report cited in Paul Mosley, Jane Harrigan, and John Toye, *Aid and Power: The World Bank and Policy Based Lending,* vol. 1, 1991.

98   " 'driven by an ever growing list . . . ' ": Findings of Meltzer Commission, Reuters.

98   "Even when loans were evaluated": Analysts from the Bank's Operations Evaluation Department carrying out an evaluation of the Bank's environmental assessments since 1989 found that only 17 percent of projects had been modified to some degree because of findings, with more than three-quarters of staff interviewed saying that by the time the assessments were ready it was too late to use them.

98   "environmental safeguards": Robert Wade, "Greening the Bank: The Struggle Over the Environment, 1970–1995," in *World Bank: Its First Half Century: vol. 2, Perspectives* (eds. Devesh Kapur, John Lewis, and Richard Webb), Brookings Institution, Washington DC, 1997, ch. 13.

98   "an internal evaluation": Report written by the Bank's Operations Evaluation Department on the Bank's Forest Policy, January 2000.

98   "Apartheid South Africa": Catherine Caufield, *Masters of Illusion: The World Bank and the Poverty of Nations,* Henry Holt & Co., 1997.

98 "Corrupt leaders": Jeffrey Winters, "Criminal Debt," in *Reinventing the World Bank* (eds. Jonathan R. Pincus and Jeffrey A. Winters), Cornell University Press, September 2002, in which he cites various leaked World Bank documents that support this claim.

99 "so commonplace was this daylight robbery": See, for example, CNN, May 1999 ("Odious Debt" report by Patricia Adams); Charles W. Corey, "Past Corruption Is Nigeria's 'Biggest Single Problem' (But Expert Calls for Worldwide Reforms)," *Washington File*, May 2000.

99 "Corruption and tyranny simply didn't factor": The Bank commissioned no internal studies on corruption between 1983 and the late 1990s. See, for example, Heather Marquette, "Corruption, Democracy, and the World Bank," *Crime, Law, and Social Change*, vol. 36, no. 4, 2001, pp. 395–407; Stephen Riley, "The Political Economy of Anti-Corruption Strategies in Africa," *The European Journal of Development Research*, vol. 10, no. 1, 1998, pp. 129–59; "Western Policies and African Realities: The New Anti-Corruption Agenda," in *Corruption and Development in Africa* (eds. K. R. Hope Sr. and B. C. Chikulo), Macmillan, Basingstoke, 2000.

99 "the United Kingdom . . . was the IMF's largest receiver": See, for example, H. James, *International Monetary Co-operation Since Bretton Woods*, Washington DC, 1996, pp. 183–91; Alex Cairncross and Barry Eichengreen, *Sterling in Decline*, Macmillan, Basingstoke, 2003, pp. 170–72.

100 "proved to be misguided": Joseph Stiglitz, *Globalization and Its Discontents*, W. W. Norton & Company, 2003.

101 "Countries . . . were leaned upon": See, for example, *IMF World Economic Outlook 1980*.

101 "Poor countries were encouraged to switch": See, for example, Wayne Ellwood, "You Can't Eat Coffee," *New Internationalist*, September 1984.

102 "Some countries were aghast": Thailand, for example, had over one hundred conditions attached to its second structural adjustment loan. Paul Mosley, Jane Harrigan, and John Toye, *Aid and Power: The World Bank and Policy-Based Lending—Volume 1*, 1991, p. 43.

103 "the Washington Consensus": See, for example, Ngaire Woods, "The Challenge of Good Governance for the IMF and the World Bank Themselves," *World Development*, vol. 28, no. 5, pp. 823–41; "The Challenges of Multilateralism and Governance," in *The World Bank: Structures and Policies* (eds. Christopher L. Gilbert and David Vines), Cambridge University Press, 2000.

103 " 'There was within the World Bank . . . ' ": Joseph Stiglitz, *Globalization and Its Discontents*, W. W. Norton & Company, 2003.

103   " 'They used to come from Washington . . . ' ": Interview with author, October 2003.

103   "the stated goals": See, for example, Michel Camdessus, "Our Primary Objective Is Growth" (1990), in James Raymond Vreeland, *The IMF and Economic Development,* Cambridge University Press, 2003; and Horst Kohler, "The IMF Should Strive to Promote Non-Inflationary Economic Growth" (2000), also cited in Vreeland.

103   "growth declined and poverty and unemployment increased": See, for example, Saskia Sassen, "The Feminization of Survival: Alternative Global Circuits," paper presented at the conference on "Gender Budgets, Financial Markets, Financing for Development," February 19–20, 2002, by the Heinrich-Boell Foundation in Berlin.

103   "IMF programs . . . reduce growth and exacerbate inequalities": See James Raymond Vreeland, *The IMF and Economic Development,* Cambridge University Press, 2003, pp. 125, 135; Joseph Stiglitz, *Globalization and Its Discontents,* W. W. Norton & Company, 2003.

103   " 'single most consistent effect . . . ' ": Manuel Pastor (1987), cited in James Raymond Vreeland, *The IMF and Economic Development,* Cambridge University Press, 2003, p. 137.

103   "growth fell by 50 percent": See, for example, S. George, *A Fate Worse Than Debt,* Penguin, 1988; J. Schatan, *El Saqueo de América Latina,* Lom Ediciones, Santiago, 1998.

104   "fell by 2 percent a year": UN data.

104   "countries that did attain high rates of growth": Ariel Buira's introduction to *Challenges to the World Bank and IMF: Developing Country Perspectives* (ed. Ariel Buira), Anthem Press, 2003.

104   "the rich became richer": See, for example, Thomas Pogge and Sanjay Reddy, "Unknown: The Extent, Distribution and Trend of Global Income Poverty," Summary Paper, Institute of Social Analysis, Columbia University, July 26, 2003.

104   "political will": See Graham Bird, *IMF Lending to Developing Countries: Issues and Evidence,* Routledge, 1995, and also Norman Humphreys, *Historical Dictionary of the International Monetary Fund,* 2d ed., Scarecrow Press, 1999.

105   "barriers to trade": "The developing world faces trade barriers costing them $200 billion per annum—twice as much as they receive in aid," www.yellowtimes.org/article.php?sid=791.

105   "developed countries used tariffs": H-J. Chang, "Kicking Away the Ladder—Infant Industry Promotion in Historical Perspective," Oxford Development Studies, vol. 31, no. 1, 2003; H-J. Chang, "Kicking Away the Ladder—Globalization and Economic Development in Historical Perspective," in *The Handbook of Globalization* (ed. J. Michie), Edward

Elgar, 2003; *Rethinking Development Economics* (ed. H-J. Chang), Anthem Press, 2003.

105 "lack of alternatives": See, for example, Martin Feldstein, "Refocusing the IMF," *Foreign Affairs,* March/April 1998, vol. 77, no. 2, pp. 20–33.

106 "only 4 percent": *World Bank News,* September 22, 1994.

106 "an effective veto vote": It does not have a formal veto but an effective one. The reason is that a number of resolutions need 85 percent majority and the United States is the only country to have greater than a 15 percent share of vote. See Ariel Buira, "The Governance of the IMF," in *Challenges to the World Bank and IMF: Developing Country Perspectives* (ed. A. Buira), Anthem Press, 2003.

106 "power asymmetry . . . is thus institutionalized": Bartram S. Brown, *The United States and the Politicization of the World Bank: Issues of International Law and Policy,* Kegan Paul International, London, 1992.

106 *"their* weak and voiceless . . . were disproportionately hurt": Often governments could have cut state spending by cutting military expenditure instead, but didn't because of political pressures from the military and domestic elites. See, for example, James Cypher and James Dietz, *The Process of Economic Development,* Routledge, London, 2003, among other writers.

107 "Filipino women who were 'sold' ": See Saskia Sassen, "The Feminization of Survival: Alternative Global Circuits," paper presented at the conference on "Gender Budgets, Financial Markets, Financing for Development," February 19–20, 2002, by the Heinrich-Boell Foundation in Berlin.

107 "join the teeming slums": UN Habitat report on New Urban Revolution, October 2003.

108 "structural adjustment continued": Tomohisa Hattori, "Reconceptualizing Foreign Aid," *Review of International Political Economy,* vol. 8, no. 4, Winter 2001, pp. 633–60.

Chapter Seven

112 *"World Development Report on Poverty"*: Paul Mosley, Jane Harrigan, and John Toye, *Aid and Power: The World Bank and Policy-Based Lending—Volume 1,* 1991.

112 "opened up their coffers": Roland Vaubel, cited in James Raymond Vreeland, *The IMF and Economic Development,* Cambridge University Press, 2003.

113 "debt overhang": Paul Krugman, "Financing vs. Forgiving a Debt Overhang," *Journal of Development Economics,* vol. 29, no. 3, November

1988, pp. 253–68; Jeffrey Sachs, "The Debt Overhang of Developing Countries," in *Debt, Growth and Stabilization: Essays in Memory of Carlos Ias Alejandro* (eds. Jorge de Macdeo and Ronald Findlay), Blackwell, Oxford, 1989, pp. 80–102.

113 "the largest share of the debt": Senegal, for example, owes 41 percent of its debt to multilateral creditors; 35 percent is composed of bilateral debt. "Debt and Destruction in Senegal," World Development Movement, October 2003.

115 "write-off": The World Bank didn't include its own loans for write-off in the same way as other creditors. Inclusion of multilateral loans was possible insofar as bilateral donors would make grants available for this purpose—moreover, bilateral funds for the multilateral component were not additional but resulted in a decrease of other development aid—e-mail correspondence with Professor Jan Pronk, former minister for development cooperation of the Netherlands, January 1, 2004.

115 "When asked why he was demanding": Conversation with former senior World Bank official, November 2002.

115 "the Allies capped the percentage": This was under the 1953 London Agreement, but note that I am not saying that 3.5 percent should be a general guideline. And distinctions need to be made between debt service during a period of recovery in which the debt service to exports ratio would need to be far below 10 percent and a sustainability criterion for debt service in normal times—in the literature a percentage of up to 20 percent would be generally accepted. This, of course, does not take into account what a country can reasonably afford to pay out. See chapter 11.

116 "sub-Saharan debt": Nicolas Van de Walle, *African Economies and the Politics of Permanent Crisis, 1979–1999,* Cambridge University Press, 2001.

116 "paying back more . . . than they were receiving": Net flows are negative from developing countries as a whole, although there are regional variances.

116 " 'Although the international community . . . ' ": *Financial Times,* January 21, 1999, p. 18.

116 "Clare Short": Neither Clare Short nor her permanent secretary, Sir John Vereker, favored blanket debt forgiveness, fearing the effect on their department's budgets and also that the benefits of debt relief would not reach the pockets of the poor.

117 "Poverty reduction": Something Britain's Department for International Development lobbied hard for.

118 "The same is true": Because delivery is tied to a country's successful completion of the HIPC program, most of the 100 percent bilateral debt cancellation promised by the United States and other major bilateral

creditors for the world's most highly indebted poor countries in Thanksgiving 1999 has failed to materialize, although these creditors have, at least, canceled the debt of those ten countries that have passed through HIPC.

118 "Uganda . . . still pays out roughly 12 percent": International Development Association and International Monetary Fund, HIPC Initiative Statistical Update, prepared by the Staffs of the World Bank and IMF, approved by Gobind Nankani and Timothy Geithner, March 10, 2003.

118 "HIV/AIDS": "Debt Relief and the HIV/AIDS Crisis in Africa," Oxfam, July 2002.

118 "total debt service . . . increased": Romilly Greenhill and Ann Pettifor (Jubilee Research), Henry Northover (CAFOD), and Ashok Sinha (Jubilee Debt Campaign), "Did the G8 Drop the Debt," May 2003.

118 "life expectancy has declined": UNDP Human Development Report, 2003.

118 " 'sustainable' ": Although the sustainable definition is now slightly more generous than under the initial HIPC program, it remains completely arbitrary.

118 "Ethiopia": Although Ethiopia's GDP registered a reasonable growth rate of 5 percent in 1999/2000, the maintenance of 5 percent, let alone a steady 6 percent a year will be extremely difficult (one estimate is for 1.5 percent growth), http://news.bbc.co.uk/1/hi/world/africa/1476618.stm; GDP Real Growth Rate (2002 est.), www.cia.gov/cia/publications/factbook/geos/et.htmlEcon.

118 "2.1 percent per annum growth": World Bank estimates, www.nationmaster.com; World Development Indicators, 2003.

119 "rely on a small list of . . . commodities": Nancy Birdsall and Brian Deese, *International Herald Tribune,* June 27, 2002.

119 "coffee makes up the bulk of . . . exports": CIA Fact Book 2003.

119 "HIPC calculations predicted": IMF-WB Uganda country document 2000, Second Decision point document.

119 "projections had been grossly inaccurate": Romilly Greenhill and Ann Pettifor (Jubilee Research), Henry Northover (CAFOD), and Ashok Sinha (Jubilee Debt Campaign), "Did the G8 Drop the Debt," May 2003.

119 "World Bank officials concede": Brian Ngo, Senior Economist, World Bank, at the Jubilee Debt Campaign Conference, March 2004.

119 "PRGFs are essentially the same": See Tony Killick's report for ODI/DFID, November 2002.

120 "IMF's own staff admits": IMF 2001: Thirty cited in James Raymond Vreeland, *The IMF and Economic Development,* Cambridge University Press, 2003, p. 161.

120 "still told to cut their budgets": Jim Levinsohn, "The Poverty Reduction

Strategy Paper Approach: Good Marketing or Good Policy?" in Ariel Buira, *Challenges to the World Bank and IMF,* Anthem Press, 2003.

120   "Eleven countries have experienced delays": "HIPC Initiative—Status of Implementation," International Monetary Fund and International Development Association, September 12, 2003.

120   " 'We are caught . . . ' ": Conversation with President Mkapa of Tanzania at World Economic Forum, 2002.

121   "*Wall Street Journal* wrote": *Wall Street Journal,* November 11, 1999.

121   "IMF's own report": "The Enhanced HIPC Initiative and the Achievement of Long-Term External Debt Sustainability," International Monetary Fund and International Development Association, April 15, 2002, p. 27.

121   "negative impact on growth": Romilly Greenhill and Ann Pettifor (Jubilee Research), Henry Northover (CAFOD), and Ashok Sinha (Jubilee Debt Campaign), "Did the G8 Drop the Debt," May 2003.

121   "insistence on adherence": Although they now appear to at least be paring down the number of attached conditionalities, see for example, Joseph Stiglitz, "The Painful Reality the IMF Ignores," *Guardian,* October 2, 2003.

121   " 'Give me their names . . . ' ": *Sud Quotidien,* July 23, 2003.

122   "civil society has remained either ignored or sidelined': North South Coalition PRSP Program Poverty Reduction Update, February 2003.

122   "Senegalese Poverty Reduction Strategy Paper": World Bank 2003 Senegal: Poverty Reduction Strategy Paper and Joint IDA-IMF Staff Assessment of the PRSP, Washington DC, January 17, 2003.

122   "The Tanzanian government": Conversation with President Mkapa of Tanzania, January 2003.

123   " 'the shareholding principle . . . ' ": Statement by Carole Brookins, EDS2003-0389, June 20, 2003.

123   "not limited to the HIPC group": R. Chowdhury Abdur, "External Debt, Growth and the HIPC Initiative: Is the Country Choice Too Narrow?" in *Debt Relief for Poor Countries* (eds. T. Addison, H. Hasen, and F. Torp), Palgrave Macmillan, 2004, p. 19.

123   "Peru is not granted debt relief": www.perusupportgroup.co.uk/debt .htmdebtintro.

124   "Mali": World Bank, World Development Indicators.

125   "eighty people died . . . in bloody protests in Bolivia," *Guardian,* October 18, 2003.

Chapter Eight

130 "Italian bankers played on the historic and ethnic ties": See, for example, *La Nacion,* December 20, 2001.

130 " 'They told me . . . ' ": Cited in Paul Blustein, "Argentina Didn't Fall on Its Own," *Washington Post,* August 3, 2003.

130 "Italian bankers": JP Morgan, UBS, BNP, and Deutsche Bank also placed a lot of paper in Italy.

130 "defaulted on their debts": "The Hole Gets Deeper," *Economist,* November 12, 2002. Many other countries have defaulted multiple times—Spain, for example, defaulted thirteen times from the sixteenth through nineteenth centuries, France eight times, Portugal and Germany's predecessor states half a dozen times. Latin American governments defaulted frequently during the nineteenth as well as the twentieth centuries. Turkey and its predecessor the Ottoman Empire were also frequently in default during the nineteenth and twentieth centuries.

131 "consequences . . . so dire": This is because once loans provided by the Bretton Woods institutions have been defaulted upon, a country becomes a pariah state, and typically receives no aid at all.

131 "indebtedness is rising in many emerging countries": In the Middle East and Turkey, Latin America, emerging Europe and developing Asia, the absolute size of external indebtedness has risen significantly between 1995 and 2003, "Trends in Sovereign Indebtedness," *ABN AMRO Emerging Markets Fortnightly,* October 22, 2003. Looking specifically at net private lending (predominately commercial bank lending and bonds), the Institute of International Finance, www.iif.com, in its paper "Capital Flows to Emerging Market Economies," September 21, 2002, estimates this to be $45.8 billion and $49.8 billion for 2003 and 2004 respectively, of which bonds make up the largest share, with commercial bank lending slowing down. However, there is considerable regional variance. Latin America and emerging Europe, for example, saw rises in bond issues in 2003, while Asia Pacific and Africa/Middle East declines.

131 "President Kuchma": *Ukrainian Journal,* December 3, 2003.

132 "projects that will improve the economy": Borrowing for productive investment only makes sense if the rate at which the countries can borrow is less than the expected rate of return from the investment in the long run (which in the long run can be proxied by GDP growth). By this measure, some low-rated developing nations that can borrow only at rates of interest of 10 percent or more and grow at much lower rates should not be borrowing as much as they do.

132 "America's national debt": Concord Coalition, September 2003.

132 "how much debt is too much": Morris Goldstein, "Debt, Sustainability,

Brazil, and the IMF," Institute for International Economics, February 2003.

132 "advice the IMF gave Argentina": Alan B. Cibils, Mark Weisbrot, and Karl Debayani, "Argentina Since Default: The IMF and the Depression," Center for Economic and Policy Research, September 3, 2002.

133 "yields demanded from borrowers": "Trends in Sovereign Indebtedness," ABN-AMRO, *Emerging Markets Fortnightly,* October 22, 2003.

134 "fast becomes another's crisis": P. Mauro, N. Sussman, Y. Yafeh, "Then versus Now," IMF Working Paper, November 2000, Emerging Market Spreads.

134 "When one emerging market faces a crisis": Barry Eichengreen and Michael D. Bordo, "Crises Now and Then: What Lessons from the Last Era of Financial Globalization?" NBER Working Paper Series, Working Paper 8716, January 2002.

134 "Uruguay": Morris Goldstein, "Debt, Sustainability, Brazil, and the IMF," Institute for International Economics, February 2003.

134 "collapse of its tourist industry": *Economist,* March 1, 2003, p. 51.

135 "desire to default": Michael Tomz, "Voter Sophistication and Domestic Preferences Regarding Debt Default," Stanford Working Paper, March 2004.

135 "growing gap between the haves and have-nots": See, for example, Robert Wade, "Poverty and Income Distribution: What Is the Evidence?" in *Real World Economic Outlook, Vol. 1* (ed. Ann Pettifor), 2003.

135 "Lula": Sue Brandford, *Red Pepper,* October 2003.

135 "economic performance continues to be lackluster": Institute of International Finance; December 2003.

135 "attempts by creditors to recover their money": For those new emerging-market bonds that will have collective action clauses, the clauses should mitigate this problem considerably as they will put virtually everyone with an interest in the outcome in the same boat, i.e., no one will fear that someone else more clued in will have a negotiating advantage. Of course, they wouldn't address what is usually the core problem—the debtor's lack of financial resources.

136 "JP Morgan Chase announced": JP Morgan Chase 2001, 10-K filing, p. 28.

136 "telecommunication companies": Telephonic, 10-K, 2002.

136 "513,000 U.S. jobs were lost": Sara Anderson and John Cavanagh, "Bearing the Burden: The Impact of Global Financial Crisis on Workers and Alternative Agendas for the IMF and Other Institutions," Institute for Policy Studies, April 2000.

136 "likelihood of people leaving their homes." Acute poverty and unemployment problems in countries of origin are root causes of migration. See, for

example, Piyasiri Wickramasekera, "Asian Labor Migration: Issues and Challenges in an Era of Globalization," *International Migration Papers* 57, ILO Geneva, 2002, www.ilo.org/public/english/protection/migrant/download/imp/imp57e.pdf; Donatella Giubilaro, "Migration from the Maghreb and Migration Pressures: Current Situation and Future Prospects," *International Migration Papers 15E,* ILO, Geneva, 1997. Available at www.ilo.org/public/english/protection/migrant/download/imp/imp15e.pdf;http://news.bbc.co.uk/2/hi/africa/2053649.stm—story of Senegalese migrants emigrating to find employment in Italy due to lack of opportunities at home; Argentina has witnessed an exodus of 255,000 since the default, roughly six times the total number of emigrants in the seven years from 1993 to 2000—National Migration Directorate.

137 "David Blunkett": *Independent,* April 28, 2002.

137 "interests . . . potentially threatened": See, for example, Mark Copelovitch, "Domestic Interests and the International Lender of Last Resort: The Political Economy of IMF Crisis Lending," August 20, 2003.

137 "Loans in these circumstances": U.S. taxpayers, for example, provided Uruguay with a $1.5 billion loan in early August 2002 in order to avert a looming default.

137 "huge loans to Russia": "The International Monetary Fund agreed Thursday on a $10.2 billion loan package to help Russia's struggling economy over the next three years, providing an enormous boost for President Boris Yeltsin on the eve of his reelection campaign." *The Tech,* MIT, February 23, 1996. Helmut Kohl was the biggest foreign financial backer of Yeltsin, and the United States (led by Stiglitz, then head of the Council of Economic Advisors) was close behind. Basically, protracted lending was about keeping Yeltsin in power so that there wasn't a return to communism/civil unrest and stability was maintained.

138 "attempt to seize government assets": The assets they can go after in practice are typically restricted given the terms of the loans—see, for example, Anatole Kaletsky, *Costs of Default,* Priority Press Publications, June 1985.

138 "debt vultures": Of course, in practice there is little recourse available to creditors as a whole when defaults occur because of poor property rights, which is then reflected in the risk premium demanded—see, for example, Kenneth Rogoff, "Emerging Market Debt. What Is the Problem?" speech given at the Sovereign Debt Restructuring Mechanism Conference, Washington DC, January 22, 2003.

138 "Argentina already faces lawsuits": "Argentina Faces Hundreds of Lawsuits from Bondholders," Bloomberg, December 2, 2003.

138 "Brazilian banks": There are investment restrictions on Brazilian financial institutions that mean that these have little choice except to invest a

significant chunk of their resources in Brazilian government debt. Of these, banks hold the largest chunk and pension funds and insurance companies make up most of the balance.

139   "Living standards had dropped": www.wsws.org/articles/2002/aug2002/arg-a22.shtml.

139   "disproportionately on the shoulders of women": See, for example, Saskia Sassen, "The Feminization of Survival: Alternative Global Circuits," paper presented at the conference on "Gender Budgets, Financial Markets, Financing for Development," February 19–20, 2002, by the Heinrich-Boell Foundation in Berlin.

139   "Despite a horrific first twelve months": "After Default Argentina Needs a Very Substantial Reduction in Its Debt," *Financial Times,* June 30, 2003.

140   "accentuate the risk of default": Lots of studies show a link between inequality and default; see, for example, Jeffrey Sachs and Andrew Berg, "The Debt Crisis: Structural Explanations of Country Performance," NBER Working Paper Series, Working Paper 2607, 1988.

140   "leverage extra-favorable terms": In January 2003, Argentina was able to get the IMF to roll over $6 billion in debts to Argentina using threat of default as one of its main negotiating positions. It was helped by the G7, which feared the health of the international financial institutions and the contagion effect if Argentina defaulted. *Financial Times,* January 21, 2003.

141   "capital controls": See, for example, *Economist,* May 1, 2003.

141   "still not commonplace": Although, in late 2003, Argentina did introduce capital controls to prevent some speculative inflows.

141   "countries rarely use them": Reasons why they tend not to be used—apart from by some large companies, such as Anglo American and other major gold producers, which do hedge the price of their products—are that premiums are significant, especially as they need to be paid up-front and this is next to impossible for people/countries living hand to mouth. And that they tend to be soft commodities, whose producers in many cases are small farmers perhaps aggregated at a cooperative level, without access to or understanding of complex derivatives markets or transactions.

141   "bankruptcy procedure": At the end of October 2003, a new code of conduct to avoid sovereign debt defaults and financial crises was discussed in the meeting of the G20 countries. This will involve a voluntary code on transparency and a general agreement that sovereign debt should be issued with collective action clauses, allowing the terms of debt to be renegotiated even if some bondholders object. It will still not, however, address the problem of determining when a country should not have to repay its debts. Nor will it ensure, as municipal and individual

bankruptcy procedures do, that the bankruptee still has a roof over its head.

141 "timing": Jose Maria Figueres, former president of Costa Rica, tells me during a conversation, September 2003, of how during the first part of his term he had a strategy to decrease his level of debt—interest rates demanded were too high, and it didn't make sense to borrow on external markets. At the end of his term, given the rise in FDI and growth in the economy, he reversed the strategy and issued dollar-denominated bonds at a reasonable rate.

Chapter Nine

142 " 'If developing countries scourged by disease . . . ' ": Lawrence Summers, "Preventing AIDS: An Investment in Global Prosperity," testimony before the Senate Appropriations Committee, Subcommittee on Foreign Operations, Washington, DC, April 11, 2000.

143 "emergent diseases": Laurie Garrett, *The Coming Plague: Newly Emerging Diseases in a World out of Balance*, Virago, London, 1995, p. 609.

144 "By January 1, 1992": PAHO Communicable Diseases Program, www.valpo.edu/geomet/geo/courses/geo215/lab7.htm.

145 "IMF and World Bank demands": The IMF has moved from limiting how high a budget deficit a country may run up, to actually insisting that they maintain budget surpluses, resulting in ever greater budget expenditure cutting—e-mail correspondence with Rick Rowden, Action Aid USA, December 2003.

145 "fees for their use": The World Bank began promoting user fees in 1987 in response to the severe budget austerity that the IMF had begun to impose as loan conditions since the late 1970s–80s. Despite congressional opposition to user fees, U.S. pressure has not led to much more than getting the World Bank to change its official policies. While it now effectively says, "We don't impose user fees in our loan conditions anymore," apart from in a few cases, many governments are still charging them because the fees allow for substitute budget support, necessary because national budgets for health and education are still insufficient. The World Bank no longer needs to impose user fees by loan conditions, because Southern governments resort to them anyway.

145 "Studies of developing-world countries": See, for example, Addis Ababa Findings, 1997.

145 "Cutbacks in education budgets": World Health Organization, "Macroeconomics and Health: Investing in Health for Economic Development," Report of the Commission on Macroeconomics and Health, p. 10.

145 "literacy of girls": See, for example, D. Potts, "Structural Adjustment and Poverty: Perceptions from Zimbabwe," *Indicator South Africa,* Vol. 14, no. 3, 1997, pp. 82–88; L. Hulton and D. Furlong, "Gender Equality in Education: A Select Annotated Bibliography," prepared for the Educational Division, British Department for International Development, January 2001.

145 "rarely see health workers": Mariam Claeson et al., "Poverty Reduction and the Health Sector," The Health, Nutrition and Population Network chapter in the World Bank's *Poverty Reduction Strategy Sourcebook,* June 2001, available at http://wbln0018.worldbank.org/HDNet/ hddocs.nsf/c840b59b6982d2498525670c004def60/cb3e5ef9ac5d0daf8 5256b1900672592/$FILE/PovertyReductionFinalJune2001.pdf.

146 "smoking rates": F. J. Chaloupka and A. Laixuthai, "U.S. Trade Policy and Cigarette Smoking," in *Asia National Bureau of Economic Research,* Working Paper No. 5543, 1996, cited in D. Yach, S. S. Fluss, D. W. Bettcher, "Globalization and Health: Targets Met, New Needs," *Politica Internazionale,* 12:233–53, 2001.

146 "the most indebted country": www.unhchr.ch/Huridocda/Huridoca .nsf/0/082c9d7252e6ae0d8025673900388f43?Opendocument; also, Dr. Barry Bosworth, a senior fellow at the Brookings Institution, writes: "We are now the world's most indebted country, and there are serious questions about how long the rest of the world will be willing to finance American consumption," www.pbs.org/newshour/btp/odop/2004-question2 .html.

146 "African countries": Nana K. Poku, "Poverty, Debt and Africa's HIV/ Aids Crisis," *International Affairs,* vol. 78, 2002, p. 3.

146 "$5,000": This figure is for total national health expenditure per capita for the United States for 2001. Private accounted for $2,749 and public $2,286. Centers for Disease Control and Prevention, National Center for Health Statistics.

146 "$168 billion": World Health Organization, "Macroeconomics and Health: Investing in Health for Economic Development," Report of the Commission on Macroeconomics and Health, December 2001.

147 "25 percent": This particular figure refers to the South Pacific islands— e-mail correspondence with Derek Yach, World Health Organization, 2003.

147 "Ethiopia . . . Niger": "Carrying the Burden," *Jubilee 2000 Coalition,* www.jubilee2000uk.org/jubilee2000/features/women0412.html.

147 "Tanzania": A. L. Colgan, "Africa's Debt," Africa Action position paper, Africa Action, Washington DC, July 2001, p. 4.

147 "HIV/AIDS": Nana K. Poku, "Poverty, Debt and Africa's HIV/Aids Crisis," *International Affairs,* vol. 78, no. 3, 2002.

147 "forty million children": L. Heinecken, "Aids: The New Security Fron-

tier," *Conflict Trends,* vol. 4. 2000, pp. 12–15; "Living in Terror: The Looming Security Threat to Southern Africa," *African Security Review,* vol. 10, no. 4, 2001.

147   "Africa spends more on servicing its debt": Nana K. Poku, "Poverty, Debt and Africa's HIV/Aids Crisis," *International Affairs,* vol. 78, 2002, no. 3, 2002.

147   " 'Defend your people' ": Wambui Chege, " 'Fund Aids Fight, Not Foreign Debts' Sachs Says at Earth Summit," Jubilee USA Network, August 2002.

148   "links between poverty and disease": See, for example, United Nations Human Development Report 2003.

148   "can't afford to pay for 'healthy' foods": Mariam Claeson et al., "Poverty Reduction and the Health Sector," The Health, Nutrition and Population Network's chapter in the World Bank's *Poverty Reduction Strategy Sourcebook,* June 2001, available at http://wbln0018.worldbank.org/HDNet/hddocs.nsf/c840b59b6982d2498525670c004def60/cb3e5ef9ac5d0daf85256b1900672592/$FILE/PovertyReductionFinalJune2001.pdf.

148   " 'They often can't find the medicine . . . ' ": "As U.S. Balks on Deal for Medicine, Patients in Africa Feel the Pain," *Wall Street Journal Europe,* June 2, 2003.

149   "significantly more vulnerable": Alison Katz, "AIDS Individual Behavior and the Unexplained Variation," in *African Journal of AIDS Research,* Vol. 1, 2002, pp. 125–42.

149   "even sicker": Mariam Claeson et al., "Poverty Reduction and the Health Sector," The Health, Nutrition and Population Network's chapter in the World Bank's *Poverty Reduction Strategy Sourcebook,* June 2001, available at http://wbln0018.worldbank.org/HDNet/hddocs.nsf/c840b59b6982d2498525670c004def60/cb3e5ef9ac5d0daf85256b1900672592/$FILE/PovertyReductionFinalJune2001.pdf.

149   "Poverty makes people sick": G. Myrdal, "Economic Aspects of Health," Address to the Fifth World Health Assembly, WHO, Geneva, 1952, cited in D. Yach, S. S. Fluss, and D. W. Bettcher, "Targets Met, New Needs," *Politica Internazionale,* vols. 1–2, January–April 2001, pp. 233–52.

149   " 'In the field . . . ' ": Nana K. Poku, "Poverty, Debt and Africa's HIV/Aids Crisis," *International Affairs,* vol. 78, no. 3, 2002

150   "doctors and nurses are leaving in droves": Most of this data is cited in *World Markets in Focus 2002,* World Markets Research Center.

150   "African doctors and nurses are leaving": "Halting Africa's Brain Drain," *BBC News,* May 19, 2003.

150   "Zambia": World Markets Research Center, quoting the International Organization for Migration, 2002.

150   "pathogens can cross borders": D. W. Bettcher, D. Yach, and G. E. Guidon, "Global Trade and Health: Key Linkages and Future Challenges," *Bulletin of WHO*, Vol. 78, no. 4, 2000, pp. 521–34. See also WHO Communicable Diseases 2002, Progress Report.

150   "The Great Plague of London": "The Stuarts and the Civil War: The Plague Years 1665–66," *BBC Timelines*, available at www.bbc.co.uk/history/timelines/england/stu_plague_year.

150   "What makes the present situation different": "Global Health Security— Epidemic Alert and Response," 54th WHO document A 54/9, WHO, Geneva, 2001, cited in D. Yach, S. S. Fluss, and D. W. Bettcher, "Targets Met, New Needs," *Politica Internazionale*, vols. 1–2, January–April 2001.

151   "Dengue fever": Between 1980 and 1999, there were, for example, sixty-eight cases of dengue in Texas, www.epolitix.com/EN/Publications/PH7/3_1/5E41D963-193D-4D71-AD50-1DECE861710D.

151   "malaria . . . imported into the United Kingdom": www.who.int/infectious-disease-report/2000/ch4.

151   "North America": Andrew T. Price-Smith, "Ghosts of Kigali: Infectious Disease and Global Stability at the Turn of the Century," in *Plagues and Politics* (ed. A. T. Price-Smith), Palgrave Macmillan, 2001.

151   "Tuberculosis": Andrew T. Price-Smith, "Ghosts of Kigali: Infectious Disease and Global Stability at the Turn of the Century," in *Plagues and Politics* (ed. A. T. Price-Smith), Palgrave Macmillan, 2001.

151   "Leishmaniasis": www.who.int/infectious-disease-report/2000/ch4.

151   "West Nile virus": www.westnilemaps.usgs.gov.

151   "subtypes of the AIDS virus": Rory Carroll, "Hope Rises in Africa for AIDS Vaccine," *Guardian*, May 20, 2003.

152   "impact upon economic growth": Robyn Pharaoh and Martin Schönteich, "AIDS, Security and Governance in Southern Africa—Exploring the Impact," Institute for Security Studies, Occasional Paper no. 65, January 2003.

152   "more than a quarter": L. Heinecken, "Aids: The New Security Frontier," *Conflict Trends*, vol. 4, 2000, pp. 12–15; "Living in Terror: The Looming Security Threat to Southern Africa," *African Security Review*, vol. 10, no. 4, 2001.

153   "security": Mark Schneider, "A Clear and Present Danger: HIV/AIDS Threatens Global Security," keynote address, Conference on HIV/AIDS as a Threat to Global Security, Yale University, New Haven, CT, November 8, 2002.

153   "almost half": In 2001, sub-Saharan Africa spent $14.5 billion repaying debts. World Bank, "Global Development Finance 2002," April 2002. The annual net financing gap it faces in 2007 is $18.7 billion and, in 2015, $27.5 billion. World Health Organization, "Macroeconomics and

Health: Investing in Health for Economic Development," Report of the Commission on Macroeconomics and Health, December 2001.

154 "could stop people dying": When we compare poor countries in general with those categorized as HIPC, we see that among poor countries the more indebted a country is the more likely it is to have higher rates of infant mortality and lower rates of life expectancy.

154 "nearly fifteen hundred poverty-stricken children unnecessarily died": According to Amnesty International, 35,000 children die every day throughout the world because of poverty—this equals 1,460 per hour.

155 "fourteen countries": In 2001, these fourteen paid out $9.1 billion in debt service. Jubilee USA Network, "Debt Relief Increases Impact of U.S. Efforts to Fight HIV-AIDS," cited in "The DATA Deal: An Emergency G7 Package for Africa," 2003.

Chapter Ten

156 "Uzan": For more on the Uzan story, see, for example, "Everyone Knows This Is a Political Lynching," *Time Europe,* August 4, 2003.

159 "Treaty of Versailles": Paul Birdsall, *Versailles Treaty Twenty Years After,* Reynal and Hitchcock, New York, 1941.

159 " 'Vengeance I dare predict . . . ' ": John Maynard Keynes, *The Economic Consequences of the Peace,* Harcourt, Brace & Howe, New York, 1920.

159 "Mugabe . . . Rais": See *The Times,* September 2, 2000; "Solution Leaves Legacy of Bitterness," *Financial Times,* August 2, 2002.

160 "Eva Perón as Saint of the Poor": Gabriella Gamini, "Argentina Finds Solace in Evita as Hardship Goes," *The Times,* November 16, 2002.

161 " 'financial tools of imperialism' ": See, for example, www.geocities.com/CapitolHill/1131/support_peru.html.

161 " 'We have to recognize . . . ' ": Michael Fortin, "Reflections on the Occasion of an Act of Terrorism," *Africana Plus,* October 2001, http://pages.infinet.net/africana/terrorism.htm.

161 " 'And then we got television . . . ' ": Conversation with Owens Wiwa, Ghent, October 30, 2001.

161 "870 million 'global desperados' ": Source UN Stats: http://216.239.59.104/search?q=cache:bPCySOL_c3sJ:unstats.un.org/unsd/accsub/2002d ocs/mdg-habitat.pdf+%22total+slum+dwellers%22&hl=en&ie=UTF-8.

162 "Lashkar-I-Taiba": Jessica Stern, "Pakistan's Jihad Culture," *Foreign Affairs,* vol. 79, no. 6, November/December 2000.

164 "Hobbesian nightmare": Thomas Hobbes, *Leviathan,* Everyman's Library, Dutton, New York, 1950, pp. 103–4.

164 "Pablo Escobar": R. Crandall, *Driven by Drugs: U.S. Policy Toward*

Colombia, Lynne Rienner, London, 2002; F. Thoumi, *Political Economy and Illegal Drugs in Colombia,* Lynne Rienner, London 1995; G. Murillo, "Narcotráfico y Política en la Década de los Ochenta: Entre la Represión y el Diálogo," in *Narcotráfico en Colombia* (eds. C. Arrieta, et al.), Tercer Mundo Editores, Colombia, 1990, pp. 203–76.

165 "Rafael Caro": F. Mejía, "La Idea de Almoloya," *La Jornada,* May 19, 1996.

165 "Pakistan": Robert Looney of the Center for Contemporary Conflict, www.ccc.nps.navy.mil/rsepResources/si/dec02/southAsia2.asp.

165 "open invitation for radical Islam": See, for example, www.brook .edu/dybdocroot/views/papers/singer/20020103.htm.

165 "attendant problems": Sometimes very serious ones—Catholic influences, for example—have blocked use of contraceptives in places where AIDS/HIV rates are high.

165 "thirty-nine thousand madrassas": Thomas Friedman, *Chicago Tribune,* November 14, 2001.

166 "hundreds of thousands of Holy Warriors": Jack Beatty, *The Real Roots of Terror,* The Atlantic Unbound, December 5, 2001, Politics and Prose; Thomas L. Friedman, "In Pakistan It's Jihad," *New York Times,* November 12, 2001; Jeffrey Goldberg, "Inside Jihad University: The Education of a Holy Warrior," *Hamilton Spectator,* September 22, 2001; International Crisis Group (ICG) Report, "Pakistan: Madrassas, Extremism and the Military," Asia Report 36, July 29, 2002, p. 16.

166 "Darul Uloom Haqqania": P. W. Singer, "Pakistan's Madrassahs: Ensuring a System of Education Not Jihad," Brookings Institution, November 2001.

166 "75 percent of students are from abroad": Alex Alexiev, "The Pakistani Time Bomb," Center for Security Policy, March 2003, www.center forsecuritypolicy.org/index.jsp?section=static&page=alexievpakistan.

166 "feed, house, and clothe them": Pakistani president Pervez Musharraf, press conference with President George W. Bush, The White House, February 13, 2002, www.yale.edu/lawweb/avalon/sept_11/president_137 .htm.

166 "Muslim Brotherhood": Although some of these groups have diminished in size over recent years, they still typically provide some combination of these.

167 "significant Muslim population": This is something the United States is realizing. As of January 2004, it announced that it was sending in troops and defense contractors to West Africa to open a new front on the war on terror. Despite the fact that West Africa is not known as a hotbed of support, and that Al Qaeda has so far concentrated its African operations in the East, Washington is taking no chances in a region with strong Arab

and Muslim ties. Especially as Mauritania, Mali, Chad, and Niger, highly indebted poor countries, all have sizeable populations, porous borders, and disgruntled opposition groups. See "U.S. Opens New Front in War on Terror by Beefing Up Border Controls in Sahara," *Guardian*, January 14, 2004.

167　*"relatively* benign": But not completely benign. The quid pro quo they can implicitly or explicitly demand for their benevolence can have seriously negative consequences. And the legitimacy they can enjoy as a consequence can be seriously problematic. But relative to drug runners or extremist groups providing these services, they can be thought of as benign.

167　"majority Muslim populations": Muslim Population Statistics, the Institute of Islamic Information and Education.

167　"The danger of extremism": Let me stress that I am not saying here that all extremism is Islamic; of course, it is not. Nor that all Muslim countries are proviolence; of course, they are not. Nor am I dismissing geopolitical or religious reasons for extremist violence. But what I am saying is that when the preconditions for Islamic extremism exists—i.e., a country is Muslim or there is a significant Muslim enclave, *and* the economic situation is dire, *and* the state weak—the odds of extremism gaining ground do shoot up.

168　"Under IMF and World Bank": See, for example, Michel Chossudovsky, *The Globalization of Poverty and the New World Order*, Global Outlook, 2003.

168　" 'we are unavoidably side by side' ": Immanuel Kant, *Perpetual Peace: A Philosophical Sketch*, 1795.

168　"development aid": In 1990, development aid was $560 million.

168　"Liberia": See, for example, *Observer*, December 1, 2002, and *The Times*, December 30, 2002.

168　"Sierra Leone": See, for example, *Financial Times*, October 30, 2002, and April 17, 2003.

169　"Sudan and Somalia": See, for example, *Financial Times*, December 12, 2001.

169　"poor and debt-burdened countries": Saudi Arabia is a notable exception. It is neither poor nor debt-burdened, yet terrorism is alive and kicking.

169　"terrorism is able to breathe and breed": For an excellent analysis of terrorism, see Mary Kaldor, "Global Terrorism," in A. Giddens, ed., *The Progressive Manifesto: New Ideas for the Centre Left*, Polity Press, 2003.

169　"costs of global warming": Sharon Beder, "Insurers Sweat Over Global Warming," *Engineers Australia*, August 2001, p. 41.

169　"debt and rates of deforestation": In Brazil, razing of the rain forests has increased since Lula assumed power—in this case so as to make space to grow soya, one of the few ways for him to find the monies he needs to retain the favor of the international capital markets, and repay his loans while also meeting his electoral promise of delivering on social justice. Elsewhere we see forests razed or lands cleared to grow other cash crops like palm oil, coffee, cocoa, and flowers. For more generally on this, see, for example, James Kahn and Judith McDonald, "Third World Debt and Tropical Deforestation," *Ecological Economics,* vol. 12, 1995.

169 "deforestation is a key driver": www.earth-policy.org/Indicators/indicators5 .htm.

170 "extinct within the next twenty years": Evan Bowen-Jones, David Brown, and Elizabeth Robinson, "Assessment of the Solution-Orientated Research Needed to Promote a More Sustainable Bushmeat Trade in Central and West Africa," January 2002, produced for DEFRA Wildlife and Countryside Directorate, 1998; Bowen-Jones also reviewed the situation in West and Central Africa in a report written for the Ape Alliance, "The African Bushmeat Trade—A Recipe for Extinction"; see also Dale Peterson, *Eating Apes,* University of California Press, 2003.

170 "more environmental risk": For sources on the impact of SAPs on the environment, see, for example, A. Gueorguieva and K. Bolt, "A Critical Review of the Literature on SAP and the Environment," World Bank Environment Department, April 2003; H. Mainhardt, "IMF Intervention in Indonesia: Undermining Macroeconomic Stability and Sustainable Development by Perpetuating Deforestation," WWF, Washington DC, 2001.

170 "mechanized fishing fleets": See, for example, http://archive.greenpeace .org/pressreleases/oceans/2001oct3.html.

171 "shrimps": "World Bank Funds Destruction of Protected Wetlands: Devastation of Mangrove Swamps for Industrial Shrimp Aquaculture Must End," November 21, 2002, Valencia, Spain, www.greenpeace.org/news/ details?campaign%5fid=4025%&intem%fid=71640;www.christian-aid.org.uk/indepth/9605praw/prawn.htm; "Smash and Grab: Conflict Corruption and Human Rights Abuses in the Shrimp Farming Industry," June 19, 2003, www.guardian.co.uk; report by the Environmental Justice Foundation in partnership with Wildaid. www.eifoundation.org/pdfs/ smash_and_grab.pdf; Eileen Maybin and Kevan Bundell, "After the Prawn Rush: The Human and Environmental Costs of Commercial Prawn Farming," Christian Aid, 1996.

172 "OPIC and Ex-Im are currently in the dock": For more on the suit, see, for example, www.climatelawsuit.org.

173 "global warming is now a greater threat": Arianna Huffington, "The Pentagon Sounds the Alarm on Global Warming; Why Isn't President

Bush Listening?" February 25, 2004. Some sources on the looming ecoapocalypse include Martin Rees, *Our Final Century. A Scientist's Warning: How Terror, Error, and Environmental Disaster Threaten Humankind's Future in This Century—On Earth and Beyond,* Basic Books, 2003; Robert Nadeau, *The Wealth of Nature: How Mainstream Economics Has Failed the Environment,* Columbia University Press, 2003.

174   "Debt . . . exacerbates poverty": In some of its own publications, even the IMF recognizes that debt worsens poverty's impact; see, for example, "Debt Relief for Poverty Reduction: The Role of the Enhanced HIPC Initiative," IMF 2001.

Chapter Eleven

179   "the concept of illegitimacy": Key sources on illegitimate or odious debts include: Patricia Adams, "The Doctrine of Odious Debts: Using the Law to Cancel Illegitimate Debts," paper delivered at the Conference on Illegitimate Debts, June 2002; Michael Kremer and Seema Jayachandran, "Odious Debt," April 2002; Jeff King, Ashfaq Khalfan and Bryan Thomas, "Advancing the Odious Debt Doctrine," working paper, Center for International Sustainable Development Law, McGill University, February 2002; Jeff Rudin, "Odious Debt Revisited," January 2002; Joseph Hanlon, "Defining Illegitimate Debt: Understanding the Issues," Norwegian Church Aid, 2003.

179   "international human rights law": Beginning with the United Nations Universal Declaration on Human Rights, but also including the European Convention for the Protection of Human Rights and Fundamental Freedoms, 1950, and the UN International Covenant on Civil and Political Rights, 1966, among others.

180   "an important precondition": David Held, "Law of States, Law of Peoples: Three Models of Sovereignty," *Legal Theory,* vol. 8, 2002.

180   "less clear": A judgment has to be made when considering whether consent of people is democratically engendered, and I can accept that some discretion is necessary. But the general point is that we *can* distinguish between different types of political regimes according to their degree of representation and democratic accountability and this would be a matter for the arbitral panel to decide. For distinctions among authoritarian dictatorships, partial democracies (which have some procedures for competitive elections and have adopted some forms of guarantees of civil and political rights) and full-fledged democracies, see *Democratization* (eds. David Potter, D. Goldblatt, M. Kiloh, and P. Lewis), Polity Press, 1997.

180   "the monies borrowed were not used in the interests of the people." There

are several legal principles—unjust enrichment, quasi-contract, money-had-and-received, etc.—that could apply in a domestic equivalent.

180 "President Juarez repudiated": J. N. Pomeroy, *Lectures on International Law in Time of Peace,* Houghton Mifflin, Boston, 1886, p. 75; see also J. King, "The Doctrine of Odious Debt under International Law," www.woek.de/pdf/kasa_mcgill_kap1.pdf.

180 "judge Dr. Jorge Ballestero ruled". See Alejandro Olmos Gaono, "The Illegal Foreign Debt: The Value and Likelihood of a Legal Ruling," www.jubileeplus.org/analysis/articles/olmos_illegal_foreign_debt.htm.

181 "Royal Bank of Canada": Chief Justice Taft of the U.S. Supreme Court in 1923: "The Royal Bank . . . must make out its case of actually furnishing the money to the government for its illegitimate use. It has not done so. The bank knew this money was to be used by the retiring President, Federico Tinoco, for his personal support after he had taken refuge in a foreign country. It could not hold his own government for the money paid to him for this purpose."

182 "Less straightforward . . . quite possible": There is understandably much debate by legal scholars as to whether debts should be considered illegitimate if they are lent to an illegitimate regime, or if the individual loans must be clearly linked to an illegitimate purpose.

182 "World Bank lent to the Suharto regime": Jeffrey Winters, "Criminal Debt," in Jonathan R. Pincus and Jeffrey A. Winters, *Reinventing the World Bank,* Cornell University Press, September 2002.

182 " 'odious' ": In 1927, the Russian jurist Alexander Sack defined debts as "odious" when they are contracted by "a despotic regime . . . not for the needs or in the interests of the state, but rather to strengthen itself . . . and are contracted and utilized, for purposes which to the lenders' knowledge are contrary to the needs and interest of the nation." And he stated that such debts are not binding on the nation when it succeeds in overthrowing the government that contracted them. See, for example, Patricia Adams, "Odious Debts: Loose Lending, Financial Corruption and the Third World's Environmental Legacy," Probe International, 1991.

182 "reasonable to expect": The "reasonable foreseeability" test is one well recognized in law for holding people vicariously liable for deeds of others.

183 "current class action suit": *Khulumani et al. v. Barclays National Bank et al.,* a case filed in New York, in November 2002, by the Khulumani Support Group, an affiliate of Jubilee South Africa and other plaintiffs, against several corporations and banks which the plaintiffs allege aided and abetted the South African regime. The case is filed as a tortious claim under the Alien Tort Claims Act, which allows foreign nationals to bring cases against non-U.S. corporations or persons in the United States. The United Nations identified apartheid as a crime against humanity in 1950.

184   "60 percent of loans made": Nancy Birdsall, John Williamson, and Brian Deese, "Delivering on Debt Relief: From IMF Gold to a New Aid Architecture," Institute for International Economics, 2002, p. 8.

184   "subsistence levels": For a discussion on what constitutes basic needs, see, for example, Francis Stewart, *Basic Needs in Developing Countries,* Johns Hopkins University Press, 1985.

184   "deemed ineligible": Even countries that do not service their debts are often penalized because their debt stock plus arrears makes them ineligible for aid.

184   "most basic rights": See, for example, Articles 25 and 26 of the Universal Declaration on Human Rights 1948, which pertain to food, health, clothing, housing, and education as well as the International Covenant on Economic, Social and Cultural Rights, which states that "in no case may a people be deprived of its own means of subsistence," a covenant that 145 states have signed. In international environmental law, however, environmental rights are as yet generally regarded an aspirational right (a right *statu nascendi,* i.e., a right with a nascent status). Although since 1968, a number of international declarations, resolutions, etc., have lent weight. For example, the 1968 UN General Assembly resolution identified a relationship between the quality of human environment and the enjoyment of basic rights. The landmark 1972 Stockholm Declaration (the first Earth Conference) stated: "[B]oth aspects of man's environment, the natural and man-made are essential to his well-being and to the enjoyment of basic rights—even the right to life itself." It continued that "man has the fundamental right to freedom, equality, and adequate conditions of life, in an environment of quality that permits a life of dignity and well-being." The UN General Assembly declared in 1990 that "all individuals are entitled to live in an environment adequate for their health and well-being." More clarity exists, however, in municipal law. Many countries' constitutions, especially those made from the 1970s onward, enshrine environmental rights as fundamental.

185   "chapter 9 bankruptcy procedure": On Chapter 9–type frameworks, see, for example, Kunnibert Raffer, "The Need for an International Chapter 9," www.jahrbuch2002.studien-von-zeitfragen.net/Weltfinanz/ RAFFER_1/raffer_12.HTM.

185   "Egypt's . . . Venezuelan": Both of these examples are referred to in James Surowiecki, "Dealing with Deadbeats," *New Yorker,* October 28, 2002.

186   "formally": I use the word "formally" because the G7 and other major bilateral creditors did commit at Cologne, given the pressure the debt cancellation movement was putting on them, to cancel 100 percent or almost 100 percent of bilateral HIPC debt, which does indicate a commitment to the principle of needs-based cancellation. Ireland, however, is the only

country which has formally adopted the "Millennium Development Goals"–based debt sustainability approach. As for the IMF and World Bank, they haven't recognized this principle in any way at all.

186 " 'capable' of paying back": Looking at debt sustainability on a needs basis, we see that many countries would need total debt cancellation, assuming, that is, that monies saved would be directed to basic need fulfillment. And many would require further aid on top of this. See Joseph Hanlon, "Linking Debt Service to Development," discussion paper of the unpayable debt workshop of the Jubilee 2000 Rome meeting, November 16, 1998; Jeffrey D. Sachs, "External Debt, Structural Adjustment and Economic Growth," *UNCTAD: International Monetary and Financial Issues for the 1990s, Vol. IX;* Henry Northover, Karen Joyner, and David Woodward, "A Human Development Approach to Debt Relief for the World's Poor," position paper, CAFOD; see also Henry Northover, "An Alternative Approach to Debt Cancellation and New Borrowing for Africa," CAFOD, October 2003. Moreover, if a country does not have sufficient fiscal revenues to make the necessary poverty alleviation investments and if it cannot count on sufficient foreign aid to fill its revenue gap, both of which are the norm, then the *only* available source of finance is further debt reduction.

186 "free": Although the term used in the Millennium Development Goals is "universal" rather than "free," Article 26 of the Universal Declaration of Human Rights states: "Everyone has a right to education. Education shall be free at least in the elementary and fundamental stages."

187 "one-tenth of 1 percent": Center for Global Development and *Foreign Policy* magazine, "Ranking the Rich," 2003.

187 "cancellation of *all* debt": Jeffrey Sachs estimates that at least thirty countries should have all their debts canceled on these grounds—conversation, April 2004.

188 "the IMF has mooted a proposal": See, for example, Ann Pettifor, "Resolving International Debt Crises—the Jubilee Framework for International Insolvency," January 2002; Kunnibert Raffer, "The Need for an International Chapter 9," www.jahrbuch2002.studien-von-zeitfragen .net/Weltfinanz/RAFFER_1/raffer_12.HTM.

188 "only commercial debts . . . should be considered": See the IMF's SDRM proposal.

188 "at best exaggerated": Jubilee Research has argued very convincingly that were the IMF to sell off some of its gold reserves, this could more than cover its needs with no likely drop in credit ratings, a view supported by Jeffrey Sachs among others (conversation, April 2004). With regard to the World Bank, so that it is not forced to increase the interest rates it charges on its loans, and thereby effectively make middle- and lower-

middle-income countries subsidize the lower-income countries, the governments that fund it could of course recapitalize it to the necessary degree. See, for example, "Can the World Bank and IMF Cancel 100% of Poor Country Debts?" Jubilee Research for Debt and Development, Coalition Ireland, 2003. More generally, if the multilateral institutions' claims that they cannot fund the cancellation of multilateral debt themselves are upheld, the world's rich countries could of course themselves cover the cost of writing this off. The cost of writing off all the multilateral debt of the HIPC countries after existing commitments on debt relief are covered would amount to $34.9 billion. Jubilee Debt Campaign and World Development Movement, in *Call for Change: How the UK Can Afford to Cancel Its Share of Third World Debt,* March 2004, show that the cost to individual G7 and industrialized countries of footing their share of this would be relatively low. The cost to the United Kingdom of unilaterally writing off its share, for example, would amount to only £1.3 billion.

188 "arbitration tribunals": Suggestions on how to compose arbitration tribunals have been mooted by Kunnibert Raffer, "Applying Chapter 9 Insolvency to International Debts: An Economically Efficient Solution with a Human Face" in World Development," vol. 18, no. 2, 1990; and Thomas Fritz and Philipp Hersel, "Fair and Transparent Arbitration Processes: A New Road to Resolve Debt Crises," Berlin Working Group on Environment and Development, August 2002, among others. In the recent design of the Geneva Accord (a completely different situation, of course, but one in which arbitration was still being proposed as a dispute resolution mechanism), a list of arbitrators that both sides agreed to was added as an appendix.

188 "an accepted mechanism": The World Trade Organization has an arbitration-based mechanism, the dispute settlement mechanism to settle disputes between nations on the basis of trade. The International Center for the Settlement of Investment Disputes (ICSID) arbitrates between states and private parties under the auspices of the World Bank.

190 "prewarned": While subsequent regimes in the countries in question would need to be forewarned that they were to honor such inherited debts or they would become ineligible for aid; otherwise their incentive to do so would be high. See Michael Kremer and Seema Jayachandran, "Odious Debt," Brookings Institution Policy Brief No. 103, July 2002.

190 "a fresh start": See, for example, Kenneth Rogoff, "Emerging Market Debt, What Is the Problem," speech given at the Sovereign Debt Restructuring Mechanism Conference, January 22, 2003; Ann Pettifor, "Resolving International Debt Crises—The Jubilee Framework from International Insolvency," New Economics Foundation, January 2002.

190   "dead in the water": Further deliberations on it were suspended indefinitely at the IMF Spring Meetings in 2003.

192   "When Poland canceled its debts": Conversation with Jeffrey Sachs, April 2004.

194   "$170 billion": The $170 billion figure is for the official debt of sub-Saharan Africa as of the end of 1999. To reach the $24 billion figure, I have used John Garrett and Angela Travis's method of calculation as laid out in "Unfinished Business—Millennium Debt Challenge," Jubilee 2000 Coalition, September 1999. The authors assume that bilateral, IMF, and World Bank loans can be written down by about 90 percent, which is what the United States already does with its bilateral debts, but that regional development banks cannot write them down by the same amount. Of course, the Bretton Woods institutions are unlikely to accept that their outstanding debt in HIPC countries should be priced as low as 10 percent, although a rational observer could think that the way in which the IMF agreed to lend Argentina (not an HIPC) $3 billion in the afternoon having got them to agree to repay $3 billion in the morning might mean that in some cases it is actually 0 percent. But even if multilateral debts are not written down, the cost of canceling these *is* within our reach. The latest data show that after existing commitments on debt relief are delivered, the forty-two HIPC countries, for example, would still owe $34.9 billion to the multilateral institutions. The world's rich countries could easily afford to cover this.

194   "don't have a very good track record": The rich world must take some of the blame for this institutionalized corruption, ill management of funds, and disregard of the needs of the poor. You will remember how, until recently, the IMF and World Bank made an explicit condition of their granting of loans to Third World governments that they slash social services, health and education expenditure, thereby actively preventing them from addressing the needs of their vulnerable; the West continues to bankroll governments that do not put the interests of the vulnerable in the forefront where their geopolitical support is deemed necessary, also providing loans that enable them to skew their spending toward military hardware and status-symbol white elephant projects. They also continue to insist that developing countries adopt numerous measures such as the privatization of public utilities that tend to exacerbate the lot of the poor. If, instead, they had been vocal on the issue of equitable redistribution of funds, perhaps we would not be seeing such huge income differentials as we do in many of these countries.

195   "Pakistan spends approximately 5 percent": In 1998, Pakistan spent about 5 percent of its $61 billion GDP on defense, yielding an active

armed force only half the size of India's. Jessica Stern, "Pakistan's Jihad Culture," *Foreign Affairs*, Nov./Dec. 2000, www.foreignaffairs .org/20001101faessay940/jessica-stern/pakistan-s-jihad-culture.html. In 1996, Pakistan spent 3 percent of its GNP on education: World Bank, "Entering the 21st Century: World Development Report 1999–2000," Oxford University Press, New York, 2000, www.worldbank.org/wdr/ 2000/fullreport.html. Pakistan's public expenditure on health from 1990 to 1997 was 0.8 percent of GDP. World Bank, "Entering the 21st Century: World Development Report 1999–2000," Oxford University Press, New York, 2000, www.worldbank.org/wdr/2000/fullreport.html.

195 "dedicated to launching a satellite": There was, for example, a provision of $28 million in the 2002 federal government budget for a satellite program.

195 "Bolivia": "Bolivia: Deflection of Resources from the Fight Against Poverty," AIS-CODEDCO, La Paz, April 17, 2003.

196 " 'Even with the best of commitment . . . ' ": World Bank/IMF Meetings, September 2003.

196 "good governance extremely hard to achieve": See, for example, Rafael La Porta, Florencio Lopez-de-Silanes, Andrei Shleifer, and Robert Vishny, "The Quality of Government," *The Journal of Law, Economics, and Organization*, vol. 15, no. 1, 1999.

196 "monies thereby saved": To those of you who may be under the belief that most poor countries are not actually servicing their debts and thus there will be no actual savings, while this was once true, today it is not. Given that in order to graduate from the HIPC program a country has to "regularize its relations with creditors"—i.e., service its debts—85 percent of debts owed by HIPCs are now being serviced. Non-HIPCs, however, are on average paying only about 40 percent of what they owe, but this is still a significant amount.

196 "National Regeneration Trusts": What projects would these trusts support? The details would be determined by the board of trustees. There should be no replication here of the "one size fits all" micromanagement—which we saw is doomed to fail—so beloved of the Bretton Woods institutions, and the board would be best placed to be able to determine national priorities. But projects would be mandated to be demonstrably pro-poor, take into account women's needs, and be geographically dispersed. The Millennium Development Goals could provide a good steer.

197 "nonnationals": The point of including a few from relevant United Nations bodies such as UNICEF (which deals with children's needs) or the World Health Organization is to be able to leverage their particular expertise and hands-on experience.

197 "having to take money out of its budget": In many cases, the only way a country has been able to pay back its creditors is because it was receiving new loans.

197 "pledge to continue financing": This would be in keeping with the international communities' pledge to reach the Millennium Development Goals.

197 "capacity to pledge to the Trust": If a debtor country does not have the money to repay the debt, and therefore would not have monies available for channeling into the Trust, the international community must be willing to commit requisite funds so that the Trust can function. And arbitration could determine the extent to which a debtor government has the capacity to pledge to the Trust. It should be noted that such capacity is, by definition, greater than the capacity to pay back internationally, because, while the capacity to repay to the international community should be calculated on the basis of what is left after a country has met the basic human needs of its people, the capacity to pledge to the fund is a first call on their resources. Also, the latter is in domestic currency, the former in foreign exchange.

198 "trustees will be elected": Civil society organizations could propose trustees, and the nominees could be voted upon with each organization being given one vote—regardless of size. The process would need to be open and transparent so as to have credibility. An internal check and balance system would also be needed in order that the Trust not be dominated by one constituency. Marianne Guerin-McManus of Conservation International suggests, in the context of conservation trusts, that a Trust could rotate its members and employ special voting systems such as requiring super majorities on certain decisions or giving certain members veto power on certain issues so as to prevent one group from gaining power at the expense of the objective of the funds. Most important, we must recognize that the hiring, training, monitoring, and capacity building of civilian trustees will come at a cost, which the rich world should be happy to finance because of the positive feedback effects.

198 "transformed into annual cash flows": While, for the creditor, my proposal would essentially mean debt cancellation, for the debtor it does not imply cancellation from the beginning, but the restructuring of the debt service in foreign exchange into an allocation in domestic currency.

198 "hold both the Trust and the country to account": One could envisage this being underpinned with a treaty like the OECD's Convention on Bribery that seeks to make bribery of foreign public officials an offense in all signatory countries and binds countries to extradition once they sign the treaty.

198 "In this way, funds would be protected": Although HIPC itself pays lip service to a much enhanced role for civil society, and the IFIs have stated that civil society will now be very much involved in both the design of poverty reduction programs and the monitoring of how funds released by debt relief are disbursed, to date these pledges have on the whole not been met. National Regeneration Trusts, on the other hand, provide a real and viable mechanism of turning such rhetoric into meaningful reality.

199 "Oil Revenue Permanent Trust Fund": See, for example, Steve Clemons, "Sharing, Alaska-Style," *New York Times,* April 9, 2003.

199 "Lessons can be drawn": Lessons can also be drawn from debt for environment swaps, which have occasionally been used in the past.

200 "social spending": Some countries receiving debt relief have increased social spending between 20 and 50 percent.

201 "$38 billion a year": "Remittances to Latin America and the Caribbean reach a record $38 billion," Inter-American Development Bank, March 27, 2004.

201 "securitized": Another way to securitize remittances might be for the host country of the migrant workers to securitize these workers' income tax payments, and create out of these a bond that can then be used to finance development.

201 "secrecy of debt": Debt in the form of bonds is notionally in the public domain, of course, from the time the government announces its proposal to issue bonds.

201 "held . . . legally to account": The case Ex-Im and OPIC are facing in the United States courts, referred to in Chapter 10, is a case where government agencies are already being held legally to account for alleged negligent lending practices.

202 "a bank can be held liable": See, for example, the BCCI case.

202 "grants": It should also be noted that countries that are not highly indebted but still poor must not lose out as a consequence of debt relief. Any grants provided to highly indebted countries or debt relief must be additional, not a replacement for aid flows to other such countries.

202 "long-term investment and growth": They could, for example, provide subsidized insurance to developing countries to help them cope with the unexpected plunges in commodity prices that have so often knocked them for a loop.

203 "offshore accounts": Although most of this money is in Western offshore havens—the Cayman Islands, Bahamas, etc.—some is now in Iran, Iraq, China, Kuwait, Saudi Arabia and Eastern Europe, where this will obviously be harder to effect. But we are talking serious money here:

Mobutu's personal fortune, mainly in assets abroad, is estimated at around $10 billion, while $3.5 billion of Nigerian monies stolen by the Abacha family have already been located in overseas banks.

203   "innovative financing schemes": See, for example, Gordon Brown on IFF; Joseph Stiglitz and George Soros on SDRM.

Index